THE INTERNATIONAL
DRUGS TRADE

THE INTERNATIONAL
DRUGS TRADE

GUY ARNOLD

Routledge
Taylor & Francis Group

NEW YORK AND LONDON

Published in 2005 by
Routledge
Taylor & Francis Group
270 Madison Avenue
New York, NY 10016

Published in Great Britain by
Routledge
Taylor & Francis Group
2 Park Square
Milton Park, Abingdon
Oxon OX14 4RN

Printed in the United States of America on acid-free paper
10 9 8 7 6 5 4 3 2 1

International Standard Book Number-10: 1-57958-396-2 (Hardcover)
International Standard Book Number-13: 978-157958-396-5 (Hardcover)
Library of Congress Card Number 2004015152

Library of Congress Cataloging-in-Publication Data

Arnold, Guy.
  The international drugs trade / Guy Arnold.
    p. cm.
  Includes bibliographical references and index.
  ISBN 1-57958-396-2 (hb)
  1. Narcotics, control of. 2. Drug traffic. 3. Narcotics, control of —
international cooperation. I. Title.
  HV5801.A725 2004
  363.45 — dc22

             2004015152

Taylor & Francis Group
is the Academic Division of T&F Informa plc.

Visit the Taylor & Francis Web site at
http://www.taylorandfrancis.com

and the Routledge Web site at
http://www.routledge-ny.com

Contents

Introduction   vii

Chapter 1   The World Pattern: An Overview   1

Chapter 2   The Role of the United Nations   11

Chapter 3   The Drugs   25

Chapter 4   Statistics and Comparisons (Britain)   39

Chapter 5   British Attitudes to Drugs   51

Chapter 6   The U.S. Drug Scene   67

Chapter 7   U.S. Statistics   77

Chapter 8   The U.S. Policy of Certification   87

Chapter 9   Colombia: Key to the Cocaine Trade   99

Chapter 10   Colombia's Neighbors   121

Chapter 11   Central America, the Caribbean, and Mexico   135

Chapter 12   The Golden Triangle   149

Chapter 13   The Golden Crescent   159

Chapter 14   The Involvement of All Asia   169

Chapter 15   The Growing Involvement of Africa   179

Chapter 16   Europe   195

Chapter 17   Money Laundering   209

Chapter 18   The Cannabis Debate   219

Chapter 19   Conclusions   229

Notes   239

Index   245

Introduction

It would be impossible to cover all aspects of the international drugs trade in one volume. Three areas are dealt with here: the principal markets for illegal drugs and official and public attitudes to the problem; the principal drug-producing countries; and the business of trafficking—how illegal drugs are moved from countries of origin and production to their markets.

The illegal drugs trade is now so widespread and affects so many countries and communities that it makes little sense for governments, politicians, or the United Nations to claim, as they periodically do, that they are successfully combating the trade and reducing its incidence. They are doing nothing of the kind. They may be combating the drugs trade, yet despite successes—huge hauls of drugs by police or customs, the capture of leading drug barons, the closing of drug export routes—the trade continues, constantly finding new outlets, while the number of drug users also continues to rise. The greater the effort put into combating the trade by authorities of all kinds, the greater the efforts directed at evasion and at the continuation of one of the world's three most profitable economies. If we examine the evidence of the last decade of the twentieth century, we find that while more and more political and media attention, and more and more money and policy initiatives were focused on the "drugs" problem, the effort was not attended by commensurate successes in reducing the numbers who used drugs—the willing market. Indeed, the opposite would appear to have been the case; as the anti-drugs effort increased, so did the consumption. What, then, is the answer?

If we look first at the side of law and order—that is, the constituencies opposed to any form of drug culture—these divide into a number of often conflicting or disparate interest groups. Governments want to control or prevent drug use because this is politically acceptable. On the other hand, some governments and plenty of banks are lukewarm about fighting money laundering because large sums of money are involved that are welcomed and "needed" by poor countries or greedy banks. The U.S. concentration on fighting the drugs war in the producer countries (such as Colombia), rather than tackling the social and economic problems that give rise to the home demand, has produced a new North–South political equation; that is, the "poor" countries of the South (which used to be described as the Third World) seek revenge for past exploitation by the North and do so by supplying the drugs that undermine the moral integrity of peoples of the principal drug markets—the United States, Europe, and Russia. Drug enforcement agencies, the police, customs, and other institutions responsible for combating the distribution of drugs have their own vested interests, apart from sometimes being corrupted themselves, because they can demand increased budgets and enlargement in the name of fighting the drugs war. They are part of a career and structural growth industry. And there are glaring anomalies. Prisons, in theory, represent some of the most controlled environments in the world, yet drugs are readily available in them. The reason is simple enough: the prison authorities find it easier to control the inmates, many of whom were convicted for drug offences in the first place, if they allow drugs into the prisons. The alternative might be far more unruly prison populations and a much harder role for the authorities.

Scapegoating, whether in democracies or dictatorships, is an integral part of political life while most societies need enemies to focus upon; during the 1980s and 1990s, drug addicts, drug traffickers, and drug barons came to fulfill this role, enormously assisted by such colorful villains as Colombia's Pablo Escobar or Panama's General Manuel Noriega. The result, by the beginning of the new century, is a perception of the drugs problem that puts it on a par with keeping the peace. The money involved in the illegal drugs trade, which now has an estimated annual turnover of \$5,000 billion,* is so great that it acts as a magnet for the greedy and provides the means to corrupt on a massive scale, affecting governments, senior ministers and police or military personnel, and more junior officials down the line, and this takes place in every country affected by the international drugs trade. Hypocrisy also plays a part. The young in schools are lectured about the evils of drugs, and the poor young drug offenders of the West's many ghettoes are the particular targets of the police, yet too often the same Western societies turn a blind eye to the use of drugs by celebrities, the rich, or the secure middle classes.

The sheer size of the drugs trade and its endless ramifications suggest that the market is too vibrant to be eliminated. Whether or not the West believes in market forces, in fact such forces always operate where people want something enough and are determined to obtain it. And so we have to face a number of awkward questions, some of which are consistently ignored by politicians who are fearful of upsetting their constituencies. Does the criminalizing of drugs make the problem better or worse? Is the present approach the best way to tackle the problem? Would decriminalization make more sense? Since the illegal drugs business has grown in recent years, even as the anti-drugs crusade has been expanded, the evidence would suggest that the huge anti-drugs war is counterproductive. If this is the case, in what other ways can the problem be tackled, and should it be tackled at all? Why are so many people, at all levels of society, so anxious to have drugs, and why are

---

*In general, financial figures are given in U.S. dollars unless they refer to drug activities in the U.K., in which case figures are given in pounds sterling.

so many governments and other social or political groups so determined to stop people from taking drugs? Can we differentiate between people who are able to take and enjoy drugs yet control their use and people who become addicts once they have taken drugs? Do governments criminalize drugs as opposed to tobacco or alcohol because they wish to set up social scapegoats? In "free" societies, should not individuals have the right to decide for themselves? Drugs have been used and abused throughout history; is it realistic to suppose that their use can be stamped out? Does not prohibition merely act as a spur to those determined to take drugs and a godsend to the criminal organizations that distribute them? Drug syndicates, for example, simply write off police or customs hauls of a percentage of their drugs as a necessary tax. They are not deterred.

The current debate on drugs—in the United States, Britain, and Europe (the big markets)—has been confined by the politicians to a series of set answers to set questions. Drugs have been designated as a "problem" or as a series of linked problems—moral, social, medical, criminal, political, and economic—and must be treated as such, with the result that solutions are confined to prohibition, punishment, and coercion. Despite the fact that this approach has failed and is still failing, the accepted wisdom has not allowed alternative discussions to take place. The international war on drugs was and continues to be primarily an American operation, and it is of recent origin. During the Cold War, when the enemy was international communism, drugs were often used as a weapon in Washington's anticommunist armory. By the beginning of the new century, with the Cold War ended, the war on drugs targeted minorities and dissidents at home and allowed the United States to intervene in the affairs of other countries, especially in the Americas, where the Drug Enforcement Administration (DEA) has become an arm of U.S. foreign policy. The whole West now lives in a drug culture and is likely to continue to do so into the foreseeable future. The war on drugs ignores this social, political, and economic fact and, as a consequence, it is creating more problems than it is likely to cure.

The drugs business is now the third biggest economy in the world and is growing. Like all modern businesses, organized crime is now conducted on a global basis and the drugs trade is its most profitable sector. In 1999 the Financial Action Task Force (FATF) of the Group of Seven (G7) estimated that at least $120 billion (£73 billion) from the drugs trade was annually laundered through the world's financial system.[1] This sum, which is in the nature of a guesstimate and is a conservative one at that, is equivalent to the total funds invested legally in the world's emerging markets during the same year. Such a comparison shows how much is at stake and also gives an indication of the impact on world development that drugs money might make if it were the outcome of legitimate trade. Much of that huge sum passes through London, which is the world's biggest foreign-exchange trading center. The

G7 established FATF to combat money laundering, bribery, and other financial aspects of organized crime, and, as yet, there is not a great deal of evidence to suggest that FATF is getting on top of these problems. There is
another cost side to the international drugs business: the growing bill for
medical, social, and policing operations. In the United States, according to
the National Drug Strategy (the official government policy on drugs), the annual social cost of combating drugs now stands at about $67 billion. About a
third of new human immunodeficiency virus (HIV) cases in the United States
are linked to the injection of drugs. In Britain, which has achieved the dubious distinction of becoming the most drug-affected country in Europe, the
cost of dealing with serious drug abuses has passed £4 billion a year, while
the Office of National Statistics estimates the size of the British drugs economy as 1.2 percent of official gross domestic product (GDP), which in 1999
stood at $1,290 billion (equivalent to £8.5 billion today).

Now, the official view of the drugs trade may be tabulated as follows:
Apart from the psychological and health damage to drug users and the cost of
rehabilitation, there are the huge costs of combating drug-related criminal activities and the consequent diversion of resources, which could be employed
in more productive activities, to deal with this problem; there is also the dis-
ruption of legal activities by the impact of drug-associated crime levels and
the way the drugs business degrades and corrupts institutions of politics and
society. Several questions are simply not addressed at all. First, if the entire
drugs trade were to be eliminated, would this also eliminate the amount of related criminal activity, or would the drug criminals simply turn to other illegal
trades such as moving migrants or organizing international prostitution?
Second, what happens to those economies that are heavily dependent on income from the drugs trade, whether directly as producers or indirectly as
money-laundering centers? Drugs are the most important export for Latin
America; and drug crops, principally the coca leaf, are its most lucrative cash
crop. Drug barons, despite constant pressures on them, control the most liq-
uid-cash assets and can and do move these assets in and out of the continent.
The Medellín cartel in Colombia once offered to pay off the country's entire
foreign debt in return for legitimacy. In post-communist Russia, the illegal
economy, much of it drug-financed, has become as powerful as, or more powerful than, the newly privatized official economy. According to FATF, money
laundering does not just take place through offshore financial centers; it is
also conducted through high-street lawyers, accountants, banks, and *bureaux
de change*—it is, in fact, the biggest of big businesses.

There is a distinct world pattern. The main drug syndicates are solidly established in the principal drug production areas such as Colombia, the
Golden Triangle, or the Golden Crescent; they are to be found operating in
the main transit centers such as Istanbul, Mexico, southern Italy, or Spain;
and in the main consumer markets of North America and Western Europe.
They are not going to disappear as long as the markets for their products

exist, at least not unless there is a change of attitude toward the consumption of drugs. And this is where comparisons are important. Why are the lessons in relation to the consumption of alcohol never related to the problems of drug consumption? In Britain, for example, the police have lobbied for the deregulation of licensing hours so that large numbers of drinkers do not feel the need to consume extra alcohol quickly before the pubs close, because the majority of disturbances requiring police intervention take place at closing time. We talk of sensible drinking, why not of sensible drug taking? If a large proportion of the British (or American or French) public can drink sensibly and enjoy doing so without becoming alcoholics, why do the authorities in the same countries act as though the idea of comparable behavior in relation to drugs is an absurdity and insist that drugs of all kinds have to be controlled and forbidden? Excessive alcohol is bad, as is excessive smoking, yet neither alcohol nor smoking are forbidden in Western societies; there are restraints relating to their consumption by minors and there are warnings on cigarette packets about the dangers to health, but they are not forbidden. Why, then, have drugs been placed in a different category, and why is it assumed that anyone who smokes cannabis or its equivalent is bound to end up a heroin addict? The high-profile fight against drugs has provided the authorities with ammunition about the brutal cartels, the international distributors, the corruption of authorities, and the greed of the crime syndicates involved, which is used to demonize drug taking. The same scenario was available early in the last century in relation to the prohibition of alcohol in the United States. That attempt at regulation was counterproductive; it led to a massive increase in criminal activities and did not work. There is more evidence to suggest that the attempted prohibition of drugs will not work any better than did the prohibition of alcohol, while there is plenty of evidence to suggest that the authorities worldwide will not win their war against drugs. The licensing laws to control alcohol consumption were introduced during World War I as a measure to prevent munitions workers from drinking too much and then failing to turn up to work the next day. Control of drugs was introduced about the same time (although attempts to control the distribution of drugs go back to the nineteenth century). Draconian controls almost always lead to worse excesses than those they were intended to contain.

Banning drugs does not work in the inner-city ghettoes of the United States or in the sink estates of Britain; if anything, prohibition simply exacerbates existing problems. In Britain the class factor, despite hypocritical pretenses that class is no longer important, makes a distinction between the middle-class drug taker who supposedly can control his or her habit and the drug or alcohol addict of the sink estates. There is indeed excessive drug use and alcoholism in U.S. inner-city ghettoes and the British sink estates. What the authorities in both countries have failed to do is address the real problems of those benighted communities by providing employment, better housing, and social amenities. Taking drugs should not be regarded as any more of a criminal offense than drinking alcohol or smoking, and it is time that fact was recognized.

In opposition to the law-and-order approach to drugs is a wide range of ordinary people who simply do not see drugs as a problem, or, at least, as a problem on the scale envisaged by governments. A British Broadcasting Corporation (BBC) television program, *Chemical Britannia*, shown in the spring of 2001 had people claiming that taking cannabis, cocaine, ecstasy, and even heroin was not dangerous but extremely enjoyable. Smoking a cannabis joint is as relaxing as drinking a glass of wine, they said, while many people find that taking ecstasy is the most pleasurable experience of their lives. Such views may be anathema to the law-and-order lobbies, yet it is time they were taken into account, especially in North America and Europe, where governments so often claim that they are democratic.

In dozens of interviews in the BBC program, drug users explained why the popularity of drugs is increasing despite the almost totally negative attitude toward drugs displayed by the media and governments. In Britain the number of people taking illegal drugs has risen dramatically from about 1 million in the 1960s to 3 million in the 1980s to about 10 million in 2000. That is just under 17 percent of the population. A majority of people under 40 years old have taken drugs at some point in their lives, or so the program claimed. It is unrealistic to suppose that all these people took drugs as a result of pressure from pushers; they took them because they wanted to and because they liked the sensation. Drugs for most of these people were a means of relaxing in the same way that alcohol and tobacco are used. Why, then, are drug users liable to be imprisoned, while alcohol users or heavy smokers do not face the same penalty? The people who claimed that taking cannabis, ecstasy, or cocaine is an acceptable way of relaxing and should be treated as such, were, however, lambasted as irresponsible by John Griffith, the chief executive of the group Drug Abuse Resistance Education, which works in schools to warn children of the dangers of drugs. He argued: "It is very disturbing that any program is produced in such a way that it makes people think there are benefits to taking drugs that may harm them in the long run. It makes our work harder in making young people realize that most people don't get involved in drugs."

On the other hand, the presenter of this program, Mat Southwell, a former employee of the National Health Service who regularly takes ecstasy, said: "As a drug user, I am sick of having my life attacked and being forced outside the law. It's time to turn the spotlight on the politicians who, despite all the evidence, refuse to accept that the war on drugs has failed and, in fact, has done more harm than good." A simple fact in support of Southwell's claim has been the rise in cocaine production since the drug was criminalized. Global production of cocaine was 10 tonnes (9.8 tons) a year before it was criminalized; now it is 700 tonnes (689 tons). Illegal drugs account for

8 percent of global trade. One more quote from Mr. Southwell may be added to the debate. He insisted: "The principle of individual freedom linked to social responsibility lies at the heart of our democracy. As an adult and responsible member of society, I absolutely assert my right to take any mind-altering substance, be that ecstasy, alcohol, heroin, tobacco, or cannabis. No one, least of all the state, has the right to tell me otherwise."[2]

The American film *Traffic* (2000), starring Michael Douglas and Catherine Zeta Jones, is an interesting Hollywood attempt to lay bare some of the hypocrisies and contradictions in the U.S. war on drugs. Douglas plays a Midwestern judge who is appointed U.S. "drugs czar," while Zeta Jones plays the wife of a narcotics tycoon. The intricacies of the plot are not important, except for the fact that halfway through the film Douglas discovers that his daughter is involved with drugs, as are half her contemporaries at college. The messages of the film, however, are stark enough: Far from inhibiting the drugs trade or reducing the power of the cartels, the U.S. anti-drugs policy is leading to greater efforts by the cartels to penetrate the U.S. market, which they do all the time. Furthermore, demonizing drugs simply ensures that corruption pervades the entire chain of command on both sides of the U.S.–Mexican border, from police and border patrols through senior ranks of the police or military up to the politicians. The money involved is more than sufficient to corrupt most of the players. The main message of the film is that the policy is futile and breeds corruption, at the same time bringing unworkable laws into contempt.

The film *Traffic* represents a popular way of criticizing the U.S. drugs policy. In recent years U.S. governments, like their British counterparts, have closed their minds to any debate on the drugs issue that offers alternative approaches to the problem. When, for example, in 1998 Washington, DC, went to the polls for its mid-term elections, one of the ballots (the result of an initiative) called for the legalization of medical marijuana. At the time, the ballots on this subject were counted and then impounded so that the result was not made public. Only after a law professor had sued was the result of this ballot released: It showed that Washington, DC, had voted by more than a 60 percent majority to decriminalize marijuana for medical purposes. This political denial pointed up the official hysteria about drugs and the refusal of the U.S. authorities to discuss alternative approaches to the problem other than the official war on drugs. Meanwhile tens of thousands of Americans are in prison for possessing or growing marijuana despite the fact that almost anyone in the United States can obtain drugs with little difficulty. At least by 2000 there were signs of revolt; every time the decriminalization of marijuana has been put to a vote in different states, it has been carried by significant majorities, and in each case the government has intervened to nullify the local vote. An increasing number of highly respected politicians, liberal and conservative, such as former Secretary of State George Shultz or William F. Buckley, have expressed their opposition to the existing policy on drugs, while the growing U.S. intervention in Colombia has also met with widespread criticism in Congress and the press. Two aspects of the war on drugs emphasize the inequalities that it embraces. First, a disproportionate number of those sentenced to prison terms for possession of drugs are poor and African American. Second, since most people purchasing drugs do so willingly, the police—to obtain evidence for convictions—are forced to rely heavily on informers, a reliance that leads to blackmail and further corruption.[3]

In March 2001, *The Face*, a popular British magazine, interviewed 1,000 teenagers and others in their early 20s in 10 British cities about their use of cocaine (coke), now the most popular drug in the country. Among the interviewees, 45 percent said they had taken cocaine and 43 percent considered it less dangerous than ecstasy. *The Face* produced a special 24-page supplement on the subject. Much of it consisted of interviews with individuals and their stories of the drug's impact on them. Some had been hospitalized, but others took it as a normal part of the youth scene and regarded it as "no big deal." Many hard facts about the drug scene were also given: The size of drug barons' assets ranges from £20 million to £150 million; the price of a kilo of cocaine on departure from South America ranges between $1,000 and $2,000. Its price on arrival in Europe rises to £15,000, and its price on arrival in Britain to £28,000, while the cheapest price for a gram in the city of Glasgow is £35. Prices per gram vary from city to city, ranging between £20 and £35.

There is no shortage of information about drugs available for young people in Britain, and drugs programs include school visits by police. One policeman, P. C. Rowan, states: "Some of the kids I see will have personal experience of cocaine. But we don't work on any assumptions about people's drug use. We live in a drug-taking society." The British government estimates that "the social, economic, psychological, crime, and health-related" cost arising from drug misuse is £4 billion a year, while the government budget for tackling drug misuse is £1 billion a year. As one dealer explained the sale of cocaine: "Cocaine is people in a good job, a stable job, earning well and out for a social weekend. That's why I sell cocaine." And there are plenty of people with lots of money to spend on it. One factor, repeated again and again, in justification or at least explanation for taking drugs, is that of boredom: Britain is bored, people are bored with their jobs and the dullness of their lives, so they turn to drugs as a relief. In 1998 the independent drugs charity DrugScope reported that 2.8 percent of 15 and 16 year olds in England had taken coke, and 2.5 percent had taken ecstasy.

The sheer scale of drug taking in the United States and Britain, despite all the anti-drugs programs, should by now suggest two things: that the present approach to drugs is not working, and that it is time to look at the problem in new ways.

1

The World Pattern: An Overview

The worldwide trade in illicit drugs ranks, after the gross domestic products (GDP) of the United States and Japan, as the world's third-largest economy; it is a global business whose organizers constantly shift their operations so that it cannot be brought under control. An estimate in February 1999 gave the U.S. GDP as $8,108 billion; Japan as $3,973 billion; and the drugs trade as $3,230 billion. This figure was regarded as a mid-range estimate of the value of the trade, which might, in fact, be worth as much as $5,000 billion. Given a trade on this scale, it is unlikely, no matter how great the efforts of drug enforcement agencies, that it can be stopped. There are, quite simply, too many people making profits, too many making a living, and too many seeking the end products of the trade for it to be brought under control.

The difficulty in tracking world drug routes is their volatility. One export-smuggling route becomes too dangerous and is closed down, to be replaced at once by another; later, when police vigilance has been relaxed, an earlier route will be reactivated. The drugs business can be divided into three broad activities: the culture and preparation of the drugs, their transit to markets, and their distribution in the principal markets such as the United States and Europe. According to the 1997 annual report of the United Nations International Narcotics Control Board (INCB), drug trafficking then equaled 8 percent of all world trade.[1] Nearly 140 million people (2.5 percent of the world's population) smoked marijuana and hashish, 13 million people used cocaine, 8 million used heroin, and another 30 million used such stimulants as amphetamines. The report suggested that efforts at drug seizure led to the interception of about one third of cocaine shipments and no more than 10 to 15 percent of heroin shipments. All these figures, as we shall see, may alter substantially from year to year. Profits, in any case, are so large that they cover the losses represented by all seizures. The problem is beyond the ability of any single government or country to control.

The United States is internationally most active in its efforts to combat the drugs trade and has established Drug Enforcement Administration (DEA) offices in more than 70 overseas locations. The United States is also the world's largest market for drugs of all kinds, and the U.S. effort is commensurate with the problem it faces on the home front. During the 1990s the European Union, and Britain in particular, developed into another major market for drugs and, after the United States, Britain probably has the next most active anti-drugs program. Heroin, until very recently, has been the most common Class A drug to be smuggled into Britain, most of it coming from the Golden Crescent (Afghanistan, Pakistan, and Iran). The drug is routed variously through the Netherlands, Germany, the Czech Republic, Slovakia, Bulgaria, and Hungary, with about 10 percent being intercepted en route. By the end of the century, however, cocaine had overtaken heroin as the leading Class A drug entering the British drug market, not least because of a major push by the Colombian cartels.

Programs sponsored by the United States or the United Nations in such countries as Peru, with the aims of destroying coca crops and providing funds for farmers to grow alternative and profitable marketable crops such as wheat, have had indifferent success—not least because farmers have agreed to grow such crops and have then moved elsewhere to grow the more profitable coca leaf as well. The United States has put huge effort into fighting the drugs trade and sometimes appears single-handedly to be waging a world war on the trade—and losing that war. The basic U.S. strategy is to tackle the drugs business as close to the source as possible, and this means persuading countries that are principal sources of drugs, such as Colombia, to cooperate in destroying a trade from which they derive huge profits. The DEA was established in 1973 to replace earlier drug enforcement agencies such as the Bureau of Drug Abuse Control or the Bureau of Narcotics and Dangerous Drugs. The DEA has two roles: domestic enforcement of federal drug laws and the coordination of U.S. drug investigations abroad. To succeed outside the United States, the DEA must work closely with other foreign law enforcement organizations.

Colombia, Bolivia, and Peru are the principal source countries for cocaine. In the mid-1990s about 200 tonnes (197 tons) of cocaine were exported annually from Colombia. Peru then had approximately 121,000 hectares (300,000 acres) of land producing the coca leaf, with Bolivia expanding its coca production and Ecuador also producing it, though on a smaller scale. The Colombian cartels, Medellín and Cali, were mainly responsible for processing the coca leaf into cocaine in the laboratories they controlled, although by the 1990s Colombia also had about 37,000 hectares (91,000 acres) of land producing the coca leaf. In addition, it was beginning to produce heroin. Despite huge U.S. efforts to persuade Colombia to control and curtail its drug production, by 1996 the coca farmers in Colombia were estimated to be supplying 85 percent of the U.S. market. At U.S. insistence, the Colombian government pursued a crop eradication program, although the coca farmers vigorously opposed its implementation. In the four southern provinces of Colombia, where most of the coca is grown, 50,000 protesters turned out in Puerto Asís to oppose the government program. In addition, the armed forces found themselves fighting left-wing guerrillas who supported the coca farmers. As U.S. pressures mounted, Colombia switched some of its attention to the European market, and especially Britain, in an effort to expand its heroin business. By mid-1996, for example, the Cali cartel boasted that it was smuggling 100 kilograms (221 pounds) of heroin into Britain every month.

Government anti-drugs operations in Peru during 1996 revealed that both army and navy officers were deeply involved in drug smuggling (200 army officers had been prosecuted for smuggling offenses over the previous few years); the increase of activity in Peru followed U.S.-inspired anti-narcotics sweeps in Colombia, which had resulted in substantial hauls of coca paste and refined cocaine. In the early 1990s the Peruvian army had succeeded in bringing an end to the activities of the left-wing Shining Path (Sendero Luminoso) guerrillas. However, the army merely replaced the guerrillas by setting up its own bases in the remote former guerrilla-controlled areas and extracting quotas from the drug lords in return for leaving their coca fields intact. In 1995 Peru, as the leading producer, harvested 186,000 tonnes (183,000 tons) of the coca leaf. Traditionally the Peruvians make the coca paste, which is shipped to Colombia for refining into cocaine; beginning in the mid-1990s, however, the Colombian cartels moved some of their operations into Peru to avoid the escalating U.S.-inspired crackdowns in their own country. Much of the drug smuggling from Peru to Colombia is along the Amazon by speedboats, first to Brazil and then on to Colombia.

In the 1980s Bolivia was largely content to grow the coca leaf and ship it north to Colombia, where it was converted into paste in the laboratories of the cartels. During the 1990s, however, with the decline of the Colombian cartels, Bolivian drug dealers began to make their own cocaine, and by the middle of the decade, Bolivian drug exports were earning $600 million a year, more than the country's legitimate exports, and the figure was rising.

Transit routes for drugs change all the time, and a cocaine assignment for Britain from Colombia, for example, might cross the Atlantic to Lagos in Nigeria and then pass through Poland, Germany, and the Netherlands before reaching its final destination. Panama acts as both a transit country and money-laundering center. Jamaica acts as a transit country for cocaine and cannabis to both the United States and Britain, and Jamaican "yardie" gangs have become an important part of the drug-distribution network in London. The Caribbean islands lie conveniently between the main cocaine source in South America and either the leading world market for the drug, the United States, or the European market. In the 1990s tougher attitudes toward drug trafficking and the closure of cocaine conduits to North America persuaded the South American cartels to extend their operations from Central America and the western Caribbean to the 29 countries of the eastern Caribbean, which stretch from Surinam to the British Virgin Islands. Small islands with minimal infrastructures and tiny economies had no experience and little capacity in dealing with highly sophisticated drug-smuggling operations. Poverty meant that officials were easily open to bribes, and from these islands new routes were opened up for transit to the United States, Britain, and Europe.

The United Nations International Drug Control Programme (UNDCP; based in Barbados) reported that 180 tonnes (177 tons) of cocaine, equivalent to 50 kilograms (110 pounds) a day, had been smuggled from South America via the eastern Caribbean into Europe during 1996. Of this amount, 60 percent passed through Britain. It was carried by cargo ships or by couriers on passenger flights. About one fifth of this Europe-bound cocaine traveled with couriers on as many as three air runs of returning vacationers a week. As the director of this UN program, Dr. Sando Calvini, explained, "You squeeze it here and it pops up over there. As their routes have been closed down, the narco-traffickers have been pushed further and further east, so these islands [of the eastern Caribbean] are now beginning to see a lot more drug activity."[2]

Despite its tough drug laws, Barbados was dealing with 60 or more drug cases a month starting in the mid-1990s. Other Leeward and Windward islands were drawn into the drugs business, often for money-laundering purposes, with the Internet being widely used to "advise" about operations. These small islands are very vulnerable to takeover as drug-smuggling transit posts; they have weak economies, high unemployment, underpaid and demoralized officials, and only small anti-narcotics budgets available. Such mini-states, which are fearful of being marginalized in the new climate of world economic globalization, may look upon money laundering for the drugs business as a life-saving economic windfall not to be passed over. Cuba, on the other hand, has maintained a strict anti-drugs stand. However, as a consequence of the U.S. blockade, Cuban waters are barred to the U.S. Coast Guard, with the result that drugs are dropped into these waters from the air in watertight packaging and then picked up and taken ashore for shipping to Europe through Cuban ports. Fidel Castro has denounced drug trafficking as against the revolution and, for example, cooperated with British police in order to prevent Cuba from becoming a transit stop for drugs between South America and Europe. Much of the cocaine destined for Europe from South America enters Europe through Portugal and Spain.

Mexico is the most important link country between the drug producers of South America and the North American market. Not only has Mexico long acted as a transit country for drugs from south to north, but it is also itself a growing source of drugs, and the U.S.–Mexican border area has become one of the most active drug-transit regions in the world. Mexico has supplied marijuana to the U.S. market for generations, while in recent years it has become a major producer of heroin. It has the advantage of a long border with the United States that has always been extremely hard to control. During the

1990s Mexico switched from producing cheap, low-grade heroin, which supplied only a small part of the U.S. market, to producing some of the world's most potent heroin. By the late 1990s it was taking over a rapidly increasing share of the U.S. market and, with Colombia, had taken over distribution in the United States from Asian organizations. The Asian share of the U.S. heroin market, meanwhile, dropped after 1992 from 90 percent to only 28 percent. In the United States the incidence of heroin users rose sharply during the 1990s from 500,000 to 600,000. According to U.S. anti-drugs officials, Mexican drug syndicates have taken over many of the cocaine distribution routes that were once dominated by the Colombians and have come to control nearly all heroin sales in the United States west of the Mississippi River. By the late 1990s the DEA estimated that 42 percent of heroin smuggled into the United States originated in Mexico; at the same time, it appeared that Colombian and Mexican drug operators were forming an increasingly close alliance.

On the other side of the world, the Golden Triangle—consisting of Myanmar (Burma), Laos, and Thailand—has always been one of the two traditional sources of heroin, with Myanmar as the leading producer country (overtaken in recent years by Afghanistan in the Golden Crescent). Most of the heroin-producing region of Myanmar has been plagued by wars over many years between the Karens and other ethnic groups and between various drug warlords, as well as between these groups and government forces. The government of Myanmar has always been prepared to allow the drugs trade to continue as long as it could obtain a major share of the drug revenues for itself. Neither Laos nor Thailand compete with Myanmar, and Thailand has carried out drug-eradication programs, largely inspired and financed by the United States, with the result that heroin from Thailand now makes a relatively small contribution to total output from the Golden Triangle. Even so, Bangkok is both a transit and money-laundering center.

The 1996 heroin harvest in Myanmar was 2,560 tonnes (2,520 tons), which represented a 9 percent increase over 1995. That year witnessed a deal between the government and the warlord Khun Sa, who, with his 20,000-man army, controlled much of the opium trade. Khun Sa surrendered and went into retirement. He handed over the day-to-day running of his drug fiefdom to Tatmadaw, the military wing of the State Law and Order Restoration Council (SLORC). Consequently, as of 1997, the Myanmar military controlled the taxation of heroin production and subsequently established heroin farms manned by forced labor. So near to legitimacy did the drugs business in Myanmar then become that during the years 1995–1997, four different ethnic groups with their own drug-trafficking armies opened offices and private banks in Rangoon from which, over this period, SLORC borrowed some $500 million. The Myanmar economy is underpinned by the proceeds of drug trafficking and, since the country has obstinately kept itself free of entanglements with the wider world community, the government cannot easily be pressured into changing its policies. (See also chapter 12.)

The second traditional region for the production of the opium poppy for heroin is the Golden Crescent—Afghanistan, Pakistan, Iran, and Turkey— with Turkey also producing heroin legally for the pharmaceutical industry. Afghanistan has overtaken Myanmar as a source of heroin; its eastern Nangarhar province is responsible for 80 percent of the country's poppy production, with an output of 1,300 tonnes (1,280 tons) of dry opium in 1995. During 1996, heroin-processing laboratories were transferred from Pakistan to areas within the Afghanistan frontier. These have been "fortified" and produce about 100 kilograms (220 pounds) of heroin a day. The then-Taliban government made a show at eradication, and over the years 1994–1996, some 30,000 hectares (74,130 acres) of opium and hashish fields were destroyed; this made little difference to the level of drug production, however. The Khyber Pass has become a two-way conduit for the drugs business: Pakistan supplies weapons for the drug mafias, and these are sent via the pass railway and are paid for with heroin. Production in Afghanistan has been turned into a highly organized and efficient agrobusiness. Technical advisers help with both crop control and drug production, while workers in the new factories have facemasks to protect them, and some of the producers even offer health insurance to their workers. Thus, in Taliban-ruled Afghanistan the drugs business was turned into a sophisticated capitalist enterprise to meet a growing world demand. Despite a Taliban statement that it would stamp out the drugs business, in 1997 Afghanistan produced 2,800 tonnes (2,760 tons) of opium. Together with Myanmar, it became the largest producer in the world. Little of the drug is consumed in Afghanistan itself; most of it, after refining in either Afghanistan or Pakistan, is moved to Europe through the countries of Central Asia. By 1997 heroin production in Afghanistan had spread into five provinces— Takhar in the north and Laghman, Parvan, Kabul, and Lowgar in the east. According to UN estimates, there are about 50 heroin laboratories operating in the country, which has become the center of the trade in the Golden Crescent. Turkey is the most important transit country for the Golden Crescent. (See also chapter 13.)

Heroin from the Golden Triangle travels by sea to Vladivostok and then is transported overland through Mongolia and the Russian Federation to Europe; the countries of the former Soviet Union have become transit countries for both heroin and cannabis, while Russia itself is also a big consumer. Malaysia, of all Asian countries, has the strictest laws regarding drugs, including flogging for soft-drug offenses and the death penalty for hard-drug offenders. Singapore, with similar tough laws, nevertheless has become a money-laundering center for the trade. Eighteen Chinese provinces are drug importers, and there is a big demand for heroin and other drugs.

Many Central and South Asian countries are involved in the transit trade. These include Bangladesh and India, which is also a hashish-consuming country, and the tier of former Soviet republics—Armenia, Azerbaijan, Tajikistan, Turkmenistan, Uzbekistan—which act principally as transit countries to the European market; some are also involved in the production of cannabis. Following the political upheavals that signaled the end of the Cold War and the disintegration of the Soviet Union, drug cartels moved into Eastern Europe. A new route for cocaine from South America was established via Russia and then into Poland and southeastern Europe. The Commonwealth of Independent States (CIS) has become a principal source of synthetic drugs such as speed, and these are also produced in laboratories in Poland, the Czech Republic, and Latvia, although the major ecstasy producers are still in Western Europe, especially the Netherlands. Lebanon, which has long been in a state of turmoil as a result of the Middle East confrontation between Israel and her neighbors, and which is situated on the western fringe of Asia with access to Africa and Europe, is a producer of heroin and cannabis, a money launderer, and the center of a major distribution system.

During the 1990s a number of African countries were drawn into the international drugs business. These included Nigeria as a major distribution center for cocaine from South America; Ivory Coast, Ghana, and Senegal as producers and distributors of cannabis; and Egypt (Cairo) as a transit center. There is the long-established trade in the narcotic leaf qat from Saudi Arabia to Somalia, and this habit has spread to Kenya. Most important, however, are the roles of Nigeria, South Africa, and Morocco.

Lagos has become a major receiver and subsequent distributor of cocaine from Colombia. Couriers take the drug to London and elsewhere in Europe; or it is routed to the northern Nigerian city of Kano and then sent north to Europe or east to Cairo, which is also a big transit center for drugs en route to Europe, especially to Amsterdam. Although Nigeria has a National Drug Law Enforcement Agency, it has been blacklisted by the United States, with Myanmar, Syria, and Iran, for refusing to cooperate in the fight against drug smuggling. Until 1995 Nigeria was primarily a center for couriers who moved drugs onward to European destinations, but since that date it has become involved in the trafficking and distribution aspects of the trade. Moreover, from being a transit center for drugs from South America to Europe it has, in addition, become a midway transit center for heroin from Asia to the U.S. market. By the mid-1990s it was estimated that 40 percent of heroin entering the United States was being smuggled in by Nigerian drug rings. Nigerians are now believed to control 80 percent of drug distribution in Atlanta and other U.S. cities with large African American populations, and they have also begun to take control of drug distribution in the northwest of England.

Nigerian drug traffickers became major players during the 1990s in competition with cartels in Brazil, Colombia, and Turkey. According to the United Nations, Nigeria has become one of the world's leading drug-trafficking nations, buying directly in the drug-producing countries and shipping to countries such as Britain, where Nigerians then sell the drugs on the streets. The Nigerians use their ethnic connections, particularly in cities such as London, Manchester, Johannesburg, or Atlanta, where there are substantial and growing Nigerian communities.

The opening up of South Africa following the end of apartheid, both to its African neighbors and to a wider world (airlines and the volume of air traffic passing through Johannesburg have more than tripled since 1994), has also meant the rapid development of Johannesburg as a drug-trafficking center. The drug Mandrax (methaqualone) represents big business in African townships; this is for local consumption, and the trade in it was largely left unhindered by the former apartheid authorities as a weapon of control in the volatile townships. The Mandrax market grew rapidly from the early 1980s, and by the late 1990s, an estimated 75 percent of the market was in South Africa. Johannesburg has become an important drug-transit and distribution center for Mandrax and also for cocaine from Colombia—for distribution in South Africa itself; for transit through to other African countries such as Zambia; and as a halfway transit point for drugs from South America en route to Europe.

Morocco is a leading world producer of cannabis; in 1996 its cannabis harvest was valued at $5 billion, and though there was a massive government clampdown on the drugs business that year, it made little impression on cannabis production. In the northern Rif region, some 74,000 hectares (182,860 acres) are normally under cannabis production and an estimated five million Moroccans depend directly or indirectly either on the cannabis industry or on the wider smuggling business. According to a European Union report by the Paris-based organization Observatoire Géopolitique des Drogues, Morocco is the world's biggest producer of cannabis, with an output of approximately 1,000 tonnes (984 tons) a year. It dominates the supply to Europe. Moreover, much of the country benefits from the income arising from the drugs business, including what are known as senior protectors of the business—"state networks" and the politicians. Other networks in Morocco have turned to the production of hard drugs and have brought in Colombians and Italians to assist them.

Cannabis is smuggled into the Spanish enclave of Ceuta, whose economy depends on such smuggling, and is then moved to Spain from where it is distributed to other European destinations. Given the wealth accruing to this illegal cannabis business, Morocco has no economic motive to stop the trade, no matter what pressures are brought to bear on the government, while stamping out—or trying to eradicate—the trade would lead to major social unrest. (See also chapter 15.)

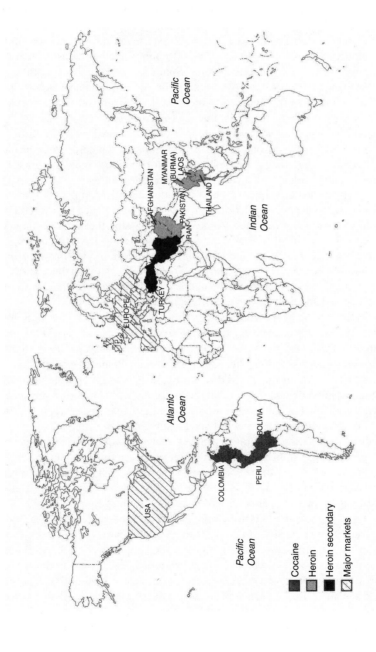

Figure 1.1 The main source-countries of drugs. (Cartography by Map Creation, Ltd. Maidenhead, Berkshire, U.K.)

Europe is the main market for drugs after the United States, and the suppliers are constantly trying to find new routes of entry. The end of the Cold War opened up Eastern Europe, with the result that drugs from the Golden Triangle and Golden Crescent can probably be moved into Europe through such countries as Bulgaria and the Czech Republic far more easily than in the communist era. In Western Europe, Spain and Portugal are points of entry for cocaine from South America, while Spain has also become the route for cannabis from Morocco, which exerts pressure on the European Union to ease anti-drugs moves against the trade.

Ireland has been targeted as a backdoor entrance for drugs into Britain, which has developed into one of the largest markets for hard drugs in the world. Dublin drug gangs are responsible for moving consignments to Manchester and London. Ireland has more than 3,220 kilometers (2,000 miles) of largely unguarded coastline, much of it wild and thinly populated, offering easy sea access to the country. During the 1990s the Irish police uncovered evidence of a rapid increase in the volume of drugs passing through the country en route to Britain; most of these drugs were believed to have originated in North Africa. One smuggling method discovered by the police involved the dumping on the seabed near Cork of sealed bales of drugs that would be relocated later by means of sophisticated satellite navigation equipment. The drugs would be landed and then sent onward through Ireland to Britain.

The Netherlands, apart from its experiments in licensed coffee bars for soft drugs, is the European center for the production of ecstasy. In 1997 it was estimated that 500,000 people in Europe had taken ecstasy, with six dying from its side effects. Britain is the Netherlands' main client for ecstasy.

The above profile of the world drug scene deals with the middle years of the 1990s.[2] It must be understood that this is a constantly changing scenario. Each year the UNDCP publishes a report covering the latest developments in the world war on drugs: the extent of seizures; the countries that have agreed to conduct eradication programs; the estimated numbers of drug users worldwide; and, given the nature of the illicit trade, the figures change all the time. (Chapter 2 looks at the report for the year 2000.) What does not appear to have happened is any falloff in demand for and use of illicit drugs. If one source of supply dries up, another will appear to fill the gap.

The three biggest markets for drugs are the United States, Europe, and Russia (see Figure 1.1). The drugs business is driven by market forces, a fact that the principal drug-consuming countries often appear to ignore. Attempts to end drug production, especially in poor countries, are counterproductive if there is no alternative and there are no other sources of income. The failure of anti-drugs measures to reduce the traffic in drugs, despite particular victories in different regions, suggests that the huge expenditure of money on combating the illicit drugs trade is not achieving results remotely commensurate with the effort involved.

2

The Role of the United Nations

During the twentieth century a series of international treaties or agreements were adopted with the aim of implementing a worldwide system for the control of drug abuse. Drug use and abuse at the beginning of the twentieth century was mainly seen as a local phenomenon in such countries as China, Myanmar (Burma), Persia, India, Egypt, Morocco, or among tribes in South America. Only the export of opium from Asian countries—or morphine, heroin, and cocaine from European countries to China—was seen as part of an international problem. China, which was a major consumer of drugs, was unable to deal with the problem on its own until agreements between China and Britain limited the export of opium from British India to China. Other sources of opium, however, replaced British India, and, when it became clear that bilateral agreements between countries were insufficient to prevent the traffic in drugs, the first international conference on narcotic drugs was held in Shanghai in 1909. This led to the adoption in 1912 of the International Opium Convention. It was soon realized that reporting and monitoring would be a necessary aspect of any drug control activity, and in 1925 a compulsory reporting system was created and a Permanent Central Board was established to monitor and supervise the compliance of governments that had entered into treaty obligations. Despite endless political and other confrontations between countries and governments, drug control measures were often excepted. For example, during the Cold War the two sides cooperated to develop and adopt the Single Convention on Narcotic Drugs of 1961, the Convention on Psychotropic Substances of 1971, and the United Nations Convention against Illicit Traffic in Narcotic Drugs and Psychotropic Substances of 1988.

Such conventions and treaties did not solve the growing problem of the drugs trade, but they did provide a framework for cooperation. As the International Narcotics Control Board[1] (INCB) claims: "Ratification of or accession to the three main international drug control treaties can be regarded as the first sign of a government's determination to contribute to the implementation of international drug control regulations." A brief examination of UN involvement follows.

The United Nations established an Office for Drug Control and Crime Prevention (ODCCP) on November 1, 1997, to enable it to focus on the international issues of drug control, crime prevention, and international terrorism. The ODCCP consists of the United Nations International Drug Control Programme (UNDCP) and the Centre for International Crime Prevention (CICP). The UNDCP, which was founded in 1991, is the central drug control entity responsible for coordinating and leading or initiating UN drug control activities. It assists governments in adopting and implementing drug control laws, helps with training for anti-drugs activities, and provides advice and technical assistance to member states on drug control matters. It supports its mandate at national, regional, and global levels through a network of field offices. As with most UN divisions, the ODCCP budget is limited; in 1998–1999 the UNDCP share of the total budget was $16.1 million. The first executive director of the ODCCP was the Italian Pino Arlacchi.

The Commission on Narcotic Drugs, a working body of the Economic and Social Council (ECOSOC) of the United Nations, is the main intergovernmental policy-making body on international drug control, consisting of 53 member states that meet annually. It analyzes the world drug abuse situation and puts forward proposals to strengthen international drug control. It directs the activities of UNDCP.

The INCB works to restrict the availability of drugs to medical and scientific purposes and to prevent their diversion into illegal channels. This is an independent body to assist and monitor the compliance of governments with the various international drug control treaties. The INCB has 13 members elected by ECOSOC who serve in their individual capacities. The INCB sends missions to drug-affected countries and sets limits on the amount of drugs countries may acquire for medical and scientific purposes.

In June 1998 a special session of the UN General Assembly met to consider the world drugs problem. The Assembly developed a global drug control strategy whereby governments committed themselves to work together to streamline existing strategies and strengthen international cooperation in curtailing illicit production and consumption. Proposed activities included campaigns to reduce the demand for drugs, programs to restrict the availability of materials that can be used in the production of illicit drugs, efforts to improve judicial cooperation among countries to improve the control of drug trafficking and punishment of offenders, and stepped-up efforts to eradicate illicit drug crops.

The United Nations has been responsible for promoting a number of treaties dealing with the drugs problem. These include the following:

The Single Convention on Narcotic Drugs (1961), which codifies the use of more than 116 natural or synthetic narcotics, including cannabis and cocaine.

The Convention on Psychotropic Substances (1971), which covers hallucinogens, amphetamines, barbiturates, nonbarbiturate sedatives, and
tranquilizers.

The 1972 Protocol Amending the Single Convention, which highlights
the need for treatment and rehabilitation of drug addicts.

The United Nations Convention against Illicit Traffic in Narcotic Drugs
and Psychotropic Substances (1988), which is designed to deprive drug
traffickers of their ill-gotten financial gains and freedom of movement.
This convention provides the framework for tracing, freezing, and con-
fiscating the proceeds and property derived from drug trafficking.

The object of these treaties is to limit the supply of drugs to medical and
scientific purposes. In order to break the economic hold that drug traffickers
establish in various regions, the UNDCP helps opium poppy and coca bush
farmers find alternative legal crops or other equally lucrative employment.
Most of its assistance under this heading has been in South America. The
UNDCP also assists governments in their efforts to counter money laundering and to confiscate assets gained from drug trafficking.

In a draft report of March 2000, ECOSOC

Reaffirms that countering the world drug problem is a common and
shared responsibility that must be addressed in a multilateral setting,
requiring an integrated and balanced approach, and must be carried
out in full conformity with the purposes and principles of the charter
of the United Nations and international law, and in particular with full
respect for the sovereignty and territorial integrity of states, the principle of nonintervention in the internal affairs of States and all human
rights and fundamental freedoms.

Calls upon all States to take further action to promote effective cooperation at the international and regional levels in the efforts to counter the
world drug problem so as to contribute to a climate conducive to
achieving that end, on the basis of the principles of equal rights and
mutual respect.

The United Nations, through its various treaties and conventions, is fully
committed to a worldwide program to combat the illegal drugs trade. This is
certainly acceptable to member states such as Britain or the United States,
though it is less certain that smaller states, whose involvement in the drugs
business is, at least in part, to their advantage, are quite so happy with these
sweeping UN mandates.

In mid-1998 the head of the ODCCP, Pino Arlacchi, pointed out that it is
just as important for drug-consuming countries, such as the United States, to

pay equal attention at home to reducing the demand for drugs as they do to tackling the production of drugs elsewhere. He argued that the barriers between drug enforcement agencies and those who argue for rehabilitation and a relaxation of the laws should be lowered. He also pointed out that two drug-producing countries, Iran and Pakistan in the Golden Crescent, had each registered in the region of one million drug addicts in their own populations, so that drug addiction was ceasing to be only a Western—that is, American and European—problem.

In June 1998, 500 leading international figures addressed an open letter to the United Nations calling for a complete rethinking of the "war on drugs." Signatories included the former UN Secretary-General Perez de Cuellar, the former U.S. Secretary of State George Shultz, the former independent South African Member of Parliament (MP) Helen Suzman, a number of South African churchmen, the Chilean writer Ariel Dorfman, the Italian Nobel Prize-winning playwright Dario Fo, the international financier and philanthropist George Soros, the retired head of Scotland Yard's drug squad Edward Ellison, the Greek Foreign Minister George Papandreou, and a number of other Nobel Prize winners. The open letter,[2] addressed to Kofi Annan, the UN Secretary-General, said, "We believe that the global war on drugs is now causing more harm than drug abuse itself," and it condemned "decades of failed and futile drug war policies." South African Helen Suzman said in relation to the letter: "I think it is time there was a proper international investigation. I don't go for the theory that a puff on a dagga cigarette leads to hard drugs. I have a glass of scotch every night and I'm not an alcoholic. It is no use simply keeping the use of drugs illegal, knowing that people will get hold of them, and that it gives rise to criminal syndicates and gangsterism." Suzman also said: "Often the fact that something is prohibited makes it desirable. We should explore alternative methods of dealing with the problem. If people are addicted, they should be treated as a medical problem. None of this is easy; there's no overnight solution. But the manner in which drugs have been handled seems to be causing more trouble than solving the problem." A shortened version of the letter reads as follows:

Dear Secretary-General,

On the occasion of the United Nations General Assembly special session on drugs in New York on June 8–10, 1998, we seek your leadership in stimulating a frank and honest evaluation of global drug control efforts.

We are all deeply concerned about the threat that drugs pose to our children, our fellow citizens, and our societies. There is no choice but to work together . . . to reduce the harms associated with drugs. The UN has . . .

an important role to play—but only if it is willing to ask and address tough questions about the success or failure of its efforts.

We believe that the global war on drugs is now causing more harm than drug abuse itself.

Every decade the United Nations adopts new international conventions, focused largely on criminalisation and punishment, that restrict the ability of individual nations to devise effective solutions to local drug problems. Every year governments enact more punitive and costly drug control measures. Every day politicians endorse harsher new drug war strategies.

What is the result? UN agencies estimate the annual revenue generated by the illegal drug industry at $4,000 billion, or the equivalent of roughly 8 percent of total international trade. This industry has empowered organised criminals, corrupted governments at all levels, eroded internal security, stimulated violence, and distorted both economic markets and moral values.

In many parts of the world, drug-war politics impedes public health efforts to stem the spread of HIV, hepatitis, and other infectious diseases. Human rights are violated, environmental assaults perpetrated, and prisons inundated with hundreds of thousands of drug-law violators.

Persisting in our current policies will only result in more abuse, more empowerment of drug markets and criminals, and more disease and suffering. Too often those who call for open debate, rigorous analysis of current policies, and serious consideration of alternatives are accused of "surrendering." But surrender is when fear as well as inertia combine to shut off debate, suppress analysis, and dismiss alternatives to current policies.

The letter was the initiative of the Lindesmith Center in New York, a reform institute financed by the billionaire philanthropist George Soros that advocates more liberal drug policies. The letter did not appear to make any difference to the ongoing UN approach to the drugs problem, although a spokesman for Kofi Annan said, "The secretary-general invites anybody who has any suggestions, proposals, or ideas that could help improve the international community's response to this problem to come forward." Official reaction to the letter in the United States was purely negative. General Barry McCaffrey, director of the Office of National Drug Control Policy under President Clinton, called the letter "a 1950s perception" of the ongoing struggle against drugs; and Donna Shalala, U.S. secretary of health and human services, said: "There's just no chance that we're going to throw up our hands and walk away from what we think is a predominantly public health issue."

INCB Annual Report

The 1999 annual report of the INCB[3] gives a general picture of how the "war on drugs" is progressing—or not. The INCB, which is the successor to earlier drug control bodies, endeavors "to limit the cultivation, production, manufacture, and use of drugs to an adequate amount required for medical and scientific purposes," "to ensure their availability for such purposes," and "to prevent illicit cultivation, production, and manufacture of, and illicit traffic in and use of, drugs." These responsibilities represent a tall order by any standards and raise questions to which we must later return, that is, how much does this UN operation make sense, and, as with any other aspects of UN work, has the international body really been given enough effective power to carry out its task?

The first part of the report is concerned with the licit drugs business, that is, ensuring that there is an adequate supply of controlled drugs for medical purposes. The second part of the report examines the international drug control system, including the number of countries that have adhered to the UN conventions: the Single Convention on Narcotic Drugs of 1961; the Convention on Psychotropic Substances of 1971; and the Convention against Illicit Traffic in Narcotic Drugs and Psychotropic Substances of 1988. Then, part three of the report analyzes the world situation by continent. Here it is possible to obtain a global picture of what is happening. Each regional analysis begins with a section on "major developments," and it is worth examining these briefly for 1999.

Africa

Particular concern was highlighted in relation to five main areas:

1. Trafficking in and abuse of narcotic drugs and psychotropic substances were increasingly linked to civil conflicts, and in these situations the spread of drugs particularly affected young people. For example, in the conflicts in the Congo and Liberia, child soldiers were provided with drugs to induce them to face dangerous situations with impunity. It was also believed that illicit drugs were being used to finance civil conflicts and the purchase of arms in Angola and Rwanda.
2. Western and southern Africa have emerged as important areas both for the transshipment of drug consignments for markets elsewhere (that is, outside Africa) but also as areas where both cocaine and heroin were increasingly consumed. As a result of increased law en-

forcement efforts in Nigeria, traffickers were using other countries in the region as transit points for shipments to Europe and North America.

3. The main drug to be trafficked and abused in Africa was cannabis, although other drugs—including cocaine, heroin, and amphetamines—were becoming increasingly popular.

4. The INCB also found that in many countries, seized drugs subsequently disappeared and known drug traffickers were frequently acquitted or disappeared while on bail.

5. There appeared to be an increasing link between AIDS and the injection of heroin, mainly in capital cities and tourist destinations.

Central America and the Caribbean

Two major developments were noted:

1. The region of Central America and the Caribbean was increasingly being used to transship cocaine and cannabis from countries in South America to the United States and Europe, and this traffic had increased the availability of cocaine in Central America and the Caribbean, where cocaine abuse was growing.

2. The INCB expressed concern at the increasingly liberal approach of some governments in Central America and the Caribbean to the offshore banking and gambling industries because of their potential use for money-laundering purposes.

North America

Four developments were especially noted:

1. Cannabis continued to be the most popular drug of abuse in Canada, Mexico, and the United States.

2. The government of the United States had issued new guidelines to ease the availability of cannabis for medical research, and both the National Academy of Sciences and the National Institutes of Health recommended a more extensive program of scientific research on cannabis.

3. According to a national survey covering 1997–1998 in the United States, drug abuse declined among young persons aged 12 to 17 and remained stable among the general population, while drug abuse appeared to be at a lower level in Canada than in the United States. There was increased cocaine and heroin abuse in Mexico, although at a much lower level than in Canada and the United States.

4. The INCB noted the increased efforts being made by the governments of North America to reduce illicit drug demand.

South America

Three major developments were noted for South America:

1. The INCB noted that in spite of exceptional coca bush eradication efforts in Bolivia in 1998 and 1999 and a significant reduction of coca bush cultivation in Peru, the availability of coca leaf for the illicit manufacture of cocaine hydrochloride and its supply to markets in Europe and North America did not appear to have been reduced.
2. In Colombia, the deterioration of public safety in general and the fact that substantial illicit coca leaf production and cocaine manufacture were taking place in areas beyond government control hampered government efforts to control drug-trafficking activities.
3. The INCB claimed that all countries in South America had increased their efforts to intercept shipments of potassium permanganate destined for the illicit manufacture of cocaine.

Asia

Two major developments were noted:

1. In 1999, there was a major reduction in the total area under illicit opium poppy cultivation in Laos, Myanmar, Thailand, and Vietnam. China, Malaysia, and Thailand remained important illicit markets for heroin and also served as transit points for heroin destined for other parts of East and Southeast Asia, North America, and Oceania.
2. Both abuse of and trafficking in amphetamines were spreading quickly across the entire region of East and Southeast Asia. In the Golden Triangle, facilities that were once used exclusively for the refining of heroin were increasingly being used for the manufacture of methamphetamine as well. China, moreover, had remained a major source of amphetamine-type stimulants.

South Asia

Three major developments were noted for this region:

1. Because of the region's proximity to Afghanistan and Myanmar, the two principal opium-producing countries, drug trafficking and drug abuse were mainly transit-related. There had been a rise in drug abuse in the region, where there appeared to be millions of drug abusers, and,

while cannabis and opium had traditionally been the main drugs consumed, the abuse of heroin and synthetic drugs was increasing rapidly.

2. Certain areas had emerged as major drug-trafficking centers: these included the Chittagong port area in Bangladesh, the northeastern part of India (the states of Manipur, Mizoram, and Nagaland), and the Indo-Pakistan border area, especially Punjab and Chandigarh, as well as Mumbai and New Delhi.

3. Both India and Sri Lanka were being confronted with increasing numbers of drug-related court cases and prisoners, and their systems were unable to cope, with the result that both governments were considering the increasing use of alternative measures for drug abusers, such as treatment and rehabilitation.

West Asia

This region appeared to face a range of acute and growing problems:

1. In Afghanistan, cultivation of the opium poppy spread into areas that had previously not been used for this purpose, and there was a sharp increase in opium production in 1999 over 1998 to a record level of 4,670 tonnes (4,600 tons), making Afghanistan the principal world source of supply.

2. The proclaimed commitment of the Taliban in Afghanistan to ban opium poppy cultivation and heroin manufacture remained open to question. Furthermore, heroin manufacture had moved from Pakistan to Afghanistan.

3. Most countries in West Asia were used as transit points for opiates originating in Afghanistan and destined for Europe. Cannabis and precursors were also being transited through these countries.

4. There was a rapid spread of illicit crop cultivation and trafficking in the Central Asian countries of Kazakhstan, Kyrgyzstan, Tajikistan, Turkmenistan, and Uzbekistan, and the Caucasus countries of Armenia, Azerbaijan, and Georgia.

5. The largest share of drugs from Afghanistan was being transported through Iran to Turkey or from Pakistan to Iran and then to other countries in the Gulf for further transshipment. Turkey remained the major transit country for heroin destined for Europe.

6. Iran had made significant efforts to intercept illicit consignments of drugs en route from Afghanistan to Turkey, member states of the CIS, and Europe.

7. The Caspian Sea was being used increasingly for the transit of drugs from Afghanistan through Turkmenistan to Russia and Europe.

8. The abuse of opiates continued to rise in Afghanistan and Iran, while heroin abuse in Pakistan remained at a very high level.

Europe

Europe remained one of the two principal drug-consuming regions of the world:

1. There had been a considerable increase in the availability of cannabis.
2. There was an increase in cocaine seizures, but lower prices had led to an increase of cocaine abuse.
3. There was a rise in the abuse of synthetic drugs, particularly amphetamine and amphetamine-type stimulants.
4. The INCB was satisfied that the number of heroin abusers in most Western European countries was declining, although heroin abuse was becoming an increasing problem in Eastern Europe.

Oceania

Four major developments were noted:

1. In Australia, the average age of first-time users of heroin had fallen below 18 years of age.
2. There was an extensive public debate in Australia regarding the drugs problem.
3. In 1999, the government of New Zealand passed legislation to control benzodiazopines.
4. A survey of drug abuse in Papua New Guinea showed that the level of cannabis abuse was quite high.

UNDCP *World Drug Report*

The United Nations *World Drug Report 2000*[4] might be described as an attempt to promote hope against a background that precludes optimism. Like all UN reports, it is well produced, is supported by a wealth of research and detailed information, and covers an astonishing range of subject matter. The first chapter provides an overview covering recent trends in production, trafficking, and consumption. Throughout the latter half of the 1990s, we are told, global illicit production of opium, the raw material for heroin, remained stable, while production of the coca leaf declined. This might be seen as good news, when in fact, it is an acceptance of a saturated market; certainly, anyone seeking these drugs had no problem finding them. Despite a huge increase in Afghanistan's opium production in 1999, the general increase in opium during the 1990s was far more moderate than that of the

1980s, when output tripled. Coca leaf production had also tripled during the 1980s, and cocaine manufacture had quadrupled. Given that the real surge in drug consumption got underway in the 1970s and soared during the 1980s, such figures are unsurprising. The real question is whether the leveling off in the late 1990s means that drug-taking is on the wane, or whether it has leveled out for the time being, which would seem a more likely explanation.

The extent of drug abuse is examined, and here the report admits the difficulties involved in attempting to estimate hidden populations (of drug abusers). It provides the following figures for the late 1990s: Globally, on an annual basis, there were 180 million people who were drug abusers and of these, 144.1 million used cannabis; 28.7 million used amphetamines, including ecstasy; 14 million used cocaine; and 13.5 million used opiates (and of these, 9.2 million used heroin). (Note that the total number of drug users is more than the sum of users of individual drugs because users often take more than one substance.) This indicates that 3 percent of the world population were deemed to be drug abusers by the United Nations. However, such figures must be examined with care when the term "abuse" is considered. Are all cannabis smokers abusing the drug or are some, probably a majority, simply enjoying it? The same query must be applied to the other, hard drugs. How many of the 180 million people are in control of their drug-taking as opposed to being controlled by the drugs they take? In relation to cannabis smoking, the numbers of people in Oceania, the Americas, and Africa are above the global average (at least double the global prevalence rate), while Europe and Asia are close to the global average. In relation to amphetamine abuse, only Oceania is seen as above the global average in its consumption. The picture for ecstasy abuse is markedly different, with Oceania, Europe, and the Americas above the global average, while Africa and Asia are below it. There is another shift in relation to cocaine abuse, with consumption in the Americas and Oceania above the global average, Europe and Africa at the global average, and Asia below it. The estimated number of opiate abusers shows Oceania, Europe, and Asia above the global average, while the Americas and Africa are below it. If heroin abusers are taken separately, consumption in Oceania, Europe, and Asia is above the global average; in the Americas consumption is at the global average level, while in Africa it is below it.

Chapter 2 of the report deals with questions of demand reduction: epidemiology, prevention, and treatment. Most research to date, unsurprisingly perhaps, has been conducted in Northern America, Europe, and Australia; those areas certainly face all the modern problems of drug taking, and the largest funds made available for research have been in the United States. The term "epidemiology," meaning a disease in a society, has been applied to the drug habit. The difficulty here is that it is applied to all the people who take drugs, thus bringing the discussion into a highly emotional and political arena. The official U.S. reaction to the 1998 letter quoted above (the initiative of the Lindesmith Center), signed by 500 eminent people worldwide, was to dismiss their opinion that the current war on drugs was causing more problems than it solved and to imply that their view was too "liberal" (harking back to the 1950s), but did such a dismissive attitude make sense? Are the world's 180 million "drug abusers" all diseased? Or are at least a significant proportion of them doing what they want to do in exactly the same way as smokers or drinkers? This is a debate to which we must frequently return.

Arguments about vulnerability are a crucial and highly emotional part of the overall debate since these begin with children or young persons. As the report outlines the case, the strongest influences on initial drug use are the family and peer groups. The influence of the family, the style of parenting, the quality of the parent–child relationship—each plays a part, as do factors such as poverty. Young people are liable to be most at risk at adolescence, when they switch from family-oriented values to peer-group values. Children, youths, parents, and families, therefore, are major targets for early prevention efforts. Here we face major social problems, often peculiar to rich Western societies, which have witnessed severe weakening of family ties and parental controls, although such trends are spreading rapidly to other parts of the world where Western materialism has become if not the norm, at least the aim. The report also deals with social reintegration and aftercare following treatment for drug addiction.

The United Nations puts great emphasis, rightly, on alternative development (to producing drugs), and this is the subject of the report's third chapter. The chapter begins: "Today the possibility of any sustained eradication of illicit crops is usually met with a skeptical response." The report claims a growing and sustained success in crop elimination. Interestingly, at the beginning of the twentieth century, the annual opium output was 20,000 tonnes (19,680 tons)—as opposed to 4,800 tonnes (4,720 tons) at the end of the century—and the bulk of that was produced in China. Today China annually produces about 20 tonnes (19.7 tons) of licit opium and almost no illicit opium. Illicit cultivation has been practically nonexistent for 50 years. That, clearly, was the achievement of a totalitarian communist regime, which carried out a massive campaign between 1950 and 1952 to extinguish opium production and consumption, and as such opens up intriguing questions for consideration in countries such as the United States or Britain that are putting increasing efforts into fighting the drugs war against a political background that insists on the liberty of the individual. In 1949 newly independent India initiated a program to prohibit the nonmedical use of opium and at the end of 10 years had virtually eliminated the illicit production of opium.

In more recent years eradication programs have been successfully carried out in Iran, Thailand, Pakistan, Lebanon, and Guatemala. However, with constant or growing world demand, the elimination of one source of a drug often acts as a stimulus to open up a new source that previously had not been a player, or had been only a minor player, in drug production. Thus, when Turkey, Iran, and India largely eliminated opium production, their places were taken by Afghanistan and Pakistan. Demand, or market forces, will usually ensure that the closure of one source is replaced by the development of another.

Alternative development projects achieved considerable success during the 1990s. In Bolivia, for example, 50,000 hectares (123,560 acres) of land were under coca production in 1997 and of these, 12,000 hectares (29,650 acres) were licit cultivation. A program of elimination meant that Bolivia began the year 2000 with only 10,000 hectares (24,710 acres) of illicit cultivation remaining, which also meant that the country had reduced illicit coca cultivation by 78 percent over three years, with income from illegal coca falling from $425 million in 1988 (8.5 percent of GDP) to $86 million in 1999 (about 1 percent of GDP). Peru also achieved a comparable reduction over the 1990s. In 1992, 129,000 hectares (318,770 acres) were producing illicit coca leaves; by 1999 the figure had been reduced to 38,000 hectares (93,900 acres). In Pakistan, opium poppy cultivation was reduced from about 800 tonnes (787 tons) in 1980 to 9 tonnes (8.9 tons) in 1999. There were other success stories in Laos and Thailand. To be effective, alternative development programs must fit in with national development priorities. They will be most likely to succeed if there is a sustainable economic environment that makes illicit cultivation unattractive; if the government is in full control of the areas that formerly produced illicit crops and insurgent groups that might thrive on illicit production have been eliminated or reduced; and if there is constant government pressure not to produce illicit crops in the form of law enforcement measures, eradication programs, and alternative sources of income.

These relatively upbeat messages from the United Nations have to be offset against what is actually happening on the ground. Successful eradication programs have to be measured against the continuing availability of drugs, the number of drug abusers worldwide (have their numbers increased, decreased, or remained static?), the level of drug-related crimes, the easy availability of drugs, and so on. During the course of a particular year, the British authorities, for example, may claim record seizures of cocaine or cannabis, but does this mean that those who seek these drugs have been unable to obtain them? Leaving aside, for the moment, the debate as to whether the war on drugs as waged by the United Nations, the United States, Britain, and other countries is the best way of tackling the problem, have the momentum of the war and the successes recorded in country eradication programs made any real difference to the flow of drugs to the main drug markets? This is not to decry the achievements of anti-drugs programs, but any examination of UN documents and reports relating to the international drugs trade suggests two ongoing phenomena: an entrenched state of warfare not unlike the stalemate trench warfare of World War I; and an expectation that the present state of affairs, though changing tactically from one country or region to another, is going to be with us for a long time to come.

As an addendum to the above consideration of the UN approach to the problems associated with drugs, the United Nations Special Session on HIV/AIDS, held in New York over June 25–27, 2001, considered the relationship between drug use and HIV/AIDS and pointed out that the spread of the HIV/AIDS pandemic was often closely related to drug use. In its preparatory papers for the special session, the United Nations made the following points:

1. The use of drugs is a universal phenomenon, and there is increasing evidence that drug use is playing a major role in the spread of HIV/AIDS.

2. Those most at risk are injecting drug users who share needles and other contaminated equipment, which is a highly effective way of transmitting the virus from one person to another.

3. Mind-altering drugs are also associated with behavior that can increase the risk of HIV infection, and the lack of inhibition that goes with the use of some drugs may result in unprotected sex or coerced sex.

4. Alcohol, perhaps the most widely used drug of all, is also associated with risky sexual behavior and the spread of HIV.

5. In reverse, drug use may arise from HIV infection, since people living with the infection may resort to drugs as a way of coping with the problems arising from their infection.

6. Injecting drug users rank among the groups most vulnerable to HIV/AIDS, since they are often also poor and marginalized.

7. Injecting drug use is a rapidly growing phenomenon in all regions and, most recently, in Africa. It is now estimated that about 10 percent of HIV infections globally result from injecting drug use, and in some European and Asian countries, more than half of HIV infections result from injecting drug use.

8. In 1992, 80 countries reported injecting drug use within their borders; the figure had risen to 136 by the year 2000.

9. Countries should implement a comprehensive package of care for HIV prevention among drug users.

10. A project to prevent drug use and HIV infection has operated successfully in Brazil since 1994. It targets at-risk teenagers as well as injecting drug users and has reached more than 100,000 students.

Few problems can be isolated; they impinge upon each other. The relationship between drug use and the spread of AIDS has become increasingly clear; it is an area where education and preventive action rather than criminalization are most likely to have an impact.

3
The Drugs

Principal Illicit Drugs

The range of illicit drugs is wide, and new drugs, usually created by adding synthetic substances to an existing drug, periodically increase availability and provide another name and a new experience to add to the list. The principal illicit drugs that feature in the "war on drugs" are listed below—beginning with soft drugs, and moving on to hard drugs—with brief details of their alternate names, prices, availability, and effects.

Cannabis

The most popular drug worldwide, cannabis is also known as blow, dope, ganja, grass, hash, marijuana, pot, skunk, and weed. It is principally used by teenagers and young people, often in combination with other substances. Hash is the brown solidified resin of the cannabis plant; grass is the dried leaves of the cannabis plant. Small numbers of cannabis smokers are now believed to take it with heroin. It is usually smoked in a joint or spliff; it is also eaten in cakes, and a dose will give a high of between one and two hours and induce a sense of relaxation, enhanced well-being, and happiness. Users claim it gives them increased intuitive insights. The aftereffects or lows include lethargy, paranoia, and the weakening of short-term memory. Under the Misuse of Drugs Act 1971, it is currently controlled as a Class B drug in Britain, but in July 2002 the home secretary, David Blunkett, announced plans to downgrade it to a Class C drug by July 2003. Perhaps one-fifth of the population (in Britain) has smoked cannabis; it is the most commonly used illegal drug. Many people do not consider cannabis to be dangerous, and often users will smoke it openly. It is widely available, and at the end of the 1990s, £15 (in Britain) would purchase enough resin for 10 to 20 joints or smokes. There are many—and apparently increasing—sources of cannabis, which is produced in countries across the globe.

Campaigns in the United States and Britain have been mounted to legalize cannabis, and the medical professions in both countries claim it has medicinal uses and benefits. A British Medical Association (BMA) report claims that 400 chemical constituents of cannabis can help control nausea and that it is helpful for cancer sufferers.[1] It assists in pain relief. Further claims suggest it can help control convulsive movements and glaucoma. Despite a growing number of public figures in both the United States and Britain arguing for the legalization of cannabis, the authorities in both countries have maintained a steady opposition to the suggestion (see chapter 18). Millions of people worldwide smoke cannabis for recreational purposes, and they have little difficulty in obtaining supplies.

LSD

Lysergic acid diethylamide—acid, blotter, flash, Lucy, tab, or trips—is generally available in the form of brown tablets or blotting paper soaked in chemicals and is taken by swallowing. LSD became popular in the 1960s and is still popular with that (older) drug-taking generation. It is widely available and used by about 14 percent of young people worldwide because of its low cost—in Britain, £1.50 to £3 a dose. Users achieve heightened perceptions, aural and visual hallucinations, and a sense of profundity. It can also result in "bad trips"—depression, acute paranoia, and anxiety. Its regular use may affect long-term mental health. It also causes flashbacks and may lead users to believe they have superhuman abilities and can fly, resulting in death or injury. It is a Class A drug, carrying in Britain a maximum penalty of seven years in prison.

Hallucinogens

Hallucinogenic mushrooms, mushies or magic mushrooms, or liberty cap mushrooms are picked in the wild. They are usually dried and swallowed raw, or cooked in food, or made into tea. Their effect is similar to that of LSD, while their "hangover" effect, if regularly used, may be depression or paranoia. They are only illegal if prepared for eating. They are picked rather than purchased.

Hallucinogenic drugs from the Amazon rainforest may be used as a powerful medicine against gut parasites and have been prescribed by tribal medicine men to meet both medicinal and spiritual needs. Professor Eloy Rodriquez of Cornell University, New York, gave details in 1998 of his work in a part of the Amazon jungle in Venezuela where he and his researchers identified more than 100 species of plant that were used for purposes other than food: deterring parasites and predators, fighting disease, and putting people into a trance. Two such plants are the passiflora (passion flower), whose leaves are used to make a drink; and a legume, the yopo, which produces bean pods that are ground into a snuff and snorted. They are both hallucinogenic and act as powerful purgatives.

Solvents

Solvents or gases such as glue or lighter fuel are cheap and sold in retail stores; their fumes are inhaled to give a high that may last from 15 to 45 minutes and result in feelings of euphoria or unreality, similar to drunkenness. Solvent or glue sniffing can lead to dependency, while heavy use may lead to brain damage. It is illegal to sell such solvents to minors knowing they intend to use them as a drug. They are mainly used by schoolchildren since they are inexpensive. They can cause death, or damage to the liver, kidneys, or brain.

Amphetamines

Amphetamines are referred to as speed, sulphate, whizz, or the poor man's cocaine. They are usually provided in wraps of powder, which is snorted up the nose, smoked in a cigarette, or taken as a pill or capsule. Hardcore users inject it. The high may last from six to eight hours. It is a powerful stimulant, which produces a rush of energy, delays sleep, diminishes fatigue, and heightens endurance (amphetamines were developed to improve troop performance in Vietnam). Regular use may cause nervousness, anxiety, and paranoia. Lows resulting from the use of amphetamines include lethargy and depression. It can be psychologically addictive and may cause panic attacks and sometimes heart failure. Amphetamines are illegal unless prescribed medically and are normally designated a Class B drug unless prepared for injection, when they are classified as an A drug. They cost between £10 and £20 a gram.

Ecstasy

Ecstasy is referred to, among other names, as Adam, brownies, burgers, E, MDMA (methylenedioxymethamphetamine), rhubarb and custard, or XTC. It comes in capsule and tablet form and is swallowed. Frequently used in clubs to improve dancing, ecstasy creates sensations of universal love and boundless energy. It is mainly taken by youths in their late teens or early twenties. The ecstasy available to users is often of poor quality, and this has led them to search for alternatives. Some high-profile deaths as a result of taking the drug led to a falloff in demand in Britain during the late 1990s. The main danger from ecstasy is overheating caused by frenetic dancing. Tablets typically cost between £10 and £25 each, but the price can be much lower. Ecstasy is an illegal Class A drug.

There has been little detailed study of the effects of ecstasy in Britain, far more in the United States. Dr. John Henry of the National Poisons Information Unit at Guy's Hospital, London, is the only scientist in Britain with a license to provide pure ecstasy. He claims that the polarization of the debate between

opponents and those who would legalize drugs, or at least soften the laws relating to them, is inhibiting necessary research. As Dr. Henry claims, "It's a
very important subject that deserves study. If we have anywhere between
50,000 and 500,000 people taking it every weekend, there's a need to know
what it does in the majority of cases."[2] Other studies have revealed that mid-
week depression between weekend ecstasy taking is common.

A powerful derivative of ecstasy, known as "DOB" or "Golden Eagle"
and up to 33 times the strength of ecstasy, began to be sold in Britain in 1998
and caused several deaths. According to the National Criminal Intelligence
Service, an increasing number of dealers were reported to be manufacturing
and selling the new drug. It was developed in the United States as a possible
antidepressant and is sometimes called "flatliners" because it provides an
out-of-body experience. Recipes for making synthetic drugs can be found on
the Internet. There are 36 derivatives of ecstasy that are currently legal to
possess, but in 1998 the British government's Home Office considered placing them all under the control of the Misuse of Drugs legislation and making
them Class A drugs.

Cocaine

Cocaine is known by a number of names—C, Charlie, coke, dust, lady,
snow, white—and typically costs between £50 and £70 a gram. It is usually
taken in the form of white powder, which is snorted, injected, or rubbed on
the gums. Crack is a smokeable form of cocaine made into small lumps or
"rocks." Cocaine has made a comeback in recent years, is fashionable, and is
often used by celebrities and media people. Crack rocks, costing around £10
to £20 each, on the other hand, are considered a loser's drug and are popular
among addicts and the poor. One gram of powder may last the night, depending on the user. A high will give feelings of omnipotence. The drug re-
duces the need to eat and sleep and leads to subtle changes of behavior.
Cocaine can be highly addictive, and constant use can cause exhaustion,
anxiety, weight loss, collapsed nasal passages, and heart failure. Crack is
more addictive than powder. By the beginning of the new century cocaine
had dramatically increased in popularity, and the huge profits from the drug
allowed the price to come down despite periodic hauls of large cocaine assignments by police and customs on both sides of the Atlantic. The profit
margins make it very popular with dealers. Cocaine is a Class A drug.

Heroin

Also known as boy, brown, china white, dragon, H, horse, skag, and smack,
heroin comes in the form of a white powder that is derived from the opium
poppy. Street heroin has a brownish tinge. It can be smoked, sniffed, injected, or inhaled. A high will last up to three hours and induces an instant

sense of pleasure, cocooned warmth, euphoria, and contentment, while mind and body functions remain unimpaired. It is highly addictive and a low can lead to withdrawal symptoms, including sweats, vomiting, or coma; a pure dose can kill. The sharing of needles carries a high risk of spreading HIV. A gram will typically cost between £80 and £100. It is a Class A illegal drug.

Heroin's popularity has risen in recent times, and the flow of the drug into Europe increased sharply during the last years of the twentieth century. Most of the heroin entering Europe comes from Afghanistan and Pakistan via Turkey, while Colombia and Mexico are increasingly becoming sources of heroin for the North American market.

Opium is the natural drug from which heroin is derived and is one of the most important of all medicinal drugs. A description of opium from the nineteenth-century *Imperial Dictionary* of the English language is worth quoting in full:

> The inspissated juice of the white poppy (cultivated principally in Hindustan and Asiatic Turkey). It flows from incisions made in the head of the plant and the best flows from the finest incision. It is one of the most energetic narcotics and at the same time one of the most precious of all medicines. It is employed in a great variety of cases but most commonly for the purpose of procuring sleep and relief from pain. Its habitual use is attended by similar or worse effects than the intemperate use of ardent spirits. A full dose is intoxicating and exhilarating but its effects are dangerous and fatal if taken in large quantities. It is heavy, of a dense texture, of a brownish yellow color, not perfectly dry, but easily receiving an impression from the finger; it has a faint smell and its taste is bitter and acrid. The chief active principle of opium is morphia, or morphine in combination with meconic acid. Opium also contains narcotine, narceine, codeine, gum resin, extractive matter, and small portions of other proximate principles. The principal part of our [British] supply of opium comes from Turkey. It is imported in flat pieces or cakes covered with leaves, and the capsules of some species of Pumex.

In 1998 it was revealed that scientists were working to create a fungus to destroy opium poppies as part of the war against the heroin trade. The strain, while allowing the poppies to grow, would decimate the quantity of opium they can produce. At the Institute of Genetics in Tashkent, Uzbekistan, a strain of the fungus *Pleospora papaveracea* has been developed; it would be sprayed over opium fields, and there are plans to produce large quantities of the fungus in industrial fermenters. Uzbekistan is situated on the edge of the Golden Crescent of Afghanistan, Iran, Turkey, and Pakistan, where much of the world's supply of opium is grown and turned into heroin. Both Britain and the United States are involved in this anti-heroin initiative. As always, in the drugs war, nothing is as simple or as straightforward as it might seem. A

Western-developed fungus that destroys crops in an Islamic country may well come to be described as part of an attempt to wage biological warfare against poor farmers in those countries. According to the director of the International Institute of Biological Control at Ascot in England, Dr. Jeff Waage, the United Nations has been investigating a range of fungi to be used against opium poppies or other illicit drug crops. Dr. Waage said, "In principle, you could produce the naturally occurring diseases of poppies artificially, and I understand this is what they are doing. There are about four or five commercially available fungal herbicides which do much the same job on weeds."[3]

Yaba

Periodically a new drug enters the world market. Toward the end of 1999, for example, a drug called "yaba," which had become more popular than heroin in the Far East, began to traverse Asia to the European market. The drug, which creates an intense hallucinogenic effect and enables users to stay awake for days, is derived from work carried out by German chemists during World War II under instructions from Hitler to find a stimulant that would make it possible for his soldiers to fight around the clock. In 1999 experts warned that the producers of yaba in the Golden Triangle were targeting the drug at Britain in particular. Samples of the drug were seized in Britain, France, and Ireland, and there was also some evidence that illegal laboratories in Britain were attempting to make it. Regular use of the drug leads to lung and kidney disorders, hallucinations, and paranoia, while those coming off the drug are subject to severe depression and suicidal urges. Demand for yaba in Britain has been fueled by the reports of returning vacationers who have claimed that it produces intense highs. Yaba is a derivative of synthetic amphetamines such as speed and can be manufactured far more quickly than other traditional forms of amphetamine. All its principal ingredients—salt, household cleaning products, distilled cold medicines, and lithium from camera batteries—can be purchased legally. It was thought that at the end of 1999, it took £300 worth of raw materials to produce yaba valued at £2,000, British street value. The drug can be made easily in a couple of casserole dishes, so the possibility of the police tracking a laboratory is slight.

Possession and supply of yaba was criminalized in Thailand in 1970, forcing the market underground. By the mid-1990s seizures of yaba had overtaken those of heroin. In Thailand the Public Health Ministry revealed that the number of students requiring rehabilitation as a result of taking yaba had risen by 970 percent over two years, and by 1999 about five times more yaba than heroin was being produced in the Golden Triangle, most of it in Myanmar (Burma), while approximately 400 million pills of yaba were smuggled across the border into Thailand in a year. The Thai authorities esti-

mated that up to two-thirds of the crimes committed in Bangkok were related to the use of yaba.[4]

Ketamine

Ketamine hydrochloride, known as K or special K, is a general anesthetic for
human and veterinary use. Ketamine has been likened to the synthetic drug
PCP (Phencyclidine; also originally manufactured as a veterinary anesthetic)
and produces effects similar to LSD. Users tout its trip as better than that of
PCP or LSD because its overt hallucinatory effects are short, lasting an hour
or less. However, the drug can affect the senses, judgment, and coordination
for a period of 18 to 24 hours. Ketamine sold on the streets comes from diverted legitimate supplies, primarily veterinary clinics. Its appearance is
similar to that of pharmaceutical-grade cocaine, and it is snorted, placed in
alcoholic beverages, or smoked in combination with marijuana. The incidence of ketamine abuse is increasing, and accounts appear in reports of rave
parties attended by teenagers.

Ritalin

Ritalin, or methylpheridate, is an amphetamine-type drug. It is prescribed
for children with attention deficit hyperactivity disorder (ADHD) in order to
calm them down. Early in 1999 the UN INCB claimed that the use of Ritalin
had risen by 100 percent in more than 50 countries over the preceding year.
The INCB warned that without checks, the use of Ritalin in Britain could
reach the same as U.S. levels. In the United States an estimated 4 million
children take the drug, including some as young as 1 year old, and in some
schools up to 40 percent of children in some classes are using it. Critics of its
use in Britain argued that doctors were creating classrooms of zombies. The
number of prescriptions for the drug rose from 2,000 in 1991 to 92,000 in
1998. In its report the INCB called on the governments of Britain and 10
other countries to "seek out possible over-diagnosis of ADD [attention
deficit disorder] and curb excessive use."

The results of a study, published in *The Observer* of September 9, 2001,
demonstrated that Ritalin exercises a more potent effect on the brain than cocaine. Using brain imaging, scientists found that in pill form Ritalin occupies
more of the neural transporters responsible for the "high" experienced by addicts than does smoked or injected cocaine. Dr. Nora Volkow, a psychiatrist
and imaging expert at the Brookhaven National Laboratory in Upton, New
York, who led the study, said that Ritalin, if injected into the veins as a liquid
rather than taken as a pill, produces a rush that "addicts like very much."
Interviewed in the *Journal of the American Medical Association*, she said:
"They think it is like cocaine." In pill form, Ritalin still blocked more of the

brain transporters that affect mood change, and had a greater potency in the brain, than cocaine. Researchers were shocked by these findings, which clearly showed that the notion that Ritalin is a weak stimulant is completely incorrect. Cocaine blocks about 50 percent of the brain transporters to leave a surfeit of dopamine (a chemical transmitter produced in the brain's "pleasure centers") in the system, and it is this surfeit that provides the "hit" that addicts seek. Now it appears that Ritalin has the effect of blocking 20 percent more of these autoreceptors. As Nora Volkow said: "As a psychiatrist I sometimes feel embarrassed [about the lack of knowledge] because this is by far the drug we prescribe most frequently to children." What was not clear was why Ritalin, which has been administered to children for more than 40 years, had not produced large numbers of addicted schoolchildren. Indeed, opponents of Ritalin believe it may be addictive as well as having dangerous side effects.

Unease about the use of Ritalin appeared to be growing in the light of these and other disclosures about the drug. Janice Hill, of the Overload Support Network, a British charity for parents of children with behavioral problems, said: "Now we have thousands of children in Scotland taking a drug that is more potent than cocaine. What does it take before the situation is thoroughly investigated?"

ADHD has been described as a fraudulent title for a nonexistent condition that would once have been put down to the natural exuberance of youth. It could be argued that Ritalin is simply a drug designed to keep lively children quiet, presumably for the benefit of educators and adults more generally. The application of a drug to force children (or anyone else) to pay attention by "dumbing down" their hyperactivity seems most dubious and comes close to the application in Aldous Huxley's 1932 novel *Brave New World* of the soma pill to keep the masses happy.

Arguments about Ritalin will undoubtedly continue. The use of the drug does raise acute questions about our entire Western drug culture. To prescribe young children a drug whose psychopharmacological effects have been described as similar to cocaine would seem to be the antithesis of everything the war on drugs is supposed to be about. It could be said that the use of Ritalin represents one of the most glaring anomalies in the Western approach to drugs: On the one hand adults take drugs to help them relax, and this is against the law; on the other hand responsible adults prescribe Ritalin to children to make them less exuberant and more pliable. If the first use of drugs is wrong, the second use cannot be right.

A Few Considerations

In Britain, in the nine years preceding 1998, the street price of most drugs either fell or remained fairly static, which suggested that the authorities—customs or police—were failing to prevent traffickers from saturating the market. Moreover, during the same period the number of people sentenced for drug smuggling dropped from 1,500 a year to 1,000 a year. The National Audit Office suggested that customs and excise had not succeeded in restricting the supply of drugs, even though in the last year of this nine-year period they had seized drugs valued at £3.3 billion and broken 130 smuggling rings. Despite these achievements, their efforts did not appear to have impaired the street availability of drugs, and it was estimated that the authorities had only managed to seize 10 percent of the drugs coming into the country. Furthermore, prices of drugs, in most cases, had either dropped or remained stable: The price of synthetic drugs had dropped by 40 percent (after inflation), cocaine by 20 percent, and heroin and herbal cannabis prices had remained the same. Only cannabis resin had increased in price, by approximately one-third. In contrast, the prices for alcohol and tobacco over the same nine years had increased by about two-thirds. This price pattern, when more people were known to be taking drugs, indicated an expanding supply. Despite the number of traffickers arrested, it was clear that other operators could be found without difficulty to replace them. The Office of National Statistics estimated that the illegal drugs market in Britain had reached an annual value of £8.6 billion and that drug dealing had become Britain's largest illegal activity.

Meanwhile, in a few selected countries the expansion of illegal drug activities had led to a noticeable hardening of government attitudes. Thus in the Netherlands, where those over age 18 had been allowed up to 30 grams (1.1 oz.) of cannabis for personal use in 1976, this was cut back to only five grams (0.2 oz.) in 1996. In Sweden, which had relaxed laws relating to soft drugs in 1968, with no penalty for personal use of cannabis, in 1995 the government announced some of the toughest drug laws in Europe, including stringent penalties for the possession of even small quantities of all controlled drugs. In 1982 Spain had decriminalized all soft drugs for personal use, but in 1995, recognizing that 70 percent of violent crimes were drug-related, the government introduced stiffer sentences for dealing in soft drugs and for possession of hard drugs, although personal possession of soft drugs remained legal. In Switzerland, in the early 1980s, the Zurich authorities had set up a "needle park" for hard-drug users where drugs and equipment could be exchanged without prosecution. In 1995, however, the police stormed "needle park" when the Swiss authorities decided to end their liberal policy and made all possession and use of all controlled drugs illegal. In 1975 the state of Alaska decriminalized the personal use of cannabis, but in 1986 (an earlier reversal than those in Europe) the law was reversed after it was found that drug usage among teenagers was three times the U.S. average.[5]

The 2000 U.S. movie *Traffic* demonstrated, among other things, that drug addiction is anything but sexy. In all the debates about drugs, addicts are either depicted as morally corrupt, weak-willed, and both a drain on society's resources and the cause—directly or indirectly—of crime; or they are seen to be victims suffering from a disease who are targeted by criminals. As Dr. Alan Leshner of the National Institute on Drug Abuse at the National Institutes of Health, Bethesda, Maryland, has said: "If we're to get a handle on this problem, we have to rise above our moral indignation and this kind of duality—biology versus culture, a victim versus a morally corrupt person." Dr. Leshner points out that addicts are compelled to use drugs and have no control over their use, even in the face of negative consequences. Moreover, he suggests that more and more scientific research indicates that drugs really do alter the mind to create an unnatural brain state by changing brain chemistry. Another expert, Dr. Roy Wise, from the Intramural Research Program at the National Institute on Drug Abuse in Baltimore, Maryland, says, "One way to understand the biology of drug-taking is to look at the brain," and he refers to the chemical transmitter dopamine, which is produced in the "pleasure centers" of the brain: "Dopamine plays a critical role in the ability of various pleasures of the flesh to motivate behavior." Dr. Wise argues that experiments with mice show that the same pleasure repeated many times does not continue to be as rewarding as in the first instance and that this is the key to drug addiction: Only more of the drug can provide pleasure equivalent to the first experience. A third scientist, Dr. Nora Volkow studied dopamine levels in human beings by imaging people's brains. She said: "We would all feel pleasure if we took drugs, but we would not all keep taking the drug until addiction." She was undertaking research to determine what gets addicts hooked in the first place and why addicts are addicts. In an experiment, Dr. Volkow found that half the people to whom she gave an amphetamine liked it and half did not, and that those who did not like it had a high level of dopamine receptors, while those who did like the drug had a low level of dopamine receptors and took to the drug to increase their natural dopamine. Thus, in part at least, reaction to drugs depends on individual chemistry. These and other researchers sought to discover ways to control or prevent addiction. However, Dr. Charles O'Brian from Penn State University, Philadelphia, Pennsylvania, has suggested that there might never be a cure for addiction. He believes that drugs used to help addicts—Naltrexone for alcoholics and heroin addicts, Baclofen for cocaine abuse, or Bupropion for smokers—have to be used in conjunction with therapy and support groups and that "the best they can do is buy time to help addicts learn new, more helpful responses to their addiction."[6]

The European Scenario at the End of 1999

Europe as a market for illicit drugs is rapidly catching up with the United States and is being increasingly targeted by drug traffickers from all the main source regions. Despite strong anti-drugs measures in some European countries, the picture is by no means an even one, and the multiplicity of borders as well as the open borders within the European Union make the work of traffickers easier and that of customs controls harder. Moreover, the rapidly changing economic and political scene—increasing wealth, the easing of movement following the end of the Cold War, the huge disruptions caused by the Balkan wars following the breakup of Yugoslavia, as well as rapidly altering social values—makes Europe an especially vulnerable region for increased drug consumption, which grew at significant rates throughout the 1990s. If we take the four main drug groups, it is possible to see the extent to which new conditions have encouraged a growth of drug trafficking.

Heroin

Southwest Asia, especially Afghanistan, is the principal source of heroin entering the European market and probably now accounts for 90 percent of the total; seizures from the countries of the Golden Triangle have dropped off and as yet not much is reaching Europe from Latin America. Most of the heroin reaching Europe comes overland through Pakistan and Iran, and across Turkey to Istanbul, which is the main gateway for heroin into Europe. The drug syndicates to either side of Istanbul coordinate their activities carefully, and most of the drugs are carried by road on the auto routes that cross Europe. The breakup of Yugoslavia and the chaotic conditions that have affected that part of the Balkans through the 1990s into the new century have been of enormous importance to drug-trafficking operations; often drug gangs are based on ethnic affinities, and the Balkans have become the forward distribution area for Western Europe. A number of Balkan drug routes are used: Istanbul through Greece, Bulgaria, or Romania to the Czech Republic, Hungary, or Slovakia and then to the main Western European markets; or through Montenegro, Bosnia, Croatia, and Slovenia into Western Europe. Greece also acts as the transit country for drugs destined for Italy and Southern Europe. Turkish seizures in 1998 of drugs on the border with Georgia pointed to the development of a new Caucasus route for traffickers. The principal markets for the heroin are Belgium, Britain, France, Germany, Italy, the Netherlands, Spain, and Switzerland, as well as the Nordic countries. Centrally placed between the Balkans and Western Europe, Germany has become a major crossroads for the traffic in heroin, while the Netherlands is another principal transit and redistribution center. The French Channel ports and the Channel Tunnel form a vital part of the network that supplies Britain. Much of the distribution in Britain is handled by Turkish gangs with direct links to the distributors operating out of Istanbul. Ethnic Albanian groups control the distribution of heroin in Switzerland, which is a lucrative market for the drug. The four Nordic countries—Denmark, Finland, Norway, and Sweden—have become growing heroin markets. European airport seizures became less common at the end of the 1990s, although new air routes were being developed through Moscow and the Central Asian countries of Kazakhstan, Turkmenistan, and Uzbekistan, which are increasingly used by couriers. Nigerians gangs, which have emerged as significant players in drug trafficking, have organized courier and express mail services from Thailand and Pakistan to recipients in North America, Africa, the Caribbean, and Europe.

Cocaine

Europe is the second-largest market for cocaine after the United States. The great bulk of the world's supply of cocaine comes from South America, and though cultivation of the coca leaf has declined sharply in Bolivia and Peru, where alternative crop substitution programs have achieved considerable success, this decline in production has been offset by a 50 percent increase in coca cultivation in Colombia, where between 610 and 711 tonnes (600 to 700 tons) of cocaine are produced on an annual basis. This has occurred despite the near collapse of the former all-powerful Cali and Medellín cartels due to successful law enforcement action by the government, backed by the United States. Separate groups now control the supply of cocaine for the North American market, where Mexico has become of increasing importance, and the supply of cocaine to Europe; this remains in the hands of the old cartels, which have established links with European networks. Four principal supply routes have been established across the Atlantic from the cocaine source in Colombia to Europe. The first route is through Spain, whose special ties with Latin America—history, language, and dual nationality arrangements—are used to assist this traffic, and shipments to Spain arrive as maritime cargo through its many ports. In some cases cocaine cargoes are transferred from cargo ships to speedboats, which can easily find offloading places on Spain's long coastline. The second route is through the various Caribbean islands, first as maritime cargo to Rotterdam, Europe's largest container port, in the Netherlands. These assignments are shipped through Surinam, Aruba, and the Dutch Antilles. Second, cargoes arrive in Britain through the container port of Felixstowe as well as being carried by couriers (returning vacationers) from such islands as Barbados. The size of this trade has been revealed by the extent of customs seizures and the uncovering of cocaine depots in the Netherlands and elsewhere. Third, the Colombian traffickers developed the Balkan route during the troubled 1990s, partly in response to increased British and Dutch controls at their main ports. Cocaine supplies have been shipped through Russia, Ukraine, Bulgaria, Croatia, and other Balkan countries or, sometimes, from Russia through the Baltic ports. The fourth route that has been developed passes through West Africa, mainly Nigeria, and growing ties have been established between the Colombian traffickers and Nigerian gangs. These latter groups have excellent links with Nigerians in major British towns such as London, Birmingham, or Manchester. In the period since 1994 and the end of sanctions, the opening up of South Africa has allowed Johannesburg in particular to develop as a major transit point for drugs from South America into Africa or north to Europe.

In 1998 the top 10 seizures of cocaine in Europe were in Amsterdam (2,808 kg/6,190 lb), Madrid (1,121 kg/2,470 lb), London (686 kg/1,510 lb), Rome (455 kg/1,000 lb), Frankfurt (298 kg/657 lb), Lisbon (290 kg/639 lb), Barcelona (177 kg/390 lb), Brussels (165 kg/364 lb), Paris (137 kg/302 lb), and Zurich (83 kg/183 lb). Other lesser seizures were made at many airports in Western Europe.

Cannabis

The most widely used drug in Europe is cannabis, whether in its resin form (hashish) or herbal form (marijuana). Morocco is Europe's first source of supply, and in 1998, for example, 80 percent of cannabis seizures in Europe came from that country. Most herbal cannabis comes from a number of other sources (as well as Morocco): Colombia, Nigeria, South Africa, Jamaica, and Southeast Asia (Thailand, Cambodia, and Laos). Albania provides substantial amounts of cannabis for Greece and Italy. In addition, a number of European countries—Britain, the Netherlands, Sweden, and Spain—have turned to the home hydroponic cultivation of cannabis. Source countries, particularly Morocco, are closer to Europe than are sources of other drugs such as heroin, and this makes the movement of the drug easier. The principal entry points into Europe are Spain, Italy, and France when the drug is imported by ferry or along auto routes. When it comes by container, the main ports of entry are Antwerp, Bremen, Dover, Felixstowe, Hamburg, Marseilles, and Rotterdam. The drug is transported in virtually all categories of road vehicles and most types of sea-going vessels. There appears to be no shortage of cannabis supply despite record hauls of illicit cargoes that are periodically made by the police. In 1998, for example, the Spanish authorities seized 396 tonnes (390 tons) of cannabis. Although particular countries can be singled out for extensive importing, distribution, and use of cannabis, in fact almost every European country is involved in the trade and use of this drug. Hashish from Southwest Asia is routed through Afghanistan, Iran, and Turkey, and also from Afghanistan through Uzbekistan and Turkmenistan and then through the Caucasus to Western Europe. As pressures by the authorities make a particular route more hazardous for the traffickers, a new route will be opened, for example, from Kabul to Sharjah in the Gulf and then to Frankfurt and Amsterdam. Herbal cannabis from Southeast Asia (Cambodia, for example) may be routed through Eastern Europe and the Balkans before it reaches its main Western European market. The different routes and the extent to which they are used, as well as the sources of the cannabis, are revealed by the official seizures that take place, yet despite the often frequent announcement of large consignments seized by customs or police, the drug keeps coming and the market for it is satisfied.

Synthetic Drugs

Synthetic drugs form the second-largest category of drugs consumed in Europe after cannabis. They include amphetamines and ecstasy. The countries of the European Union are the major producers of amphetamines and ecstasy, with the Netherlands, Belgium, Spain, Britain, and Germany as the principal producers, although the Netherlands is regarded as the leading source country. However, certain countries in Eastern Europe—Poland, Bulgaria, the Czech Republic, and the Baltic countries—are also emerging as increasingly important source countries. The Netherlands, in particular, is regarded as the biggest source country for ecstasy, while Britain is a major market for the drug. In addition, the Netherlands has now become a source country for ecstasy exported to the Far East, including Australia, Malaysia, Indonesia, Singapore, Thailand, and Hong Kong. There is also a growing U.S. market for ecstasy from the Netherlands. The various precursors and chemicals used in the production of cocaine, heroin, amphetamines, or ecstasy are widely produced in Europe as part of the legitimate pharmaceutical trade and, as such, are easy to obtain for illicit purposes.

The European market for the range of all the main drugs is growing and, despite highly successful hauls of illegal drugs by the authorities, this does not appear to make any difference to a flow of drugs that is enough to satisfy demand. As the war on drugs has been stepped up, so have the drug traffickers become more sophisticated and ingenious in the methods they employ to ensure that the drugs reach their markets. Drugs such as cocaine and heroin can be disguised by pigment, while the use of express mail and courier services for sending drugs increased rapidly over the last years of the twentieth century. Heroin has been sent by this means from Asia to Africa, North America, and Europe. The more the European Union relaxes control of communications and transport between its members, the easier it will become for drug traffickers to operate.

The disappearance of the Iron Curtain and the end of the Cold War, the breakup of the Soviet Union into 15 component parts (many of which are poor and underdeveloped), the collapse of Yugoslavia into a number of unstable successor states, the easing of boundary restrictions throughout Europe and greater emphasis on the easy movement of goods by means of container transport, and the globalization of the world economy each work in favor of greater ease of smuggling. This has occurred, making it easier for the drug traffickers to respond to the escalating demand for drugs throughout Europe.

4

Statistics and Comparisons (Britain)

Governments criminalize the distribution and use of drugs in order to protect their citizens from harming themselves and claim that the ill effects of drug-taking justify government actions that deny freedom of choice in this particular sphere of activity. This is, at best, a dubious argument. In societies such as those of the United States or Western Europe that on the one hand extol their belief in the freedom of the individual and leave a wide range of choices up to him or her and then, on the other hand, clamp down fiercely on one particular activity, precise justifications need to be made to explain such a specific prohibition. Other arguments are involved, for example, that it would be a mistake to legalize the smoking of the comparatively harmless drug cannabis since this, inevitably, will lead to the abuse of more harmful drugs such as cocaine or heroin. The debate about drugs—prohibition or legalization, how to fight the worldwide drugs war, whether it makes more sense to take the battle to the drug producers or the drug consumers—has become of major political importance in many countries around the world and raises strong passions, both moral and economic. In the end, however, any policy has to be judged by its results. Two questions need to be addressed. First, does prohibition stop people obtaining the drugs they wish to use? The answer to this is very clearly no. Second, does the policy of prohibition lead to a massive level of drug-related crime? The answer to this, equally clearly, is yes. Moreover, the level of drug-related criminal activities is so great that it would appear to do more damage than the damage to individuals that the criminalization of drugs is designed to prevent. There is another consideration. Given the huge costs of the war against drugs, the limited success that the drugs war appears to be achieving, and the fact that those who are determined to use drugs do so despite all the prohibitions of the law, it makes sense to compare the war being waged on drugs with the different approaches of governments to the consumption of alcohol and the use of tobacco.

Statistics for Britain of deaths and severe damage to health resulting from addiction relating to drugs, alcohol, and tobacco (as well as deaths and injuries resulting from road accidents) are shown throughout this chapter. The conclusions to be drawn from these comparisons have a far wider application than only to the one country.

Drug Use and Abuse in Britain

The subcultures that developed in Britain and elsewhere during the 1960s, principally embracing adolescents and young adults, included the widespread use of drugs for recreational purposes. Many people were attracted to a counterculture that represented a clear break with more staid and restricted British traditions from the past. Furthermore, the new culture held particular attractions for individuals, again mainly young people, who suffered from low status in mainstream society. In response to this, additional control legislation relating to drugs was introduced at national and international levels, and by the late 1960s drug treatment centers had also been set up. Later, a variety of drug counseling agencies were created. These initial reactions against the new culture had comparatively little impact as the incidence of drug taking soared during the 1970s and 1980s. In 1995 a survey of 10 to 15 year olds in Britain showed that 39.8 percent of girls and 45 percent of boys had used illicit drugs. (A caveat needs to be introduced at this point: since the use of drugs is illegal, it may be more difficult to estimate total drug use and abuse than to do so in the cases of either alcohol or tobacco use, which are not illegal except for minors.) Surveys can almost always be faulted in one way or another, and where they concern a highly controversial subject such as the use of drugs, they may be affected by under- or overreporting.

Surveys conducted in Britain since 1969 reveal a remarkable consistency in the spread of drug use among schoolchildren, university students, criminals, and the young generally. A survey of 1969 (Binnie and Murdock) found that 9 percent of a study group of students in Leicester had used some type of drug. A 1973 survey (McKay et al.) showed that 14 percent of medical students in Glasgow had taken drugs. The British Crime Survey of 1981 revealed that 16 percent of 20 to 24 year olds in England and Wales had used cannabis, while another survey gave a 19 percent figure for Scotland. A national survey of 15 to 21 year olds indicated that cannabis was by far the most commonly used drug and had been tried by between 13 and 28 percent of this age group in different regions of Britain. At the same time, amphetamines had been used by 3 to 10 percent of this age group, glues and solvents by 1 to 4 percent, barbiturates by 2 to 16 percent, LSD by 2 to 8 percent, cocaine by 1 to 3 percent, and heroin by 0.5 to 7 percent. A survey of 2,417 secondary school and college students in England and Wales (conducted in 1986) revealed that 17 percent had used cannabis, 6 percent had used glues or solvents, and 2 percent had used heroin. Another survey of teenagers in Bournemouth and Southampton revealed that 19 percent of a sample had used drugs, mainly cannabis, glue, gas, typewriter correction fluid, and amphetamines. Other surveys showed that drug use was common over a range of 5 to 40 percent of young people. By the 1990s the use of ecstasy had become widespread, while a 1992 British Crime Survey indicated that 17 percent of respondents aged 16 to 59 in England and Wales had used illicit drugs, with the implication that four million people in this age group had done so. A 1994 survey of the Western Isles of Scotland revealed that 22 percent had used cannabis.[1]

How, then, should these figures be interpreted? Two important comments are made in the report *The Health of Adult Britain*: "Most drug users do not come to the attention of 'official agencies' as a result of their drug use, which is mainly very restricted." And, "Most illicit drug use appears to be very limited and harmless." However, the rate of drug seizures from individuals has increased dramatically over the years since 1945, when only 230 people were convicted of offenses in relation to opium, cannabis, or manufactured drugs and 206 of these concerned opium. Between 1981 and 1994, the number of people found guilty of drug offenses rose from 17,921 in the former to 86,961 in the latter year. The great majority of drug offenders are men and relatively young; in 1994, for example, only 9.4 percent of offenders were women. A new factor in drug-related diseases arose with the prevalence of HIV/AIDS, since the virus can be transmitted when needles used for injecting drugs are shared between users.

In the nineteenth century, deaths associated with drug taking were recorded. Between 1863 and 1900 the annual total of such deaths varied between 90 and 206, mainly from laudanum. These figures declined in the early years of the twentieth century to 43 in 1919. The number of addicts—individuals notified by doctors as being drug-dependent—declined between 1935 and 1955, from 700 to fewer than 400. Since 1965, however, there has been a steady rise in the number of notified addicts, from 1,426 in 1970 to 37,164 in 1995 (see Table 4.1). Most addicts are relatively young; in 1995 the average age of newly notified addicts was 26.3 years for men and 25.8 years for women. The total of drug-related deaths in 1988 came to 1,212; by 1994 the figure had risen to 1,620. Drug-related deaths have increased significantly since 1979, particularly among men.

Health Statistics Quarterly (Spring 2001) gives the figures shown in Table 4.2 for deaths related to drug poisoning in England and Wales between 1995 and 1999.[2] These cover drug dependence and nondependent abuse, accident, suicide and undetermined death, and drug psychoses or assault.

The range of substances involved in these deaths included legal and illegal drugs, prescribed substances, and over-the-counter medication. Where specific substances were mentioned on the death certificate, 21 percent of deaths mentioned more than one drug, and 22 percent contained a mention of alcohol. Deaths mentioning heroin and/or morphine showed the largest increase over the five-year period, with deaths for males mentioning heroin and/or morphine increasing from 11 deaths per million in 1995 to 25 deaths per million in 1999.

Table 4.1   Narcotic Addicts Known to the Home Office, 1970–1995

Year	Males	Females	Total	% Change Over Previous Years*
1970	1,051	375	1,426	—
1971	1,133	416	1,549	+9
1972	1,195	421	1,616	+4
1973	1,370	446	1,816	+2
1974	1,458	509	1,967	+8
1975	1,438	511	1,949	−1
1976	1,387	487	1,874	−4
1977	1,466	550	2,016	+6
1978	1,703	699	2,402	+9
1979	1,892	774	2,666	+1
1980	2,009	837	2,846	+7
1981	2,732	1,112	3,844	+36
1982	3,124	1,247	4,371	+4
1983	3,601	1,478	5,079	+6
1984	4,133	1,736	5,869	+5
1985	4,952	2,100	7,052	+20
1986	5,929	2,515	8,444	+20
1987	7,766	2,950	10,716	+27
1988	9,093	3,551	12,644	+8
1989	10,479	4,306	14,785	+7
1990	12,807	4,948	17,755	+20
1991	15,138	5,682	20,820	+7
1992	18,241	6,462	24,703	+9
1993	21,036	6,940	27,976	+3
1994	25,389	8,561	33,952	+21
1995	28,097	9,067	37,164	+9

*Rounded to nearest percent

Note: 1970–1986 figures indicate addicts notified on December 31 each year; 1987–1995 figures indicate addicts notified during the year.

Source: Home Office 1979–1996. This table is taken from John Charlton and Mike Murphy, editors, *The Health of Adult Britain: 1841–1994*, Decennial Supplement No. 12 (London: Stationery Office, 1997), 123.

Alcohol Abuse in Britain

National statistics for Britain give a figure of 3,565 deaths from alcohol-specific diseases in 1992, rising to 4,907 in 1997, while the annual number of deaths in which alcohol was a significant factor was estimated to be between 25,000 and 40,000. According to Alcohol Concern, a nongovernment

---

Table 4.2   Number of Deaths from Drug-Related Poisoning in England and Wales, 1995–1999

Year	1995	1996	1997	1998	1999	Total for 5 years
Males	1,643	1,811	1,932	1,944	2,043	9,373
Females	920	910	926	978	900	4,634
Total	2,563	2,721	2,858	2,922	2,943	14,007

Source: Figures are taken from Tables 1 and 2 in "Deaths Related to Drug Poisoning: England and Wales, 1995–1999," *Health Statistics Quarterly 9* (Spring 2001).

---

body dealing with alcohol problems, alcohol misuse costs the National Health Service £3 billion a year (12 percent of total spending in hospitals), while a further £3 billion covers the cost of absenteeism, crime, and accidents related to alcohol. One person in 25 is dependent on alcohol, which is twice as many as those dependent upon drugs of all kinds (apart from tobacco). According to the Office of National Statistics, 37 percent of men and 23 percent of women aged between 16 and 24 regularly drink twice the recommended safe levels of alcohol, while the proportion of women drinking above sensible levels increased from 10 to 15 percent between 1988 and 1998. The British Crime Survey of 2000 showed that in 40 percent of violent crimes recorded in that year, the offender was under the influence of alcohol, compared with 18 percent of offenders in violent crimes who were under the influence of drugs. According to the Consumer Directorate of the Department of Trade and Industry, the number of alcohol-related accidents in the home rose by 152 percent during the 1990s, from 13,262 in 1990 to 33,345 in 1998. The average weekly alcohol consumption among 11 to 15 year olds more than doubled between 1990 and 1998, from 0.8 units a week to 1.8 units, while the proportion of 11 to 15 year olds drinking at least once a week increased from 13 percent in 1988 to 20 percent in 1998. These and other statistics have focused attention on a problem that for years was rated lower than drug taking or smoking, and the British government has pledged to introduce a national alcohol strategy.[3]

It is worth looking briefly here at historical attempts at prohibition. Various attempts to prohibit alcohol use have been recorded in ancient China, Aztec society, feudal Japan, and the Polynesian islands, while in more modern times the Scandinavian countries of Iceland, Finland, Norway, and Sweden have attempted partial or total prohibition, as have Russia, Canada, and India. Attitudes toward drink have varied from country to country; sometimes the emphasis has been on the drinker, sometimes on the provider or seller. In Britain during the latter part of the nineteenth century, the "Blue Ribbon Army" of people who had taken the pledge not to drink (and wore a blue ribbon to signify the fact) became a powerful social force arguing for abstinence. In the 1870s the Temperance Party became strong among nonconformists, and all religious movements promoted the temperance movement. In 1904 the British government passed a Licensing Act to reduce the excessive number of outlets for drink. Limited drinking hours were introduced during World War I in Britain and elsewhere with the principal objective of preventing munitions workers drinking to excess and so rendering themselves incapable of work the following day. Two countries— Finland and the United States—introduced prohibition on a national scale during the twentieth century. Finland introduced prohibition of spirits in 1919 in an effort to redirect the drinking population toward the consumption of beer with its lower alcohol content. The prohibition was repealed in 1931.

Religious revivalism in the United States during the 1820s and 1830s led to the emergence of a number of temperance movements, and the first state prohibition law was passed in Maine in 1846. Other moves toward prohibition emerged during the latter years of the nineteenth century and the first decades of the twentieth, so that by January 1920 prohibition was in effect in 33 states, accounting for 63 percent of the U.S. population. The National Prohibition Act (the Volstead Act, named after Congressman Andrew J. Volstead, who had promoted it) came into force on October 28, 1919, although enforcement varied enormously from state to state and between big towns, where enforcement was often much weaker, and in small towns and the countryside, where it was more rigidly applied. What drew almost universal attention to American prohibition was the huge crime wave that accompanied it as bootleggers illegally met the demands for liquor that had been closed off by the law. The results were gang warfare, culminating in the notorious St Valentine's Day Massacre in Chicago in 1929, and a huge network of criminal activity that was more dangerous to society than the amount of drinking that had actually been prevented. Prohibition was repealed in 1933.

In today's Britain, alcohol is a reality. It is part of the culture, with 83 percent of the population drinking alcohol at various levels of consumption. What is required, therefore, is realistic education about its effects for the young. Social workers and others concerned with the effects of alcohol argue that the war on drugs has diverted attention from the problem of alcohol, which is seen as every bit as threatening to society. According to a Market Opinion and Research International (MORI) survey of February–March 2000, 41 percent of people associate alcohol with socializing and 25 percent associate it with relaxing. On the negative effects of alcohol, 23 percent of people associate it with antisocial behavior, 22 percent with drunkenness, and 20 percent with driving under the influence. On the other hand, while 46 percent of people think that alcohol is very risky for long-term health, this percentage compares favorably with the 83 percent who think the same about cigarettes, 91 percent about cocaine, and 90 percent about ecstasy. The same

MORI survey found that 88 percent of people think alcohol misuse is a major cause of violence in Britain, while 81 percent think it is a major cause of marital breakdown. According to MORI research for the British Police Foundation in 2000, a majority of adults believe both alcohol and tobacco are more harmful than cannabis, while 60 percent of the police say that alcohol has a greater impact on their workload than drugs. In answer to a parliamentary question by Dr. Vincent Cable, MP, on April 6, 2001, Health Minister Gisela Stuart said that central government funds allocated (for the year 2000/2001) for preventive or curative work in relation to drugs, alcohol, and tobacco misuse was as follows: alcohol £1.1 million, drugs £91.45 million, tobacco £33.75 million, and alcohol, drugs, and tobacco combined £8.64 million. A 2000 MORI poll for the Youth Justice Board found that 20 percent of pupils excluded from school were suspended for drinking alcohol and that 16 percent of the excluded pupils drank alcohol every day.

According to Alcohol Concern—in its publication *Britain's Ruin?*—1.7 million men and 0.6 million women in Britain drink at very risky levels, and as many as 65 percent of suicide attempts are linked with excessive drinking. There are depressing statistics relating to the impact of alcohol on families. Between 60 and 70 percent of men who assault their partners do so under the influence of alcohol; 920,000 children live in a home where one or both parents misuse alcohol; and 23 percent of child neglect cases involve parental alcohol misuse. Unlike drugs, alcohol is legally available to all adults over the age of 18. Excessive use of or reliance on alcohol is responsible for a range of public health, social exclusion, and crime and disorder problems and these affect the home, the workplace, and society more generally, for example, by causing road accidents. In statistical terms the effects of alcohol misuse are every bit as damaging as the effects of drug misuse, but the law treats the two problems very differently. Public houses and other public establishments such as hotels and restaurants must not serve alcohol to minors, yet minors who can pass for 18 can usually obtain drink without close checks, and the sale of alcohol to minors clearly represents a substantial part of the total business.

Smoking and Its Impact

Smoking by men became well established during the nineteenth century and increased to the end of World War II, when the incidence of smoking appeared to stabilize; by that time cigarettes provided by far the most common form of smoking. Average tobacco consumption per person aged 15 or over was estimated at 2.6 kilograms (5.7 pounds) in 1871; by the early 1940s it had risen to 5.3 kilograms (11.7 pounds) per person per annum. After a steady fall in consumption from the late 1960s, by 1987 it stood at 2.4 kilograms (5.3 pounds) per annum, slightly lower than the figure for 1871. A change in the pattern of tobacco consumption may have contributed to a rise in tobacco-related diseases. In the nineteenth century most tobacco was smoked in pipes and then in cigars or used for snuff or chewing. Since the 1940s, however, cigarettes have accounted for between 83 and 91 percent of all men's tobacco consumption. Smoking by women—which became widespread in the 1920s—has been almost exclusively confined to cigarettes. In addition to campaigns to persuade people not to smoke, efforts to reduce the health risks have concentrated on reducing the toxicity of cigarettes by reducing the tar yield. On the other hand, it has been found that smokers inhale more deeply when smoking low-tar cigarettes than high-tar cigarettes.

According to *The Health of Adult Britain*, smoking tobacco introduces 4,000 different chemicals into the body and these, in various ways, help cause more than 20 diseases; they also help protect against some others. Although a range of diseases, some fatal, are caused by tobacco smoking, they all have other causes as well. Diseases defined as strongly related to smoking are those in which the mortality attributed to them is regularly reported as at least 10 times higher in heavy cigarette smokers than in lifelong nonsmokers. The figures in Table 4.3 relate to 1992.

Table 4.3   Importance of Diseases Examined as the Certified Cause of Death in Britain, 1992

	Males		Females	
Cause of Death	**Number of Deaths**	**% of all Deaths**	**Number of Deaths**	**% of all Deaths**
Strongly related to smoking—causal*				
Cancer of lung	25,429	8.5	12,541	3.9
Chronic obstructive lung disease	18,588	6.2	11,793	3.7
Subtotal	44,017	14.6	24,334	7.7
Strongly related to smoking—causal and confounding†				
Cancer of lip	29	0.01	16	0.01
Cancer of oral cavity and pyarynx (less salivary glands and nasopharynx)	998	0.3	537	0.2
Cancer of esophagus	3,668	1.2	2,427	0.8
Cancer of larynx	782	0.3	215	0.1
Subtotal	5,477	1.8	3,195	1.0
Moderately related to smoking—causal*				
Cancer of pancreas	3,218	1.1	3,419	1.1
Cancer of bladder	3,803	1.3	1,813	0.6
Aortic aneurysm	6,037	2.0	3,518	1.1
Peptic ulcer	2,135	0.7	2,674	0.8
Subtotal	15,193	5.1	11,424	3.6

Other diseases studied

Ischaemic heart disease and related conditions	89,939	29.9	78,754	24.8
Total	**154,626**	**51.4**	**117,707**	**37.0**

* Relationship reflects contribution of smoking to the causation of the disease.

† Relationship partly reflects contribution to the causation of the disease and partly confounding between smoking and some other causative factor.

Source: John Charlton and Mike Murphy, editors, *The Health of Adult Britain: 1841–1994,* Decennial Supplement No. 12 (London: Stationery Office, 1997), 129.

An analysis carried out in 1994 concluded that the death rate per 100,000 attributable to smoking was as shown in Table 4.4.

The principal diseases connected with smoking are lung cancer (see Table 4.5), chronic obstructive lung disease, cancer of the lip, esophageal cancer, laryngeal cancer, pancreatic cancer, bladder cancer, aortic aneurysm, and peptic ulcers. The impact of smoking varies for these diseases. According to *The Health of Adult Britain,* "The great majority of all lung

Table 4.4   Death Rate per 100,000 Attributable to Smoking

	Year	Number
Men aged 35–69 years		
	1955	651
	1965	732
	1975	622
	1990	379
Men aged 70–79 years		
	1955	1,310
	1965	2,160
	1975	2,640
	1990	1,890
Women aged 35–69 years		
	1955	55
	1965	96
	1975	135
	1990	153
Women aged 70–79 years		
	1955	93
	1965	191
	1975	363
	1990	635

Source: John Charlton and Mike Murphy, editors, *The Health of Adult Britain: 1841–1994,* Decennial Supplement No. 12 (London: Stationery Office, 1997), 130.

Table 4.5　Mortality Rates per Million in Britain from Lung Cancer by Age, Sex, and Calendar Year

Year	30–34	35–39	40–44	45–49	50–54	55–59	60–64	65–69	70–74	75–79	80–84
Males											
1951–55	37	102	251	5,691	1,244	2,024	2,564	2,909	2,568	2,026	1,413
1956–60	35	95	256	599	1,262	2,326	3,368	3,944	3,861	3,289	2,221
1961–65	34	95	229	575	1,241	2,319	3,716	4,882	4,974	4,494	3,367
1966–70	26	77	225	540	1,170	2,226	3,719	5,304	6,213	5,933	4,525
1971–75	23	59	180	510	1,081	2,090	3,554	5,195	6,825	7,243	6,058
1976–80	17	54	139	401	1,009	1,908	3,346	4,977	6,692	7,987	7,638
1981–85	13	42	120	322	780	1,731	3,021	4,574	6,336	7,753	8,395
1986–90	8	34	104	276	600	1,350	2,691	4,129	5,850	7,135	7,975
1991–92	9	33	91	250	612	1,135	2,241	3,936	5,312	6,542	7,518
Females											
1951–55	15	28	52	89	139	207	286	352	391	440	398
1956–60	15	31	63	105	171	243	331	387	454	496	459
1961–65	11	32	71	140	219	308	424	518	548	580	564
1966–70	11	31	82	164	286	401	512	653	729	740	671
1971–75	8	28	70	187	339	504	678	807	880	901	868
1976–80	7	27	65	164	374	583	869	1,033	1,112	1,134	1,060
1981–85	7	25	61	147	315	650	992	1,313	1,450	1,462	1,360
1986–90	6	21	63	141	276	583	1,131	1,496	1,757	1,769	1,663
1991–92	4	17	62	147	489	499	1,019	1,608	1,891	1,976	1,827

Source: John Charlton and Mike Murphy, editors, *The Health of Adult Britain: 1841–1994*, Decennial Supplement No. 12 (London: Stationery Office, 1997), 136.

cancers are caused by smoking in the sense that, in the absence of smoking, the incidence of the disease is consistently low."

Estimates for chronic obstructive lung disease (COLD), which includes bronchitis or emphysema, are more complex, although in 1992 it was estimated that 80 percent of deaths in men, and 70 percent in women from these diseases were caused by smoking. Cancer of the lip has long been associated with smoking and, while data are unreliable, smoking is probably the cause of the great majority of cases. Smoking may be responsible for about 70 percent of esophageal cancer and a similar percentage is given for laryngeal cancer, while in the case of pancreatic cancer about a quarter of such deaths in men and a third in women have been attributed to smoking. In the case of bladder cancer, it has been estimated that 45 percent of deaths in men and 30 percent in women are attributable to cigarette smoking; in the case of aortic aneurysm, about 30 percent of deaths are attributable to smoking; and in the case of peptic ulcers, about 20 percent are attributable to smoking.

An estimate for 1999 gave a total figure of 120,000 annual deaths from cancer, heart attacks, and strokes as being related to smoking. Just over a quarter of the population in Britain—27 percent—are smokers, and they consume between 13 and 14 million cigarettes, averaging 13.6 cigarettes per person a day.

An editorial in the British daily newspaper *The Independent* of June 8, 2001, commenting on the award of $3 billion in punitive damages against cigarette manufacturer Philip Morris by the Los Angeles Superior Court on behalf of an individual lifelong smoker who claimed he had not been warned of the dangers, highlighted the ambivalent attitude toward smoking in countries such as the United States and Britain. The editorial began as follows:

> Tobacco is the only legal consumer product that kills people when used as intended. That stark statement is often used by propagandists against the cigarette industry, yet it is entirely factual. In moral terms, tobacco companies are not like other enterprises. Even arms makers can argue that their products defend democracy or help to fight just wars. Cigarette makers can justify their trade by no principle whatever.

This same editorial posed two dilemmas. First, should such punitive damages be awarded to express disapproval (which seemed clearly to be the case in this Los Angeles court judgment)? Second, should tobacco be banned or should it not? In Britain it is an offense to sell tobacco to anyone below 16 years of age, although minors have little difficulty obtaining cigarettes if they want them. And, according to the law, there are health warnings on all packets of cigarettes. The government, meanwhile, takes a large slice of revenue from tobacco products, which are heavily taxed.

One other comparison, for road casualties, is worth making. In 1998 deaths and injuries resulting from road accidents in Britain came to 3,421 deaths and 40,834 serious injuries, to make a combined total of 44,255 casualties. In 1999 the figures were 3,423 deaths and 39,122 serious injuries, to make a total of 42,545 casualties. In this case there was an overall improvement for the two-year period, with traffic rising by 2 percent and the casualty rate falling by 3 percent. By comparison, for the years 1981–1985 the average number of fatal accidents a year was then 5,598 and the average number of serious accidents a year 74,534, which shows that a very substantial improvement had taken place by the late 1990s. Even so, the casualty rate for both deaths and serious injuries remained unacceptably high.[4]

A summary of these statistics for recent years shows that deaths from drugs in 1999 came to 2,943, in the same year deaths from smoking came to 120,000, and those from road accidents came to 3,423, while deaths from alcohol in 1997 came to 4,907. Furthermore, police estimates for the year 2000 indicated that 40 percent of violent crimes were due to alcohol, and 18 percent were due to drugs. These figures must raise a massive question mark in relation to the war on drugs. Casualties from alcohol, smoking, and road accidents were all greater than those from drugs, yet the national approach to the former three categories was markedly different. Why? If levels of drug addiction that resulted in 2,943 deaths in 1999 warrant a massive anti-drugs campaign that leads to prohibition and criminalization, should not the same approach be applied to alcohol (4,907 deaths in 1997) and even more to smoking, with 120,000 related deaths from the addiction in 1999? Road casualties are in a different category and are not the result of addiction, yet could almost certainly be cut drastically if, for example, more stringent speed limits were applied or if, by law, all vehicles had fitted mechanisms that controlled their speeds. Could it be that the demands of commerce and profits in this case are seen as more important than limiting the numbers of casualties from bad driving habits? If there is a case for banning all drugs and making their use illegal, there is a greater case for doing the same in relation to both alcohol and tobacco.

5

British Attitudes to Drugs

In the 1920s there were only a small number of drug addicts in Britain, most of whom were either health professionals or patients who had become addicts during a particular course of treatment. During the last 40 years of the twentieth century, however, the problem took on a different dimension as drug use was adopted by an increasing number of people for recreational purposes. By the 1960s the use of drugs such as cannabis or LSD by the young was seen as a necessary act of political dissent. Since that time there has been a major growth in drug use, particularly—though not exclusively—among the young, a pattern that is to be found in much of the industrialized world. Thus, while only 5 percent of 14 and 15 year olds had ever been offered a drug in 1969, more than 40 percent had been by 1994 (see Figure 5.1).[1]

The drugs problem constantly changes, as new drugs come into vogue, but the rise in drug use has continued steadily. In the late 1940s and 1950s, amphetamines and benzodiazepines were prescribed for adults as antidepressants and as a counter to tiredness. However, they then came to be used for extra energy by a younger generation of the new youth culture, and by the 1980s benzodiazepines were being injected intravenously.

Concern about drug use was demonstrated in 1916, during World War I, when the possession of cocaine was made illegal because British soldiers were using it while on leave from the front. Then the Dangerous Drugs Acts of 1920 and 1921 extended the prohibition to morphine and heroin. Prompted by a much more severe drugs problem in the United States, the British government set up a committee under the president of the Royal College of Physicians, Sir Humphrey Rolleston, to look at the British drugs problem, but the committee's report, delivered in 1926, concluded that there was very little opiate addiction in the country and recommended that addicted individuals should be treated as patients requiring detoxification.

Many social attitudes in Britain changed during the 1960s, a period that saw an end to traditional deference, growing political protest, and the rise of a new and startlingly self-assured youth culture. Drugs became a part of this culture, and cannabis became the most widely used drug at this time. Toward the end of the 1960s, the Advisory Council on the Misuse of Drugs set up an expert inquiry under Baroness Wootton of Abinger. Although its report did

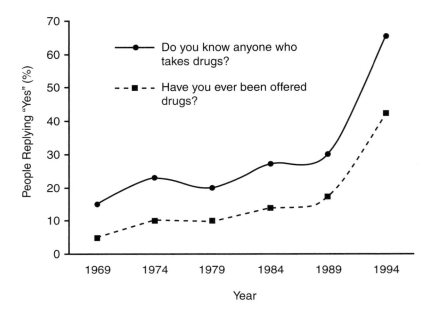

Figure 5.1 Changes over 25 years in "yes" response to two questions about taking drugs. (J. D. Wright and L. Pearl, "Knowledge and Experience of Young People Aged 14–15 Regarding Drug Misuse, 1969–1994," *British Medical Journal 310* (1995): 20–24. This figure is taken from Working Party of the Royal College of Psychiatrists and Royal College of Physicians, *Drugs: Dilemmas and Choices* (London: Gaskell, 2000), 38.

not recommend the legalization of cannabis, it did say that the dangers of its use had been exaggerated and suggested that penalties for limited use should be reduced. Meanwhile, in the mid-1960s, LSD made its first appearance, coming to Britain from U.S. universities, where the psychedelic revolution was born.

A new generation of heroin addicts appeared in the 1950s when it was found that some doctors were prescribing large amounts of the drug and that these were falling into the hands of people who were not on the list of opiate patients. Over the years 1958–1964, the number of known heroin addicts in Britain increased from 62 to 342, and for the first time addicts aged under 20 emerged. The 1967 Dangerous Drugs Act provided for special addiction treatment centers, and doctors who were permitted to prescribe cocaine or heroin to addicts were restricted to those working in the new treatment centers. In 1971 the Misuse of Drugs Act replaced the Dangerous Drugs Act to remain in force into the twenty-first century. Under its provisions, drugs were divided into classes A, B, and C (see Table 5.1).

Table 5.1   Drugs Categorized Under the Misuse of Drugs Act 1971 and Subsequent Amendments

Class A	Class B	Class C
Heroin	Amphetamines	Amphetamine-related drugs
Morphine	Barbiturates	Buprenorphine
Methadone	Cannabis	Most benzodiazepines
Cocaine	Codeine	Anabolic steroids
LSD		(under certain circumstances)
Ecstasy		
Any Class B drug when prepared for injection		

Note: Cannabis was reclassified as a Class C drug in 2002.

Source: Working Party of the Royal College of Psychiatrists and Royal College of Physicians, *Drugs: Dilemmas and Choices* (London: Gaskell, 2000), 47.

During the 1970s a new problem arose with the spread of intravenous barbiturate use, although this waned toward the end of the decade, to be replaced by the growth of a heroin problem dependent on growing imports of the new type of heroin from Southwest Asia. However, the largest increase in drug use occurred between 1975 and 1997 with amphetamines, which became the most widely used drug in Britain after cannabis.

Heroin use was to escalate during the 1980s and chiefly involved adolescents and young adults. The method of taking the drug, known as "chasing the dragon," was to heat the brown heroin powder on tin foil and then inhale the vapors through a tube into the mouth. At least this method avoided the use of needles and possible infection from multiple needle use. There was no shortage of heroin, which came from the countries of the Golden Crescent such as Iran, Afghanistan, Turkey, and Pakistan. The growth in the number of heroin addicts has been startling, rising from 100 to 3,000 or 4,000 during the 1960s, but then increasing from approximately 5,000 in 1980 to 50,000 in the late 1990s. The number of addicts is still rising.

Ecstasy, a stimulant drug, appeared and spread quickly in Britain at the end of the 1980s. It was especially associated with the growth of a new nightclub scene and played an important part in developing the so-called "rave" culture. However, surveys suggest it has been used less than other dance drugs such as LSD and amphetamines. Some drugs last; others appear as part of a fashion and then largely disappear. What had become plain by the end of the twentieth century was that Britain had developed into a major drug-using society.[2]

In 1997 Britain's new prime minister, Tony Blair, appointed Keith Hellawell, the chief constable of West Yorkshire Police, as the country's first "drugs czar." His tasks were to advise the government and coordinate the fight against substance abuse, combat foreign drug traffickers, influence youth attitudes, and oversee treatment facilities. It was a mammoth undertaking. Meanwhile, Foreign Secretary Robin Cook had announced that "full intelligence resources" would be made available to tackle the growing global threat posed by drug trafficking. On a trip to Malaysia, Cook was especially critical of Myanmar (Burma), the world's largest source of heroin (at that time), whose military government connived with drug barons. The new British policy, like that of the United States, was to concentrate on attacking the drug supply chain in order to stifle production at the source, and MI6 (British intelligence) was to use its resources in support of the police and customs to combat the trade.

The political and social problems attached to drugs were highlighted in January 1998 when William Straw, the 17-year-old son of Jack Straw, then Britain's home secretary, was given a police caution for buying 1.92 grams of cannabis in a pub from a man who turned out to be an undercover reporter. The incident sparked off a debate on the ethics of the press and the use of cannabis. Then, in April 1998, a National Crime Squad (NCS) of 1,450 police was inaugurated with the task of covering England and Wales. Its chief, Roy Penrose, said its main priority would be to target drug dealers. Also that April, a government white paper set out a 10-year strategy to combat drug misuse. It proposed, among other things, that money seized from convicted drug traffickers should be used to fund treatment for addicts and to fund anti-drugs educational programs for children. The strategy was the work of the new drugs czar, Keith Hellawell. In May 1999 Hellawell published a 10-year strategy to concentrate on reducing the use of Class A drugs such as heroin and cocaine by young people and on the provision of more treatment centers for addicts.

Periodically, the country was reminded of the widespread prevalence of drug use when a high-profile case of drug misuse occurred. One such case concerned Lawrence Dallaglio, who resigned as England's rugby captain in May 1999 after telling undercover reporters of the *News of the World* newspaper that he had taken cocaine and supplied drugs to his teammates. He admitted to having "experimented" with drugs as a teenager. Later in the year the Rugby Football Union tribunal fined Dallaglio £15,000 with £10,000 costs for bringing the game into disrepute with his tabloid revelations. Then in July 1999 *The Times* published material from leaked Foreign Office documents that included material from U.S. government agencies to show that Michael Ashcroft, the conservative party treasurer, had been investigated for possible involvement in drug trafficking and money laundering in Belize.

A quite different drugs problem emerged during the 1990s when it was found that drug dealers were targeting psychiatric homes, where the misuse of illicit drugs by patients was a growing concern. A survey by the Royal College of Nursing revealed that 70 percent of respondents from both urban and rural areas who worked in in-patient psychiatric services said the misuse of illicit drugs in their units was a problem. Findings based on a study of the high-security Ashworth Special Hospital near Liverpool showed that illicit drugs caused a "general deterioration of mental health or exacerbation of existing problems . . . which increased conflict between staff and patients and amongst patients themselves."

Jon Thompson, a correspondent for *The Independent* in February 1997, wrote to suggest that the government should legalize cannabis, tax it, and use the money to subsidize proper education and harm-reduction campaigns against hard drugs. He said: "Though the public has accepted that drug-taking is as commonplace as, and safer than, many legal activities, the government continues in its futile war on drugs, denying any debate—even on the subject of medicinal cannabis." And another correspondent, Jack Girling, chairman of the Campaign to Legalise Cannabis International Association, also writing to the same newspaper, argued:

> For thousands of years much of the human race survived from the cannabis seed, using it to make gruel and bread. Today the plant is banned almost everywhere, seemingly because those in power do not want people to get high. The many medicinal uses of cannabis are similarly ignored. Surely the "high" of cannabis is not the real reason, considering that dangerous and addictive alcohol is legal. Could it be pressures from the companies, which make ineffective synthetic drugs, pesticides and fertilisers, diesel, and plastics? Hemp grown for fabric (the word "canvas" comes from the Dutch word for hemp), paper, fuel, oil, paints, and medicines, is cheaper, better, and with no pollution.

The failure of the prison services to control the use of drugs is notorious. According to findings revealed in a 1997 report, "Persistent Drug-Misusing Offenders" by Professor Philip Bean and Diane Winterburn of Loughborough University, the amount and the variety of illegal substances used by drug offenders who are jailed actually increase a year after their imprisonment. The criminal justice system fails to have any effect on drug use by addicts. A group of 148 offenders, interviewed a year after conviction, consisted mainly of unemployed men in their twenties who had committed offenses ranging from burglary and theft to violence and drug possession. About half of them took heroin, four in 10 had tried crack, and most took a combination of drugs that included cannabis, amphetamines, tranquillizers, and LSD. Although, as a small survey, the report had to be treated with caution, it nonetheless showed that jail or community sentences failed to stop addicts from taking drugs.[3]

There was a reaction by experts against the proposed appointment of a national drugs czar when these experts argued that the policy could backfire if enforcement of the drug laws was overemphasized at the expense of treatment, rehabilitation, and prevention. Writing in the *British Medical Journal* in 1997, they warned against "war" rhetoric—the czar was to be charged with leading "the battle against drugs"—and they expressed unhappiness that the United States had been chosen as a role model. The group of experts was led by John Strang, director of the National Addiction Centre in London, while his coauthors were William Clee, chairman of the Welsh Advisory Committee on Drug and Alcohol Misuse; Lawrence Grewer, a consultant in public health medicine from Glasgow; and Duncan Raistrick, director of the Leeds Addiction Unit.[4]

A great deal of attention was devoted to the drugs problem in 1997, the year the Labour Party, restyled as "New Labour," swept to power, not least perhaps because there was much public interest as to how the new government would tackle the problem. In a wide-ranging report, London's *Evening Standard* newspaper suggested that 87 percent of young clubbers regularly took drugs and that 97 percent had done so at some time. It also reported that drug use had become widespread in the legal profession and that many young city workers were drug users. In other words, the paper said, "we must recognize that among Britain's new generation, and especially in London, drugs are a familiar social fact." Among young middle classes, drugs had achieved the social acceptability that cigarettes possessed a generation earlier. Meanwhile, the illegal industry that met these needs had become huge and lay at the root of most attempts to corrupt policemen. Therefore, people should not delude themselves into believing that the so-called "war against drugs" was being won; it was not. As the paper argued: "Despite the expenditure of huge sums of public money and police effort, drugs remain readily available all over London. The only achievement of the counteroffensive has been to drive up the price." Although the *Evening Standard* was reluctant to support the decriminalization of drugs, it did say that the possibility should be properly debated.[5]

The task of dissuading young people from taking drugs is not helped by the fact that, as with drinking alcohol or cigarette smoking, the immediate damaging effects on their physical well-being by such drugs as cannabis, amphetamines, LSD, or even ecstasy, appear minimal. Although there were several high-profile deaths linked to ecstasy during the late 1980s and the 1990s, hundreds of thousands of people used the drug every week and suffered no worse after-effects than headaches. Drug counselors have suggested that, in order to make an impact on the rising incidence of drug-taking in schools, children should be given accurate information that allows them to make informed choices, and such information should include explaining when drugs do not cause problems. Much of the youth drugs problem is exacerbated by the attitudes of members of the older generation who lecture the young on what they should or should not do. A steadily widening gap emerged throughout the 1990s on this issue, with an increasing demand for the legalization of cannabis as a starting point for a different approach to the whole problem. Politicians, fearful of upsetting their middle-class and middle-aged supporters, did not help with their anti-drugs attitude, which at times bordered on the hysterical, as the furor that greeted the call in 1996 for a debate on drugs by Labour MP Clare Short, demonstrated. The growing drugs debate that took place in the latter part of the 1990s, despite the wish of politicians to smother it, raised the question of the age at which people should be allowed to make their own responsible decisions.

On the other hand, figures published by doctors in the *British Medical Journal* in 1997 revealed a dramatic rise in deaths among teenage drug abusers over the period 1985–1995. Overall drug deaths among those aged 15 to 19 increased by 8 percent a year, and during this period 436 teenagers died accidentally from drug poisoning; of these 303 were male and 133 were female. Opiates such as heroin accounted for 21 percent of the deaths. Between 1985 and 1989, 17 teenagers died from taking opiates and related narcotics; however, in the four years 1991–1995, the figure had risen to 67. There were similar rises in the number of deaths from drugs such as ecstasy; there were eight deaths in this category between 1985 and 1989, but 32 between 1991 and 1995.

According to a 1997 report by Release, the drugs awareness charity, only a small minority of young people who went night-clubbing did not take drugs, while 87 percent of those attending dance events told the survey that they had taken or intended to take drugs, and only 3 percent of those surveyed in London clubs had never taken drugs. Of those admitting to taking drugs, 95 percent had smoked cannabis, while 85 percent admitted to taking ecstasy. Young people who were interviewed admitted to taking a range of drugs; they obtained them from friends at college or from "a dodgy pub," and they saw this as a normal part of their and their peers' culture. As Neil, a 27-year-old care worker who had been a student at Liverpool University, explained, drug culture among students is widespread, and he did not believe that drugs had interfered with his degree. As he said in a typical response: "I've never worried about so-called 'long-term effects.' I think that's rubbish. I think there was a death while I was at Liverpool and people went into comas, but it didn't worry me: it's usually due to alcohol or drinking too much water or taking too much E. I hardly ever took more than one." Neil's attitude is clearly typical of a large proportion of drug users. Since this is the case, it would make more sense to ensure that adequate information about safer usage of drugs is available. In Holland, for example, ecstasy is analyzed for impurities. Other respondents to the survey had much the same attitude. They also said that they grew out of the habit once they settled into full-time employment. As Mike Goodman, director of Release, which commissioned the survey, explained:

> I was a bit surprised by the survey's results but not shocked. . . . The plain fact is that people have always used mood-affecting substances in association with night-time dancing. These young people's parents used alcohol. Ancient civilizations used all kinds of things. And colonial officers used to take their ladies dancing pepped up on Benzedrine. So I don't put my head in my hands when I see these figures. But that said, just as we, as a society, talk about sensible drinking, we should talk about sensible drug use. This is not the same as recommending drugs. The rules are broadly:
>
> • Don't take more than one dose
> • Don't mix drugs
> • Don't mix them with alcohol
> • Stay cool—drink adequate fluid: about a pint per hour, if you're dancing
> • Have breaks from dancing
>
> The young people we spoke to had thought the issues through. They were relatively intelligent and well informed. We're not talking about a bunch of stupid people . . . you've got to take the real world as it is.[6]

In November 1997 the medical research charity Action on Addiction warned that one in three children would grow up addicted to drugs, alcohol, and tobacco, and that despite massive investment in drug education, this was failing to change young people's attitudes or behavior. Professor John Strang, the former head of the government task force on drugs, speaking on behalf of the charity, warned that there was an "epidemic still in development" with the number of heroin addicts doubling over three years, while the price of the drug had halved between 1986 and 1996. In some areas of Britain, drugs had become a way of life, and, for example, in a deprived area of Glasgow, it was found that nearly a third of 12 to 14 year olds had experimented with at least three illicit drugs. Having suggested that the best way to deal with heroin was to apply market forces to it and treat it as any other business, Professor Strang said: "It's too simplistic and convenient to isolate drugs as a social issue and blight. The Glasgow study shows the extent of drug use amongst young people, and many see this as a positive, recreational part of their lives. We need credible education initiatives, which can compete against all the other sources of information, such as friends, newspapers, magazines, television, music, and films."[7]

The 1998 British Crime Survey of England and Wales, published in September 1999, revealed that most people between the ages of 16 and 24 had taken drugs at least once, with cocaine consumption showing the most significant rise during the late 1990s, from 1 percent to 3 percent among 16

Table 5.2   The Drug Habits of 16 to 29 Year Olds (Who Have Taken Drugs)—The Percentage for Each of the Drugs

Methadone	1%
Crack	1%
Heroin	1%
Steroids	1%
Pills (various)	3%
Temazepam	3%
Cocaine	6%
Glue	6%
Smoke (unknown)	7%
Ecstasy	10%
Magic mushrooms	10%
LSD	11%
Poppers	16%
Amphetamines	20%
Cannabis	42%
Any drug	49%

Source: Figures derived from *The Independent,* April 9, 1999.

to 29 year olds between 1996 and 1998 (see Table 5.2). Moreover, links with the rich and famous boosted cocaine's image, while the use of dance drugs such as ecstasy had leveled off. London, the south of England, and Merseyside were identified as the areas where cocaine was most popular. Studies based on the 1998 British Crime Survey showed that an increasing number of young people were trying cocaine, attracted by both its low price and its association with wealth and fame.

A survey carried out by the *Evening Standard* newspaper, "Drugs in London" (April 2001), concluded that cocaine and a cocktail of other drugs had never been cheaper or more easily available. The survey showed that cocaine had become a mainstream drug used by tens of thousands of young Londoners, with an estimated 600,000 regular users in the capital. London prices in 2001 were cocaine at £60 a gram, ecstasy at £9 a pill, amphetamine at £9 a gram, and heroin at £70 a gram. Each of these prices had fallen quite dramatically over the preceding three or four years. The Metropolitan Police Authority published an annual performance plan in which it set forth its priorities and targets for the financial year; it placed "reducing damage to London's communities caused by drug dealing" as one of Scotland Yard's four top priorities. Interestingly, neither cannabis nor ecstasy merited a mention in the plan, an indication of changing police attitudes toward these drugs. A clear distinction emerges in the London drug market, with recreational drug users at one end taking cannabis, ecstasy, and cocaine, and addicts at the other end using crack and heroin and turning to crime in order to feed their habits. New Home Office figures showed that heroin, cannabis, and ecstasy have spread nationwide, with between 21 and 26 percent of seizures of these drugs being made in Greater London where 14.6 percent of the population of England lives.

In April 2001 the government pledged an extra £67.5 million to help law enforcers in the battle against drug traffickers. Initiatives included the provision of aid for transit countries such as Turkey to help them cut off heroin routes. During 1999 and 2000 hard drugs with a street value of £1.25 billion were intercepted in Britain. Even as the British authorities were stepping up their efforts to fight the war on drugs, the U.S. Drug Enforcement Administration (DEA) revealed a dramatic increase in drug production, from heroin in Afghanistan to ecstasy in the Netherlands, with traffickers stockpiling in Europe so that they can maintain an uninterrupted supply. As a result, drug seizures in Europe or Asia have come to be interpreted less as the consequence of effective policing than as a sign of increasing volume. And the European Union's drug agency reinforced this view when it confirmed, in relation to cocaine, that "the overall picture is of an expanding market with increased availability." According to Professor Mike Hough, a criminologist at London's South Bank University, among the 600,000 regular drug users in the capital, only 8,000 could be classified as hardcore addicts on cocaine or heroin. Despite the government's 10-year strategy—"Tackling Drugs to Build a Better Britain"—and endless warnings by politicians against drug use, the fact is that for a substantial proportion of the population, drugs have become so common that they are no longer even regarded as something exotic.

The police have found that dealers are increasingly able to evade detection by using mobile phones to make individual appointments rather than selling their drugs at particular locations known to buyers. And Lady Runciman, who chaired the 2000 report bearing her name (see chapter 18), accused politicians of leaving decisions about which drug users to arrest to the police and described this as "a moral cop-out." Once a week, on what is known as the "milk run" to the police, officers are sent to London's West End clubs and discos to collect drugs discovered by bouncers conducting body searches at the door. If the people carrying drugs only have a small amount—enough for personal use—they are allowed to go free; if they have more, suggesting they are dealers, then they will be held for the police. For their part the police admit that they cannot beat the problem and just hope to contain it. And the clubs are geared for drugs, with hard techno music reaching a crescendo every 10 minutes to enhance the "rush" that comes from ecstasy, while the pulsing light and laser rig is also designed to intensify the effects of the drugs. At the bars no alcohol is served, only bottled water or other soft drinks, and there are chill-out rooms. Entry is at £20 to compensate for the fact that little money will be taken at the bar.[8]

By 2001 it was clear that cocaine had become the drug of choice in Britain after cannabis. The price had decreased steadily from £200 a gram in the early 1980s to an average of £40 in the new century. A drug group, Crew 2000, conducted a survey at Edinburgh University and found that the use of cocaine on campus had increased substantially more than any other drug; its cheapness had brought it within reach of students. During 2000 some 20,000 pupils in 67 secondary schools were asked to fill in questionnaires about drugs. The results showed that more than 100 boys aged 12 had tried heroin and a similar number of 11 year olds had tried cocaine, while twice as many said they had used cannabis, or had sniffed glue or propellants and inhalants known as "gas." Such findings contradicted government claims that juvenile drug use was falling. According to one survey, carried out by Jeremy Gluck of the Adolescent Assessment Services in Swansea, Wales, drug use in schools was so high that in some cases those conducting the survey did not want to believe their findings. Furthermore, the survey suggested that smoking and drinking among adolescents was likely to initiate later drug use.[9]

Heroin is generally regarded as the most dangerous of the hard drugs, and its use among the young in Britain made dramatic advances at the end of the twentieth century, partly, it has been suggested, because it has been glamorized by the media or by films such as *Trainspotting* (1996). It appeared to be replacing both ecstasy and LSD as the main drug used by club-goers. A Home Office report of 1998, *New Heroin Outbreaks Amongst Young People in England and Wales*, found that heroin dealers were increasingly targeting young teenagers. The report highlighted four aspects of the new heroin epidemic: dealers were marketing heroin aggressively by offering cut-price drugs and affordable £10 deals and sometimes giving it away free to encourage the habit; the core group of users were 15 to 20 year olds from poor, broken families and had education problems; many young people were unaware of the dangers of heroin and began to smoke it in the belief that it was not habit-forming; and the range of people taking the drug was wide. By 1999 young heroin users were socially diverse and came from almost anywhere in the country.

Most heroin reaching Britain comes from the Golden Crescent—Iran, Pakistan, and Afghanistan—and is smuggled via Turkey and the Balkans into Britain through its seaports and airports. The drug mostly enters the country on trucks coming through Dover. It is a Class A drug and importers, if caught, face up to 20 years in prison, while couriers who bring it, often in condoms that they swallow, can face a 10-year prison sentence. Once in Britain, a consignment of heroin will be broken up among a network of dealers who sell it in small amounts after mixing it with other substances. On the streets it is known as smack, brown, junk, or skag. In 1997 there were 194 deaths from heroin, and although there were then 40,000 known heroin addicts, the real figure could be five times higher. It is commonly sold in £10 wraps, and an estimated £3 billion is spent on heroin by users each year. In 1999 the National Criminal Intelligence Service, MI5, drug squads, and customs officers involved in tracking the distribution of heroin found that over the previous few years there had been a huge increase in the amount on sale. A majority of the heroin gangs were Turkish groups in London and Liverpool, the two main distribution points for drug trafficking for the whole country. They also found that criminal gangs from Kosovo and Armenia were involved in the trade and estimated that these groups were responsible for between 85 and 90 percent of the heroin imported into Britain. The police have found it difficult to infiltrate the gangs, which are close-knit and often only employ family members or longtime friends.

By the end of the twentieth century, deaths from both heroin and cocaine had increased dramatically. In 1995 heroin was mentioned in 357 death certificates; by 1999 the figure had more than doubled to 754, while the rise in cocaine-related deaths over the same period had increased from 19 to 87. Deaths from the heroin substitute methadone remained constant at 300 to 400 a year, while deaths associated with amphetamines rose from 48 in 1995 to 79 in 1999. However, painkillers such as paracetamol or compounds that included it accounted for 2,500 deaths over the four-year period. The increase in heroin-related deaths in Britain reflected a European trend. In 1995 the European Union saw 10 deaths per million people, compared with 25 deaths per million in 1999. The causes of drug-related deaths varied, and of a total of 9,373 over this period, just under 3,000 were recorded by coroners as accidental and 3,800 as either suicide or undetermined. By 2001 the unthinkable was beginning to be voiced: Should heroin be legalized? Perhaps, if it were, it would be easier to tackle treatment at one end of the chain and all the associated crimes leading to the other end of the chain. And while Britain continued to criminalize drugs, the total cost to business from alcohol-related illness had reached an annual rate of £2 billion.

Drug prohibition has not worked in Britain any more than alcohol prohibition worked in the United States during the 1920s and 1930s. Britain has some of the toughest anti-drug laws of Europe yet, according to the European Monitoring Centre for Drugs and Drug Abuse (EMCDDA), it also has some of the highest levels of drug use and misuse. The assumption that making drugs illegal will somehow stop people using them is clearly not working and, moreover, appears to be unworkable. Keith Hellawell told *The Guardian* in 1994, when he was chief constable of West Yorkshire Police: "The current policies are not working. We seize more drugs, we arrest more people, but when you look at the availability of drugs, the use of drugs, the crime committed because of and through people who use drugs, the violence associated with drugs, it's on the increase. It can't be working." And it clearly is not working. In an article in *Druglink* (the magazine published by the charity DrugScope), Danny Kushlick, the director of Transform (the campaign for effective drugs policy), argues that the government boasts of evidence-based policymaking, yet there seems to be little or no evidence available to support the current policy of prohibiting drugs. He suggests common aims for an effective drugs policy and then poses the question of how prohibition fares in relation to them. Under seven headings—health, crime, regulation and control, expenditure and revenue, education and information, civil rights, and community involvement—Kushlick shows that the war on drugs is not working. Under health, drug-related illness and addiction continue to rise; under crime, heroin users are said to commit half of all property crime; under regulation and control, the most dangerous drugs are not controlled except by the criminal dealers; under expenditure and revenue, between £8 and £20 billion is spent on drugs by users and is untaxed, while the cost of enforcing the drug laws comes to £1 billion a year. Education about drugs is based on fear (and clearly does not work); under civil rights, the author argues that millions of people have their human rights abused; and under community involvement, the policy of outright prohibition makes it impossible for communities to play any important role except at the margins. Danny Kushlick presents a powerful plea for a top-to-bottom reappraisal of the British drug laws and, indeed, for a reconsideration of the country's authoritarian approach to a problem that is no different from problems relating to alcohol or tobacco, although these drugs are legal.[10]

The independent review of British drug laws published in March 2000 was a Police Foundation inquiry, chaired by Lady Runciman. It recommended a review of the existing classification of drugs "to take account of modern developments in medical, sociological, and scientific knowledge." It argued that the main classification criterion should continue to be that of dangerousness. Of most immediate importance to the existing drug scene in Britain, it recommended that ecstasy should be transferred from Class A to Class B, and that cannabis should be transferred from Class B to Class C under the three bands of classification from A (the most dangerous) to C (the least dangerous) that had been established under the Misuse of Drugs Act 1971. The reaction of the British government and Keith Hellawell to the review was instantly negative, insisting that there was "no justification" for any change in the categorization of cannabis and ecstasy. Lady Runciman, by contrast, said bluntly: "The most dangerous message of all is that all drugs are equally dangerous." As *The Independent* argued, should the government persist in treating the problems associated with cannabis and ecstasy as similar to those associated with heroin and cocaine, it would lose all credibility. At the time of the review, the government seemed determined to do just that and, despite its proclaimed 10-year strategy to fight drugs, appeared fearful of introducing any meaningful changes. The report also recommended that jail sentences for the possession of hard drugs should be radically reduced and that education about the dangers of drugs, rather than punishment, should be the guiding principle. The immediate reaction of the government was to sideline the report rather than act on its recommendations, but it remains as a progressive attempt to introduce a more sensible, less draconian approach to a nationwide problem that every effort at control over the preceding decades had failed to achieve.[11]

The British police are not noted for radical initiatives; rather, they are seen as a conservative if not reactionary force, yet the police rather than the Labour government made the running during 2001 in tentative efforts to reform the country's outmoded and reactionary approach to drugs. The police are at the sharp end of the war on drugs and, if only for pragmatic reasons concerning the limitations on their resources, they came to see that the war on drugs could not be won as it had been conducted for at least three decades. During June 2001, in the London borough of Lambeth, Commander Brian Paddick launched a pioneering scheme to address the widespread use of cannabis in his area. Those found in possession of the drug for personal use would have it confiscated by the police and would be warned but not prosecuted. Commander Paddick's scheme was later endorsed by the home secretary, David Blunkett (see chapter 18), as the government was induced to take its first faltering steps toward legalizing this particular drug. As *The Observer* commented:

> . . . it is truly refreshing to find senior police officers moving one step ahead of our sclerotic political process rather than their customary two paces behind. But if Mr. Paddick's approach appears courageous, it is partly a reflection of the pusillanimity of British politicians about drugs. A year after Dame Ruth Runciman's lengthy inquiry into our drugs laws, some of its key recommendations—particularly that cannabis be reclassified from a Class B to a Class C drug, thus meriting the treatment it will now receive in Lambeth—have been ignored.[12]

Statistics about drugs are flexible; that is, they are only quantifiable in part. Seizures of drugs by police or customs can be precisely tabulated, as can arrests and prosecutions, but other information is the result of estimates that rely on official surveys or university, drug charity, or press investigations. A Home Office report of 1997, *Tackling Local Drug Markets*, estimated that there were more than 30 million drug deals a year in London alone and that of these only one in every 4,000 street sales resulted in an arrest. The street deals, in any case, only accounted for between 3 and 5 million drug deals, while the majority of sales, usually of cannabis, were conducted in people's homes. Some of the people questioned spent an average of £333 a week on drugs or £17,300 a year. Of an estimated 500,000 people in London who regularly take drugs, between 20,000 and 40,000 are

Table 5.3   The Value of Drugs Seized from Passengers and Vehicles Using the Tunnel in 1996 and 1997

1996	£8.7m
1997	£16.8m

Note: Cannabis headed the list, followed by heroin, ecstasy, and cocaine.
Source: Figures extracted from *The Independent,* February 1, 1999.

"problem users," a finding that clearly suggests that the great majority of drug takers do not cause social or criminal problems as a result of their habit.

Figures for seizures of drugs from passengers and vehicles using the new Channel Tunnel during 1996 and 1997 suggest how quickly a new route will be brought into service by drug traffickers (see Table 5.3).

Figures for 1999 revealed that up to 40 percent of Britons aged 15 and 16 had tried cannabis and 20 percent had tried solvents, and that 2 percent of Britons, the highest figure for Europe, had used heroin. As for cannabis, about 9 percent of adults in England and Wales used it compared with 1 percent in Sweden, while the use of ecstasy, amphetamines, and LSD in England and Wales was also unsurpassed by any other European Union country. In every case, British drug prices over the five-year period 1995–2000 had become cheaper.

An estimate of September 2001 suggested that £6.6 billion a year was spent on drugs in Britain, equivalent to more than £113 for each man, woman, and child. These figures also imply that the government is losing the war on drugs and that the level of use is rising. The biggest market was that for heroin, worth £2,313 million, followed by crack cocaine (£1,817 million), cannabis (£1,577 million), then cocaine (£352 million), ecstasy (£294 million), and amphetamines (£258 million). Every significant report over the years 1995–2001 showed an increase in drug taking. Story after story in the press demonstrated how easy it was to obtain drugs, how they are regarded as part of the "scene" by the young or are used by middle-class and middle-aged executives as a normal aspect of recreation, and how easy it is to procure whichever drug a user desires. An article in the *Daily Telegraph* revealed that the police had turned their attention to targeting businessmen and women with recreational drug habits in London's West End. City traders, bankers, executives, and lawyers who buy small amounts of cocaine or ecstasy could see their careers ruined. As a Scotland Yard source said: "We are going to prosecute everyone caught in possession of Class A drugs."[13] It seemed that having relaxed, very mildly, their attitude in relation to cannabis, the police and the government were determined to show how tough they could be elsewhere.

Three days after this police pronouncement, a former labor minister, Tony Banks, blamed Tony Blair for slowing the pace of reform of the drug laws and described the home secretary's proposal to reduce the penalty for personal use of cannabis as a "small and timid step." In a parliamentary debate, MPs from all parties called for softer penalties for people who use drugs on a recreational basis or grow them for their own consumption. The liberal democrat home affairs spokesman, Simon Hughes, called for the decriminalization of the recreational use of all drugs by individuals, including ecstasy and cocaine, and said that the police should concentrate on prosecuting drug dealers. He said: "People who are recreational drug users we should treat as citizens. People who are addicts we should treat as victims because they need help. It's people who are the pushers, the dealers, the traffickers who are criminals. It seems to me that the personal use of recreational drugs should not be criminal." Another MP, the veteran drugs reform campaigner Paul Flynn, told the House of Commons: "In Holland, in every category, there's less use of drugs than there is here. What we are doing here with prohibition is killing our young people. Last year in this country 59 people were killed by prohibition. They were killed because their heroin was contaminated." Government reluctance to move further or faster in drug reform, stemming almost certainly from the personal views of the prime minister, was revealed in the response of the Home Office minister Robert Ainsworth, who said: "If the availability of drugs such as cocaine and heroin increases substantially, the chances of children aged 10 getting into problems with these drugs, as I did with tobacco, must increase as well."[14]

By the beginning of the new century, the drugs debate had moved to center stage in Britain, and the signs were that slowly, despite rearguard actions from a timid government, progress toward a less draconian, more sensible approach to the drugs problem would eventually emerge.

6

The U.S. Drug Scene

The Drug Enforcement Administration (DEA) is the most important U.S. federal body dealing with drugs, and it operates both at home in the United States, where it is principally concerned with fighting the distribution and consumption of drugs, and outside the United States, where it reinforces the national programs of other countries, in order to curtail the production or transit of drugs that may eventually end up in the United States. The United States is, by far, the most active country in waging a war on drugs; it also has the world's biggest drug problem in terms of consumption. Successive U.S. administrations have put huge efforts into fighting a war against the international drugs trade but, though they have registered successes in different parts of the world, the effect of these, as a rule, is rapidly annulled as a new source of supply springs up to fill the gap. U.S. strategy is to tackle the drugs business as close to the source as possible. The DEA, then, has two roles: domestic enforcement of federal drug laws and the coordination of U.S. drug investigations abroad.

A major problem facing the DEA in the United States is how to obtain information about dealers in a country where so many people deal. A court case in 2000 revealed the corrupting influence of using the services of dubious middlemen as *agents provocateurs*. Andrew Chambers worked for the DEA in its anti-drugs war for 16 years. He turned up in different towns and persuaded dealer after dealer that he was one of them, luring them into major sales of cocaine or heroin while hidden surveillance cameras captured the whole scene. In the course of his career, Chambers worked from coast to coast and helped federal officials make 400 arrests, seize 1.5 tons of cocaine, and recover $6 million in assets. Then he was "caught" because he lied in court (giving evidence) about his own misdemeanors (unrelated to drugs) with the result that he jeopardized all the evidence he had collected, since under the rigid conditions of the U.S. legal system, an irregularity of conduct by a state witness can ruin the value of his or her evidence. The scandal that arose from his exposure provoked a number of questions. Did the DEA know that Chambers had lied on the witness stand? He lied about taxes and prostitutes he had solicited; had he also lied about other matters? How did he always manage, apparently so easily, to nail drug dealers wherever he operated, and should the government have paid him, as it did, more than $4 million over the years as his cut or reward from the recovered assets and drugs? As Gerald Uelman, an ethics professor at Santa Clara Law School in California, asked, "What I worry is that it is the tip of the iceberg. How many other Andrew Chambers are there?" The revelation that Chambers had perjured himself led Janet Reno, U.S. attorney general, to press for an internal investigation into how the DEA let Chambers "slip through the cracks." More important, the government found that 12 defendants in Florida had had their cases dismissed, as had three in South Carolina, with 11 others appealing.[1] The Chambers case raised acute questions about corruption: To what extent does the DEA use doubtful methods and tainted personnel to obtain its convictions? In 1996, for example, the DEA was accused of using surveillance and informers to check on doctors who recommended the use of drugs to their patients. Pressures upon an organization such as the DEA to produce results—that is, to obtain convictions—can lead to the employment of dubious (if not downright illegal) methods that in turn produce a corruption of their own.

Cocaine first came to the United States from Peru rather than Colombia. The coca leaf was first processed into the drug cocaine in 1860 in Germany and quickly caught on as a therapeutic drug. By 1885, it had become so popular that U.S. diplomats in South America were being asked to send "full information to assure quality Peruvian coca for growing demand in the United States." This sudden U.S. interest in a plant that had been used in the Andes for thousands of years prompted the Peruvian government to convene a conference of medical and scientific personnel to examine the growing U.S. demand. Within five years, as a result, Peru had become the world's largest supplier of raw coca and was exporting 1 million kilograms of it a year. By 1901, the United States imported 863,252 kilograms (1.9 million pounds) of coca and had become the leading consumer, producer, and promoter of cocaine. The drug was used as an anesthetic and in the treatment of alcoholism, depression, and fatigue. However, in 1907 the U.S. Congress passed the Anti-Cocaine Law, which required sellers to label coca products as "poison." There was an upsurge in the use of cocaine in World War I when it was supplied to soldiers on the front line. Thereafter, the use of cocaine as an illegal drug was relatively unimportant until the 1970s, when Colombia under its powerful criminal mafias became the world's leading source of cocaine for the illicit international market; by 2001 Colombia had become the most dangerous producer of illegal drugs in the world and, despite earlier denials of any such intent, it appeared that the United States was becoming more and more involved—with money and troops and DEA programs—in fighting the drugs war on Colombian soil.

In any case, by the end of the twentieth century, the United States appeared to be locked into its anti-drugs war around half the world. In April 2000, for example, during a five-day tour of Central Asia, U.S. Secretary of

State Madeleine Albright pledged $3 million each to the presidents of Kazakhstan, Kyrgyzstan, and Uzbekistan to fight cross-border terrorism and drug trafficking.[2] In June 2000 more than 240 reputed members of the Mexican-based Nayarit heroin-smuggling ring were arrested in coordinated raids in 22 U.S. cities. In April 2001 the crew of a U.S. surveillance plane monitored the shooting-down of a seaplane carrying American missionaries after it had wrongly identified them to Peruvian fighter planes as possible drug smugglers, and a mother and her child were killed when the Cessna 185 was forced to make an emergency landing on the Amazon River. The Peruvian fighters strafed the survivors as they struggled in the water.[3] Understandably, such cavalier treatment of what at best was only a "suspect" plane caused an uproar, and the U.S. embassy in Lima announced that all drug interception flights in Peru had been suspended "pending a thorough investigation . . . of how this tragic accident took place." This small tragedy raised the astonishing question: Who controls the Peruvian Air Force—Peru or the United States?

Arguably, the most contentious aspect of the U.S. war on drugs, as far as other countries are concerned, is the U.S. practice of granting or withholding certification of countries depending on whether Washington deems they are making a proper effort to fight the international drugs trade (see chapter 8). The Clinton administration, for example, refused to certify Iran as a nonoffender, though without any hard evidence to the contrary, and adopted the same line with regard to Sudan. (Both countries had long been blacklisted by the United States for reasons unconnected with drugs.) In its annual process of certifying countries eligible for its aid, the U.S. administration report of March 1, 1995, singled out Bolivia, Colombia, Paraguay, and Peru as failing to do enough to eradicate drug production and trafficking, although they each received "partial certification" that guaranteed continuing support. The presidents of the four countries, in a joint letter of March 4 to President Clinton, said the report was unfair and proposed an Americas anti-drugs summit. In February 1998, the eighth meeting of foreign ministers from the 14-member Group of Rio and the European Union held in Panama City rejected the U.S. policy of certification by which Washington unilaterally evaluated the struggle waged by countries against drug trafficking and described the policy of "certification" as "extra territorial" and an unacceptable breach of sovereignty. The ministers argued that the policy was counterproductive and tended to weaken joint efforts to combat a common problem. Over April 18–19 of that year, at the Summit of the Americas held in Chile, officials cited the creation of a multilateral counterdrug alliance under the Organization of American States (OAS) to establish an "objective procedure" for evaluating national efforts against drug trafficking. The United States responded to this by insisting that its policy of certification would not be changed.[4] In its annual certification of countries eligible to receive its aid, the U.S. government decided on March 1, 2000, that it would endorse, as it had done in 1999, the Bolivian, Colombian, Mexican, and Peruvian governments as cooperating fully with the United States in its fight against illicit drugs. Haiti and Paraguay were declared not to be cooperating fully, but sanctions against them were again waived on grounds of U.S. national interest. In September 1999, President Clinton authorized the extension of the U.S. coastal waters control zone from 12 to 24 nautical miles to reduce drug trafficking and overfishing.

Drugs consumed in the United States are not only imported. In May 2000, a study conducted at the University of Kentucky revealed that 40 percent of marijuana grown in the United States was produced in the hills of eastern Kentucky and that it generated an annual income of $4 billion for the local economy. In July 2000, U.S. Customs service agents at Los Angeles International Airport discovered a consignment of ecstasy tablets valued at $40 million on board an incoming flight from Paris. Ecstasy, according to a New Yorker who uses the drug, is "in the 2000s what coke was in the 1980s and 1990s. It's do-able. You can get a buzz and you can work next day, better than if you'd had a night of whisky sours." The growth of the U.S. ecstasy (nonrave) market results from the fact that, compared with heroin and cocaine, it is easier to import and is as easy to buy, at between $20 and $30 a hit, as a packet of cigarettes. Most ecstasy enters New York through the JFK and Newark airports. As the U.S. commissioner of customs has said: "Ecstasy is a much neater business than cocaine or heroin smuggling. You can invest $100,000 as a distributor and get $5 million back." Arrests during 2000 revealed that Israeli crime syndicates were responsible for more than 50 percent of the ecstasy traffic; there was evidence that they were protected by the new Russian mafia that had emerged as the most powerful criminal empire in New York. In addition, Dutch smuggling rings import enough MDMA (ecstasy's base compound) into New York to manufacture millions of tablets. As the market grows, different groups jump on the bandwagon to become importers or distributors. Ecstasy has spread to a range of customers and as a customs official explained: "The drug is as common in the Bronx High School of Science as it is in *haute couture* high fashion."[5]

The Hollywood film *Traffic*, which opened in U.S. cinemas at the end of 2000, attracted a good deal of attention in both the United States and abroad; it was, as one commentator suggested, the first time Hollywood had treated the country's 30-year war on drugs realistically. Its director, Steven Soderbergh, said he hoped the film would reignite debate on America's drugs war, which costs $19 billion a year, at a time when a new administration (of George W. Bush) had been sworn in and the United States was embarking on its "Plan Colombia" at a cost of $1.3 billion; this anti-drugs aid package included military hardware that, opponents claimed, would turn Colombia into a new Vietnam. The commitment with respect to Colombia was made by the outgoing Clinton administration. Few observers believe there is likely to be a quick resolution of the Colombia drugs war, and it was feared that an escalation of anti-drugs activities in Colombia could spread to neighboring states. About 70 percent of the U.S. aid allotment will go to finance, train, and supply army antinarcotics battalions operating in southeastern Colombia, where 60 percent of the country's coca and opium is grown. Opponents of Plan Colombia argue that it will simply lead to the "narcotization" of the peace process in Colombia and escalate further the war with the guerrilla insurgents. Jorge Rocas, the director of the Consultancy on Human Rights and Displacement, claimed that under the pretext of the fight against drugs, "control over national territory, the exploitation of natural resources, and the biodiversity of the Amazon jungle are being put at risk for the benefit of the United States." Perhaps the most important point raised by *Traffic* is that the drugs issue is a problem of human nature rather than of criminal nature: at the end of 2000 there were 500,000 drug offenders in the U.S. prison system and a further million on parole or probation for drug offenses. There were some signs, though mainly muted, that a national change in attitude toward the drugs issue was underway. In five states drugs policy reform initiatives had been passed, including Proposition 36 in California, which aims to shift the focus of the criminal justice system from incarceration to treatment; the measure won more than 60 percent of the popular vote. However, the drugs issue hardly featured at all in the 2000 presidential election except for statements to the effect that both candidates planned a tougher line against drugs. As Laura Bickford, the producer of *Traffic*, said: "You cannot attack supply without attacking demand and expect to get anywhere."[6]

In downtown Los Angeles, where the 1992 riots took place, the war on drugs is likely to be carried out against young black Americans. In a routine police check, a car carrying blacks is pulled over, the occupants ordered out and made to kneel on the pavement while the police search the car and then question the men. They may then let them go. The California "three strikes" law means that two petty thefts to feed his drug habit and then a third offense can land a young man (usually black) in prison for 25 years. All too often, the result of the U.S. war on drugs is to send petty offenders to prison while the big-time dealers or money launderers stay free. It is this aspect of the war on drugs that ensures a continuing divide in U.S. society. It is easier for the police to pick on blacks or Hispanics in the inner cities than it is to arrest or check middle-class whites whose parents and lawyers know how to respond to such harassment. As Melvin Farmer, a full-time campaigner against what he sees as an inherently racist criminal justice system, claims: "They [the police] say they are looking for drugs, but that's just a pretext. They know you are on parole. Most people around here [downtown Los Angeles] are. And that gives them the right to search for anything, any little excuse to send you back to jail and perpetuate the system that keeps them all in work—the cops, the prosecutors, the judges, the prison guards, all of them." That, of course, is a view that many would reject out of hand, yet the United States has by far the highest per capita prison population of any Western country, with more than 2 million inmates of whom about a quarter are in prison for drug-related charges. This figure represents a tenfold increase over the 20 years during which the war on drugs has been waged. The statistics for prison inmates serving sentences show an unmistakable racial bias: in California, where African Americans make up 7 percent of the population, they account for 31 percent of prison inmates and 44 percent of those are serving sentences under the three strikes law, while, if Hispanics are added to the list, the 44 percent jumps to 70 percent. As it is, approximately 5 times as many whites use drugs as blacks, but the blacks are 13 times more likely to be prosecuted.

George W. Bush, despite his conservative credentials, gave little indication during the presidential election of where he stood on the drugs issue, although Colin Powell, his secretary of state, has said that the war on drugs can never be won simply by cutting off supply and arresting users. When the film *Traffic* was being made, a number of politicians, journalists, and drug experts were invited to interact with Michael Douglas (who played the film's judge character), and Orrin Hatch, the Republican chairman of the Senate Judiciary Committee, told Douglas: "This is a dirty little war with dirty little people in dirty little cities." This revealing line does not appear in the film. The evidence suggests that the war on drugs has become inextricably intertwined with a quite different aspect of U.S. politics: the issue of inner-city poverty in contrast with suburban affluence, or the ongoing race confrontation. This conflict has been ably summarized by John Kenneth Galbraith in his book *The Culture of Contentment*, published in 1992, in which he demonstrates how the United States has become two societies. He says:

> In the inner cities of the United States, as less dramatically in Europe—Brixton and Notting Hill Gate in London, areas in France where North African migrants are heavily concentrated—there is a continuing threat of underclass social disorder, crime, and conflict. Drug dealing, indiscriminate gunfire, other crime, and family disorientation and disintegration are now all aspects of everyday existence.[7]

The situation in such inner cities has become worse since Galbraith wrote those words; the relentless war on drugs is doing nothing to ameliorate that kind of situation.

During the latter half of the 1990s, a number of U.S. states voted to legalize the use of marijuana, at least for medical purposes. In November 1996 California and Arizona sought to legalize the use of marijuana in order to alleviate severe medical conditions, although the drug remained illegal under federal law. On April 14, 1997, a federal district judge restrained the Clinton administration from punishing doctors in California who recommended marijuana to patients under the terms of a new state law passed as a proposition in November 1996. The order restrained, subject to appeal, the federal government from proceeding with legal measures to restrict the practice, which had been outlawed in December 1996. On April 18, 1997, the governor of Arizona, Fyfe Symington, committed himself to sign a bill passed by 17 votes to 13 in the state senate that would neutralize the proposition of November 1996 that allowed the prescription of marijuana and other illegal drugs to alleviate severe medical conditions. In the November 1998 midterm elections in Washington, DC, voters supported a proposition to allow the medical use of marijuana by a 69 percent majority. However, the result of the ballot was held back by Republican opponents of the measure in Congress. Only by obtaining a court order did the supporters of the measure force Congress to reveal the result of the ballot. On November 5, 1999, voters in Maine passed a proposition allowing the medical use of marijuana; Maine was the eighth state to vote for the drug's use when prescribed by a physician. On April 29, 2000, the state senate of Hawaii passed a bill legalizing the medical use of marijuana by 15 votes to 10 and became the first U.S. legislature to pass such legislation. The law, which had to be signed by the state governor, allows patients with specific illnesses such as AIDS and cancer to use the drug for the relief of pain. Although prior to the Hawaii legislation voters in California, Alaska, Oregon, Washington, and Maine had passed voter initiatives allowing the medical use of the drug, none of these initiatives had been ratified by a state legislature. On September 7, 2000, a federal district judge sitting in San Francisco ruled, in a class-action lawsuit against the federal government filed in 1997, that federal officials were not obliged to prosecute or revoke the prescription license of doctors who recommended the medical use of marijuana to alleviate symptoms under the terms of a California ballot initiative approved by voters in 1996. During November 2000, voters in Colorado and Nevada endorsed the medical use of marijuana by margins of 54 to 46 percent and 65 to 35 percent, respectively. In all these instances it was clear that state sentiment was moving ahead of federal sentiment on the question of legalizing the use of marijuana. Another setback for the war on drugs came in the case of *Indianapolis v. Edmond,* in which the U.S. Supreme Court ruled by a margin of 3 to 4 that random police roadblocks set up to catch drug traffickers were an unacceptable infringement of the right to privacy as guaranteed by the Fourth Amendment to the Constitution. The court argued that roadblocks and searches had to be based on "individualized suspicion of wrongdoing."

By the beginning of the new century, with a new Republican administration in power, there were signs that—just possibly—a reconsideration of the approach to the drugs war might emerge. The problem is immense; the question is, how best to tackle it? Although the level of addiction in the United States was lower than the all-time high at the beginning of the 1980s, the drop among users was for marijuana and soft drugs, while the numbers using heroin were higher than ever, at a recorded 3 million, and more than 2 million were using cocaine. New Jersey, California, and Georgia, in the Deep South, were the main centers of heroin use. Of the country's 2 million prison inmates, between 60 and 70 percent tested positive for substance abuse (including alcohol) at the time of arrest, while drug-related offenses vary from state to state between 18 and 27 percent. The U.S. Center on Addiction and Substance Abuse estimates the cost of drug addiction, smoking, and alcohol abuse at $300 billion a year, while the amount of money spent on treatment and prevention is only a small proportion of federal and state drug-related budgets. The federal drug control budget in 2001 stood at $18.4 billion of which half goes for domestic law enforcement and only $3.6 billion for treatment. Even DEA officials admit that the flood of cocaine from Colombia or other sources has increased beyond realistic control and that nothing is likely to alter unless there is a cut in demand. One of President Bush's first summit meetings with a head of state was with Colombia's President Andrés Pastrana Arango to discuss the U.S. Plan Colombia (authorized by the Clinton administration the previous year), whereby Colombia has become the third-largest recipient of U.S. aid, after Israel and Egypt, for use in its drugs war. Whether aid at the rate of $2 million a day will make much difference to Colombia's war on drugs remains to be seen, but U.S. critics of the plan argue that it is throwing good money after bad, while Colombia's neighbors say it will spread the drugs war across their frontiers. Furthermore, they argue that the United States, which is the world's biggest drug consumer, should tackle the home problem in some other way than by its relentless policy of criminalization, which has clearly not worked. President Bush has at least said on CNN that he regards alcohol and drug addiction as "an illness" and added: "We haven't done a very good job thus far of curing people of that illness."

Early in 2001 a senior Republican figure, New York Governor George Pataki, who is a close "henchman" of President Bush, laid before the New York legislature a plan to abolish the Rockefeller Code. Introduced in 1973 by Governor Nelson Rockefeller, the code laid down mandatory jail sentences of between 15 years and life for the more serious drug offenses and lesser prison terms for nonviolent drug-related crimes. The Pataki bill aimed to cut the 15 years to 8.5 years and provide treatment rather than prison for a range of nonviolent drug-related offenses.[8] However, such signs of a change appeared to have been put aside by the start of May 2001, when it began to emerge that the conservative approach to drugs was winning the battle for presidential approval, and that a series of initiatives was on the way favoring punishment over treatment at home and possible military intervention against the drug cartels of Latin America. The U.S. Department of Education, for example, announced that it would investigate the drug backgrounds of students seeking government loans, while Congress discussed increasing penalties for the use of ecstasy. By April, reformers who had hoped for a new approach to the drugs question had become increasingly dismayed that hardliners on the issue appeared to have won the battle with the president. As Ethan Nadelmann, the director of the Lindesmith Center, the drug-reform group based in New York, said: "We have seen one step forward on mandatory minimums, but three or four steps back on other issues." John Walters, the new "drugs czar," came from a background of working in the drug control office and was seen as a hardliner; he will control an annual budget of $22 billion that will cover activities ranging from military hardware to law enforcement on the Mexican border. A comment by Mr. Nadelmann raises the most interesting issue of all in U.S. public life: "It is hard to believe," he said, "that some of the younger senior staff in the administration do not have some past experience with marijuana and other substances."[9]

Despite the apparent growth of new hard-line attitudes toward drugs, the evidence would suggest that the war on drugs is not succeeding. As Joan Smith argued in *Druglink*: "Punishing users has failed, so the United States is now exporting castigation to producers. South America is becoming the whipping-boy of drug-ravaged U.S.A." In a hard-hitting appraisal of U.S. policies on drugs, the author argued, in relation to the growing U.S. involvement in Colombia, that "Clinton even managed to persuade his European Union allies, including Britain, to offer financial support to this scheme, which has been denounced by opponents from drug reformers and human rights activists to Republicans worried by an apparently open-ended war that the Colombian government is by no means certain to win."[10] The war on drugs "legitimizes" U.S. interventions in Latin America.

A quite different approach to drugs was reported in November 2001 when the U.S. government approved the first clinical trials of ecstasy as a treatment for victims of post-traumatic stress disorder. Medical researchers at the University of South Carolina were given permission by the Food and Drug Administration to carry out a series of tests in which they hoped traumatized patients would respond better to psychotherapy under the influence of the drug, which is normally associated with teenage raves and dancing. However, Dr. Julie Holland said: "Being a popular illicit drug does not negate the potential medical benefits. MDMA (the chemical name for ecstasy) provides an opportunity to process a trauma in a more comfortable atmosphere—similar to anesthesia, which allows painful surgery to proceed."[11]

7
U.S. Statistics

The annual *National Household Survey on Drug Abuse* issued by the U.S. Substance Abuse and Mental Health Services Administration (SAMHSA) provides a wealth of information on the American drug scene, including tobacco and alcohol, as well as highlighting trends and attitudes related to the war on drugs. The survey for 1999 provided for the first time state-by-state estimates of illicit drug, alcohol, and cigarette use by age group.[1] In an upbeat introduction to the survey, the then director of the White House Office of National Drug Control Policy (ONDCP), Barry McCaffrey, said: "The survey provides extremely encouraging news that teen drug use is going down significantly. However, we must be aware that the younger a person is when first trying marijuana, the greater the risk of drug dependency later. Young people may think that they are experimenting, but, as this study shows, they are really gambling with their futures." Although there had been a decrease in marijuana use by 12 to 17 year olds between 1997 and 1999, from 9.4 percent to 7.0 percent, the use of cocaine, heroin, hallucinogens, and inhalants among the same group had remained stable. However, over the same three years (1997–1999) there had been an increase in illicit drug use among young adults aged 18 to 25, from 14.7 percent in 1997 to 18.8 percent in 1999. The rates of use for the older age groups—26 to 34 and 35 years and older—had not changed significantly.

According to the new expanded *National Household Survey on Drug Abuse* for 1999, an estimated 14.8 million Americans were current users of illicit drugs; an estimated 66.8 million Americans were current users of a tobacco product (30.2 percent of the population); and 105 million Americans (47.3 percent) were current users of alcohol. Figures for first-time users of these substances indicate just how hard it will be to change patterns that are so widespread throughout the United States. Thus, an estimated 2.3 million persons first used marijuana in 1998, equivalent to about 6,400 new marijuana users a day, of whom more than two-thirds were under 18 years old. Similarly, an estimated 1.6 million people began smoking cigarettes on a daily basis in 1998, and about half of these were under 18. And an estimated 4.9 million people tried cigars for the first time in 1998, about 13,000 a day; this represented a threefold increase in cigar smoking since 1991. In 1999 there were 554,932 drug-related hospital emergency department episodes in the United States and 1,015,206 drug mentions in episodes dealt with by hospitals.

Elaborations on these findings include the following: The rates of current (1999) illicit drug use for major racial/ethnic groups were 6.6 percent for whites, 6.8 percent for Hispanics, and 7.7 percent for blacks. Rates were highest among the American Indian/Alaska Native population (10.6 percent) and among persons reporting multiple race origins (11.2 percent), while Asians had the lowest rate of 3.2 percent (see Figure 7.1). Rates for drug use were higher for metropolitan areas than nonmetropolitan areas. Of the 66.8 million Americans who were current users of tobacco products (ranging in age from 12 years upward; see Figure 7.2), 57 million smoked cigarettes, 12.1 million smoked cigars, 7.6 million used smokeless tobacco, and 2.4 million smoked tobacco in pipes. Youths aged 12 to 17 who smoked cigarettes were seven times more likely to use illicit drugs than youths who didn't smoke, while young adults aged 18 to 25 who smoked were four times more likely to use illicit drugs than those who did not smoke. Of the 105 million Americans aged 12 and over who used alcohol (Figure 7.3), about 45 million engaged in binge drinking and 12.4 million were heavy drinkers. Though the consumption of alcohol is illegal for those under 21 years of age, some 10.4 million drinkers were aged 12 to 20 in 1999 and of these, 6.8 million engaged in binge drinking and 2.1 million were heavy drinkers.

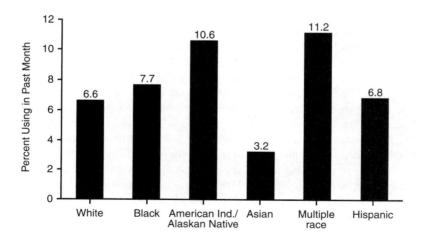

Figure 7.1 Illicit drug use in the United States, by race/ethnicity, ages 12 and older, 1999 (www.samhsa.gov/oas/NHSDA/1999/Chapter2.htm, retrieved June 13, 2001).

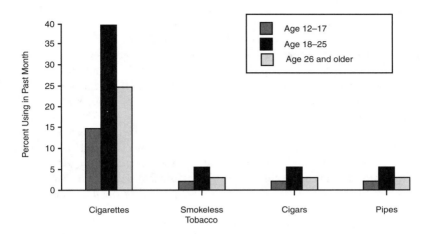

Figure 7.2 Tobacco use in the United States, by age, 1999 (www.samhsa.gov/oas/NHSDA/ 1999/Chapter2.htm, retrieved June 13, 2001).

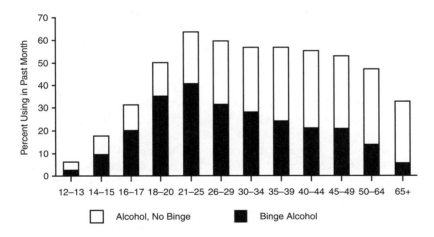

Figure 7.3 Alcohol use in the United States, by age, 1999 (www.samhsa.gov/oas/NHSDA/ 1999/Chapter2.htm, retrieved June 13, 2001).

Trends in heroin use are hard to pinpoint accurately as there is a wide variability in use. However, a large proportion of new heroin initiates are young and smoke, sniff, or snort heroin; of 471,000 persons using heroin for the first time in the three-year period 1996–1998, more than a quarter

(125,000) were under age 18 and another 47 percent (222,000) were aged 18 to 25. An estimated 1.6 million Americans used prescription-type pain relievers nonmedically for the first time in 1998; this was a significant increase over the 1980s when there were fewer than 500,000 such new users a year. The rate of such use went up sharply during the 1990s among the 12 to 17 age group, from 6.3 per 1,000 potential new users in 1990 to 32.4 per 1,000 in 1998, while the comparable figure for the 18 to 25 age group was from 7.7 per 1,000 in 1990 to 20.3 per 1,000 in 1998.

In a section of the SAMHSA survey on substance dependence and treatment, the following figures are given: In 1999 an estimated 3.6 million Americans, representing 1.6 percent of the total population aged 12 and older, were dependent on illicit drugs. An estimated 8.2 million Americans were dependent on alcohol, representing 3.7 percent of the population aged 12 and over, and of the above groups, 1.5 million people were dependent on both drugs and alcohol, with a total of 10.3 million people dependent on either drugs or alcohol. In general, adults who first used drugs at an early age were more likely to be dependent on them than adults who only came to use them at a later age. Males were more likely to be dependent on both drugs and alcohol than females—in 1999, 2 percent of males (aged 12 and older) were dependent on illicit drugs and 4.9 percent of males were dependent on alcohol; the comparable figures for females were 1.3 percent and 2.6 percent, respectively.

Statistics relating to individual states showed that of the 10 states with the highest rates of illicit drug abuse, six were in the Western region, while eight states with the lowest rates were in the Southern region, though there were variations within these figures. The state with the highest rate of binge drinking (28.7 percent) was North Dakota, while seven out of the 10 top states for alcohol abuse were in the Midwest region. The state with the highest rates of dependence on both illicit drugs and alcohol was Alaska.

A breakdown of types of drugs taken in 1999 showed that marijuana was the most widely prevalent drug, used by 75 percent of the current drug users, with 57 percent of drug users taking marijuana only, while a further 18 percent took marijuana and other drugs. The remaining 25 percent of drug users took drugs other than marijuana. Of the 6.4 million users of drugs other than marijuana, 4 million (1.8 percent of the population aged 12 and older) were using psychotherapeutics (pain relievers, tranquillizers, stimulants, and sedatives) nonmedically. An estimated 1.5 million people were cocaine users, and the estimated number of crack users was 413,000. An estimated 900,000 Americans were hallucinogen users and 200,000 were heroin users. In general, there was a correlation between drug use and educational status, with college graduates registering the lowest rate of use. Drug use was highest among the unemployed, although the majority of drug users (77 percent) were either employed full time or part time. Figures for first-time drug users in 1998 were as follows: 2.3 million Americans used marijuana for the first time; 149,000 used heroin for the first time; and 934,000 used cocaine for the first time (as opposed to 514,000 in 1994); 1.2 million used hallucinogens for the first time (almost twice the average annual number during the 1980s); 991,000 used inhalants for the first time; and an estimated 1.6 million used prescription-type pain relievers nonmedically. By comparison, in 1997 there were 4.7 million new users of alcohol (compared with 3.2 million in 1992), and the rate of use by the 18 to 25 age group had risen from 157.5 per 1,000 in 1989 to 219.3 per 1,000 in 1997, while the rate of initiation of alcohol use among the 12 to 17 age group had risen from 117.6 per 1,000 in 1989 to 216.8 per 1,000 in 1997.

A series of calculations from 1990 to 1998 for causes of death in the United States shows the following average annual rates of death: from tobacco 430,700 (1990–1994); from alcohol 110,640 (1996); from adverse reactions to prescription drugs 32,000 (1982–1998); from suicides 30,575; from homicide 18,272; from all drugs (licit and illicit) 16,926; and from nonsteroidal antiinflammatory drugs such as aspirin 7,600. The source of these figures, the Web site "Drug War Facts," also makes the following observation in relation to marijuana: "An exhaustive search of the literature finds no deaths induced by marijuana. The U.S. Drug Abuse Warning Network (DAWN) records instances of drug mentions in medical examiners' reports, and though marijuana is mentioned, it is usually in combination with alcohol or other drugs. Marijuana alone has not been shown to cause an overdose death."[2]

According to a study prepared by the Lewin Group for the National Institute on Drug Abuse, the estimated total economic cost of alcohol and drug abuse in the United States for 1992 came to $245.7 billion and of this, $97.7 billion was due to drug abuse (but not nicotine). The 1995 *National Drug Control Strategy*, produced by the ONDCP, determined how much money was spent on illegal drugs that otherwise would have been spent for legitimate purposes or savings and found that, between 1988 and 1995, Americans spent $57.3 billion on drugs, divided among cocaine ($38 billion), heroin ($9.6 billion), marijuana ($7 billion), and other illegal substances ($2.7 billion).

Alcoholism and alcohol-related problems contribute to 100,000 deaths a year in the United States. According to the National Council on Alcoholism and Drug Dependence, nearly 13.8 million Americans aged 18 and over have problems with drinking and 8.1 million of them are alcoholics. Almost three times as many men (9.8 million) as women (3.9 million) are problem drinkers, and the prevalence is highest for both sexes between the ages of 18 and 29. People who begin drinking before age 15 are four times more likely to develop alcoholism than those who begin at 21. Between 1985 and 1992, the economic costs of alcoholism rose by 42 percent to $148 billion and two-thirds of these costs related to lost productivity. According to victim reports, 183,000 (37 percent) of rapes and sexual assaults each year involve alcohol use by the offender, as do just over 197,000 (15 percent) of robberies, about 661,000 (27 percent) of aggravated assaults, and 1.7 million (25 percent) of simple assaults.[3]

The Race Question and the War on Drugs

Some revealing figures about the way the domestic war on drugs is conducted are provided by the nongovernment agency Human Rights Watch. In its report *Punishment and Prejudice: Racial Disparities in the War on Drugs*,[4] it reveals that there are five times more white drug users than black, yet relative to the population, black men are admitted to prison on drug charges at a rate that is 13.4 times greater than the rate for white men. The report claims that it is in large part due to the extraordinary racial disparities in incarceration for drug offenses, that blacks are incarcerated for all offenses at 8.2 times the rate for whites.

Ten U.S. states—California, Illinois, Louisiana, Maryland, New Jersey, New York, Ohio, Pennsylvania, Virginia, and Washington—have the highest rates of drug offender admissions to prison relative to population. There are wide variations, with only six per 100,000 residents of Maine being admitted to prison for drug offenses as opposed to 91 in California. Even more relevant to an assessment of the impact of the war on drugs is the fact that drug offenders are sent to prison at a rate relative to population that is 13 percent higher than the rate for violent offenders. Six states—Arkansas, California, Illinois, New Jersey, New York, and Virginia—send drug offenders to prison at rates ranging from 50 to 100 percent higher than rates for violent offenders. The percentage of the population using drugs in the United States varies substantially from state to state, between 4.1 and 8.2 percent of the state populations, although the estimated percentage of drug users may not tally with the rate at which users are sent to prison. Thus, states with the higher rates of drug use are not necessarily those with the higher drug offender rates of prison admissions, or vice versa. Oregon, with the third-highest percentage of drug use, has one of the lowest rates of drug offender admissions to prison. Nor does low drug use automatically correlate with low drug offender admissions.

The Human Rights Watch report examines the question of whether drug offenders are dangerous criminals, which is one of the justifications for imprisoning them. It has some revealing things to say about this question. For example, "Research to date on criminal histories of incarcerated drug offenders consistently shows, however, that most cannot reasonably be considered dangerous individuals. Three quarters of the drug offenders in state prisons in 1997 had no prior convictions for violent crimes; one third had prior sentences limited to drug offenses." Such analyses raise questions about the public or state perception that drug users are a menace to society as opposed to being a menace to themselves.

In a section of the report, titled "Racially Disproportionate Incarceration of Drug Offenders," Human Rights Watch asks why so many more American blacks, both proportionately and absolutely, are imprisoned for drug offenses than whites. Thus, 56 percent of drug offenders in state prisons nationwide are black. Figures for 1996 reveal that 62.6 percent of all drug offenders admitted to state prisons were black, while whites accounted for 36.7 percent. The disproportion between the races was much higher in certain states; 90 percent of all drug admissions to prison in Maryland and Illinois were black, and in all states, "the proportion of drug offenders admitted to state prison greatly exceeds the proportions of the state population that is black." The most alarming comparative figures are the following: The drug offender admissions rate for black men ranges from 60 to 1,146 per 100,000 black men, while the white rate, in contrast, begins at 6 and rises no higher than 139 per 100,000 white men. In 10 states, black men are sent to prison on drug charges at rates between 26 and 57 times greater than the rate for white men in the same state. In Illinois, "a black man is 57 times more likely to be sent to prison on drug charges than a white man." As Human Rights Watch points out, the high rate of black incarceration in the United States is "propelled by nonviolent drug offenses" and but for the war on drugs, the extent of black incarceration would be significantly lower. Drug offenses account for 38 percent of all black admissions to prison, but account for only 24 percent of white admissions.

The war on drugs has led to a disproportionate targeting of black drug offenders as opposed to white offenders. During the 1970s, blacks were twice as likely as whites to be arrested for drug offenses, but by 1988, when the war on drugs was in full force, blacks were arrested on drug charges at five times the rate of whites. Disparities in the rates of arrest also varied enormously from state to state: In Georgia between 1990 and 1995, relative to their shares of the population, blacks were arrested for cocaine offenses at 17 times the rate for whites, and in Minnesota during the 1980s drug arrests of blacks increased by 500 percent as opposed to 22 percent for whites. These figures do not reflect a differing rate of drug use between blacks and whites. One crucial explanation for the difference arises from the way in which the war on drugs has been conducted. As Human Rights Watch points out: "Yet because drug law enforcement resources have been concentrated in low-income, predominantly minority urban areas, drug-offending whites have been disproportionately free from arrest compared to blacks."

Although the number of women in U.S. prisons is proportionately far lower than the figure for men, the racial pattern of incarceration is similar. In 1997, black women were more than eight times as likely to be in prison than

white women. Moreover, the war on drugs has led to a dramatic increase in
the number of women in prison. Between 1990 and 1997 the number of
women in prison for drug offenses nearly doubled, while between the years
1986 and 1996, the number of women incarcerated on drug charges rose by
888 percent. In 1979, only 12 percent of women in state prison had been
convicted of drug offenses; by 1997 the figure had risen dramatically to 34.4
percent. In 2000, Human Rights Watch pointed out:

> As with men, the impact of the war on drugs falls disproportionately on
> black women. Nationwide, 42.2 percent of all black women and 36.1 percent
> of white women admitted to prison in 1996 were convicted of drug offenses.
> Even in the states with the lowest percentages of female drug offender ad-
> missions, the figure is more than one in five (with the exception of Iowa).
> Black women constitute 6.3 percent of the national adult population and 7
> percent of prison drug admissions; white women constitute 43.2 percent of
> the national adult population but only 5.4 percent of drug admissions.[5]

These figures bring out the startling difference between the treatment of
blacks and whites as a result of the war on drugs. A black citizen of the
United States who is a drug offender, whether male or female, faces a far
greater likelihood of being sent to prison for the offense than a white person.
    The widespread pattern of drug, tobacco, and alcohol use in the United
States (14.8 million drug users, 66.8 million tobacco users, and 105 million
alcohol users) would suggest that those who wish to use such drugs—a wide
proportion of the population—will continue to do so whatever programs are
mounted by the government of the day. Given the intensity of the war on
drugs over the last two decades of the twentieth century, there is little evidence that it has dented the growth of the drug use or abuse pattern. In all the
calculations regarding drugs, tobacco, and alcohol, statistics for the 12 to 17
age group are considered and the numbers of teenagers using these three
stimulants is huge, despite the fact that in all three cases they are breaking
the law. Legal or illegal availability of these stimulants and the desire of
large segments of the population to purchase and use them would appear to
outweigh all efforts by the government to cut back on their use significantly.

Comparison: The United States and Britain

In mid-2000 the population of Britain stood at 59,511,464, while the population of the United States stood at 275,562,673, approximately five times as
great as that of Britain. A comparison of figures for the two countries for
deaths from drugs, alcohol, and tobacco shows a broad similarity of pattern,
though with some interesting variations. U.S. deaths from drugs at the end of
the 1990s averaged 16,926 a year, while in Britain the figure was 2,943, so

that the U.S. rate of deaths was slightly more than five and a half times that of Britain. The larger figure for the United States is almost entirely accounted for, on a pro rata basis, by its larger population. British deaths from alcohol, at an annual average of 4,907, were vastly lower than those in the United States, which numbered 110,640—a differential of more than 22 to1. Deaths (mainly cancers) resulting from smoking showed a British rate of 120,000 a year compared to a U.S. rate of 430,700 a year, so that, proportionately to population, the United States had achieved a better scenario than Britain, with a differential of only three and a half U.S. deaths from smoking to one in Britain. What is plain from these figures is that both alcoholism and smoking do far greater damage to the populations of the two countries in terms of both deaths and avoidable sickness than does drug abuse. These figures, therefore, raise the question for both countries: Why do they conduct such highly publicized wars on drugs but not on either tobacco or alcohol? The answer in both cases is political: what is acceptable in any given circumstance. Any attempt to ban either smoking or alcohol (the U.S. government tried to ban the latter with disastrous results in the 1920s) would meet with huge uncontrollable opposition from both the consumers and the producers. Drugs, on the other hand, are principally produced in developing countries and illegally imported.

8

The U.S. Policy of Certification

One of the more controversial aspects of U.S. foreign policy is the annual determination by the U.S. government that certain countries will be certified or not certified according to whether or not they are making sufficient effort to fight the drugs war, either by limiting the production of drugs in their own countries or by combating the use of their countries for drug-transit purposes. Depending on Washington's decisions, such countries may or may not qualify for U.S. aid. The United States uses this drug certification process to force corruption to the surface. Section 490 of the Foreign Assistance Act of 1961 requires the president to certify annually that each major drug-producing or transit country has cooperated fully or has taken adequate steps on its own to meet the goals and objectives of the 1988 UN Convention against Illicit Traffic in Narcotic Drugs and Psychotropic Substances (1988 UN Drug Convention), including rooting out public corruption. This, by any standards, is a tall order; in effect, it empowers the U.S. government to decide the extent to which such countries are corrupt and the extent to which they are attempting to combat such corruption. Most countries have enough on their hands combating corruption at home. In a presidential letter of December 4, 1998, to the chairman and ranking members of the House Committees on Appropriations and International Relations and the Senate Committees on Appropriations and Foreign Relations,[1] President Bill Clinton set forth his policy for the coming year: "I have determined that the following countries are major illicit drug-producing or transit countries: Afghanistan, Aruba, the Bahamas, Belize, Bolivia, Brazil, Myanmar (Burma), Cambodia, China, Colombia, Dominican Republic, Ecuador, Guatemala, Haiti, Hong Kong, India, Jamaica, Laos, Mexico, Nigeria, Pakistan, Panama, Paraguay, Peru, Taiwan, Thailand, Venezuela, and Vietnam." This is a formidable list, and all these countries would expect to come under some form of U.S. pressure about their inability or unwillingness to curtail drug activities. The president went on to say that he had removed Iran and Malaysia from the list of major drug-producing countries and designated them countries of concern. Iran had long been a traditional opium-producing country but during the 1990s had carried out a successful policy of eradicating illicit opium poppy cultivation. Although large amounts of illicit drugs continued to transit Iran en route to Europe, the

U.S. government had no evidence that significant quantities of these drugs were destined for the United States. Similarly, in relation to Malaysia, the president said there was no evidence that drugs destined for the United States had transited Malaysia over the previous few years. The president also stated that the following countries or regions were places of concern for the purpose of U.S. counternarcotics efforts and he gave varying reasons for listing the Netherlands Antilles, Turkey and other "Balkan Route Countries," Syria and Lebanon, Cuba, "Major Cannabis Producers" (under which he listed Kazakhstan, Kyrgyzstan, Morocco, the Philippines, and South Africa, but went on to say that the cannabis produced was either consumed locally or was exported to countries other than the United States), and central Asia (Tajikistan and Uzbekistan, which were cleared of significant opium poppy cultivation). The president pointed out that Central America was the natural conduit for the transshipment of drugs from South America to the United States, and he expressed particular concern about the roles of Costa Rica, El Salvador, Honduras, and Nicaragua. This list of countries over which the president and, through him, the U.S. government expressed concern for their drug activities and their likely impact on the U.S. drug market amounted to a substantial number of countries worldwide that the United states sought to influence in terms of its war on drugs.

In its 1999 annual report known as the International Narcotics Control Strategy Report (INCSR),[2] the Department of State's Bureau for International Narcotics and Law Enforcement Affairs claimed that international counternarcotics efforts of the previous few years had narrowed the field of action of the drug syndicates and that crop reduction and chemical control programs had caused major shifts in cultivation and refining operations. The biggest change noted was the steady decline in the Andean coca crop, which is the source of cocaine destined for the U.S. market, with the most dramatic declines occurring in Bolivia and Peru. During the four-year period 1995–1999, the eradication program carried out by the Bolivian government had reduced the number of hectares devoted to coca cultivation from 48,600 hectares (120,090 acres) to 21,800 hectares (53,870 acres) and in Peru from 115,300 hectares (284,910 acres) to 38,700 hectares (95,630 acres). Such reductions, it was claimed, were the result of close cooperation between the governments of these countries and that of the United States. However, coca production in Colombia over the same period increased by 20 percent as the Colombian syndicates, to make up for the loss of production in their major traditional sources of supply, moved coca cultivation to the conflict-ridden south and southwest of the country. The implications of this Colombian move were not encouraging for that country since it made allies of the antigovernment guerrillas, who fund their activities with money from their coca crops, and the drug producers. As a result, the Colombian cocaine syndicates expanded the coca crop from 101,800 hectares (251,550 acres) in

1998 to 122,500 hectares (302,700 acres) in 1999. In addition, it was noted that the Colombian syndicates had achieved much greater levels of efficiency in extracting cocaine from their coca crops. These developments in Bolivia, Peru, and Colombia illustrate the nature of the drugs business. When successful efforts lead to a drop in production in one area, these act as a stimulus to intensified efforts to increase production elsewhere. As a consequence of these changes, the United States proposed a $1.3 billion assistance package to strengthen Colombian democracy and reinvigorate the economy while bringing new pressures to bear on the drugs trade.

The second priority for the U.S. government was to cut the flows of heroin to the United States where there were growing signs of its increasing use and popularity, particularly among young people. Stopping heroin production at its source is more difficult than stopping cocaine; at present the coca plant is only grown in three Andean countries, although in the early twentieth century the largest coca supporter was the Dutch East Indies, followed by Taiwan (Japanese Formosa). The opium poppy, however, can be produced in almost all regions of the world. Moreover, unlike the coca harvest, up to three harvests a year may be produced by opium. The U.S. effort to limit the cultivation of opium was also hampered because the vast bulk of the illicit crop was grown in two countries—Afghanistan and Myanmar (Burma)—where the United States had very little influence. Colombia, meanwhile, had also become a substantial producer of opium. The United States has embarked on a number of joint operations with other governments to limit drug production such as Operation Millennium of October 1999 between the U.S. and Colombian governments, which led to the arrest of scores of Colombian traffickers and had repercussions in Peru, the United States, and Europe.

Part of the U.S. strategy is to promote institutional changes in drug-producing and transit countries by means of training programs carried out by U.S. law enforcement agencies or by assisting governments in strengthening their judicial and banking systems. In fact, this is a highly controversial area that has produced nationalist reactions to U.S. interference. As the 1999 INCSR suggests: "There have been instances where law enforcement agencies in key drug-affected countries have captured and jailed prominent traffickers, only to see them set free by the arbitrary decision of a single judge or magistrate. Thanks to several long-standing cooperative administration of justice programs, such instances are becoming rarer." The sanction most feared by drug barons in South America is extradition to the United States, but this raises extremely sensitive political reactions and drug barons have been highly successful in exploiting national sensitivities on this subject. Nonetheless, for the first time in nine years, the Colombian government extradited one of its citizens to the United States in 1999, though there was no guarantee that such a practice would continue.

Too often in the war on drugs, successes in one area are matched by failures in another, while the closing down in whole or part of one source of production merely stimulates the creation of a new source of supply. Despite major U.S. successes in relation to curtailing the cocaine-producing sources in Latin America during the late 1990s, this did not prevent the transport of hundreds of tons of cocaine to the United States and Western Europe, as well as to markets in Latin America, Asia, Africa, and the CIS countries. As the INCSR pointed out—an ironical comparison in the age of globalization— "The major drug-trafficking syndicates are the criminal equivalent of large multinational organizations, with drug distribution centers and money laundering on every continent." Moreover, new syndicates are constantly springing up to compete for a share in the business. And the markets change as well. For example, Europe, which was once the preserve of the heroin trade, has developed a growing appetite for cocaine and amphetamines. The primary objective of the U.S. war on drugs outside the United States is to reduce the sources of supply, although, as the DEA and other government officials have discovered, crop control has huge economic and political implications in poor countries where a substantial sector of the population may depend on income from this source. There have to be alternatives, and these have to be proposed and funded and make sense in the particular environment where they are introduced. Such a process takes time, and if it is inadequately managed, there will be massive pressures from the drug-producing vested interests to persuade small farmers to revert to drug production.

Corruption, in one form or another, acts as the lubricant for the illicit drugs trade. The enormous turnover of profits attached to the trade enables the syndicates and dealers to buy immunity, and to corrupt police, border guards, customs officials, airport officials and pilots, and members of the military who are supposedly combating their activities, as well as politicians and law enforcement officers, often at the highest levels. A ton of pure cocaine has a street value in the United States of $100 million and much more if it is mixed with adulterants. The U.S. government seizes about 100 tonnes (98.4 tons) of cocaine a year (worth $10 billion), yet the loss is hardly felt by the big syndicates. In 2000 the United States denied certification to two countries—Afghanistan and Myanmar; gave four countries—Cambodia, Haiti, Nigeria, and Paraguay—certificates but under its National Interest Certification provision (that is, they were declared not to be operating fully, but sanctions against them were waived on grounds of U.S. national interest); and 20 countries certificates under its provision of Certification with Explanation (they were trying but had a long way to go). This latter group of countries consisted of the Bahamas, Bolivia, Brazil, China, Colombia, Dominican Republic, Ecuador, Guatemala, Hong Kong, India, Jamaica, Laos, Mexico, Pakistan, Panama, Peru, Taiwan, Thailand, Venezuela, and

Vietnam. A number of countries were removed from the list requiring certification during the latter half of the 1990s, including Aruba, Belize, Iran, Lebanon, Malaysia, Morocco, and Syria.

Statements of explanation from the U.S. government for its certification decisions help us to understand Washington's perspective on its war on drugs, while also presenting a broad picture of the principal drug-producing and transit countries worldwide, particularly as these are seen to have an impact on the United States. The following appraisals were presented in February 2000.

In 1999 Afghanistan cultivated a larger opium poppy crop and harvested more opium gum than any other country. Although U.S. sources indicated a 23 percent crop increase over the previous year, the UNDCP estimated a 70 percent increase. Despite U.S. attempts to persuade the Taliban government to curtail production, and the Taliban government's 1997 ban on the cultivation of the opium poppy, in fact it taxed the crop at a rate of 10 percent and also received payments from traffickers. Although the Taliban claimed that it was employing certain counterdrug measures, in reality Afghanistan had become the world's largest producer of opium and heroin.

The Bahamas, on the other hand, was seen as a major transit country for drugs from South America en route to the United States; in this case, however, there was close cooperation between the governments of the United States and the Bahamas. In addition, the Bahamas had become a center for money laundering and, though the government was seen to be taking action to curtail this activity, it had a long way to go to become effective. Despite efforts to strengthen the Bahamas judicial system, no major drug traffickers had been convicted and sent to prison, while weak bail laws allowed drug traffickers who had been arrested to obtain bail and continue operating. The Bahamas needed to adopt a comprehensive national drugs strategy.

Bolivia, in contrast, came in for high praise for having exceeded the schedule of its five-year plan to eliminate all illicit coca production; in 1999 the government eradicated a total of 16,999 hectares (42,010 acres) of coca. Even so, Bolivia remained the world's third-largest producer of cocaine. The government had also introduced successful legislation to prevent precursor chemicals from being smuggled into the country from neighboring states. It also aimed to launch an eradication program for the Yungas, where it produces its licit coca crop, but where there was evidence of coca being diverted for illicit conversion into cocaine. Of vital importance to Bolivia was the maintenance of its alternative crops, although the demand for alternative development assistance by former coca farmers was exceeding supply and that could threaten the future success of the government's eradication policy. Attempts to reform the Bolivian judicial code were less than successful in providing a mechanism to discipline members of the judiciary, and the anti-money-laundering law had yet to be used effectively.

Brazil is important in the South American drug complex as a significant transit country for drugs being moved north to the United States; it is also a major producer of precursor chemicals and synthetic drugs. In April 1999 a Brazilian Congressional Panel of Inquiry was formed to investigate drug trafficking. Its investigations led to 115 arrests, including that of many government officials, thus bringing to light the corrupt impact of the drugs trade on public institutions and civil servants. Money laundering is a major aspect of the illegal drugs business in Brazil, and the Brazilian Central Bank created a special internal agency to trace money laundering. Brazil also joined both the Financial Action Task Force (FATF) and the Egmont Group, two international bodies concerned with increasing efforts to curtail money laundering.

The United States designated Cambodia a major drug-transit country in 1999. General lawlessness and political turmoil make any credible Cambodian anti-drugs policy unlikely and the country did not warrant full certification by the United States. The levels of corruption in Cambodia also make drug law enforcement uneven or problematic. Despite these failings, the United States provided Cambodia with a national interests certification for 2000 in order to protect vital U.S. national interests in the country, including promoting democracy in Cambodia and maintaining stability in the region. Although Cambodia remains vulnerable to drug trafficking, the United States felt that, should counterdrug sanctions be imposed, it would not be possible to respond to potential crises or assist in strengthening the bases of Cambodia's democratic system.

The People's Republic of China maintains a strong anti-drugs policy and, for example, seizures of heroin in China account for the great majority of heroin seized throughout Asia. In 1999 China cooperated with the UNDCP and other states in the region to reduce the demand for illicit drugs. China and the United States signed a Customs Mutual Assistance Agreement with the aim of accelerating the flow of intelligence related to the counterdrug effort between the two countries. However, China often fails to respond to U.S. requests for information and has also failed to strengthen its anti-money-laundering legislation. Even so, it is committed to a firm anti-drugs policy of its own.

Although Colombia is the source of over three-quarters of the world's cocaine production, it met U.S. certification criteria in 1999 because it had made important strides in combating illicit drugs in full cooperation with the United States. The arguments in relation to Colombia raise many questions about the war on drugs (see chapter 9) and U.S. involvement in that country.

The Dominican Republic is an important transit country for drugs en route from South America to the United States; during 1999 its government cooperated fully with the U.S. government and, among other measures, extradited nine Dominicans to the United States and kept a number of other persons in custody while extradition proceedings were considered. During 1999 the Dominican Republic and neighboring Haiti agreed to border-control accords. The government announced various other measures, and the National Drug Control Directorate worked closely with the DEA. The U.S. government determined to continue encouraging the Dominican government to regularize its extradition process.

Ecuador is a two-way transit country: for cocaine from Colombia to the United States and for precursor chemicals going south to drug-processing laboratories in Colombia and Peru. Ecuador pursues an active anti-drugs agenda, and its government cooperates closely with that of the United States in the war on drugs. In November 1999 Ecuador entered into a 10-year agreement with the United States to allow U.S. regional counterdrug detection missions and monitoring missions to operate from the Ecuadorean air force base in Manta.

Guatemala is both a transit country for drugs from South America to the United States and a storage point for cocaine prior to its shipment through Mexico. In 1999 the government began to implement a national drugs policy, but though it is a party to the 1988 UN Drug Convention, some of the convention's provisions have not been codified into Guatemalan law. Cooperation with the United States is generally hampered by corruption and a weak administration.

Haiti is a significant transit country for cocaine destined for the U.S. market. However, as the INCSR for 1999 states, the U.S. government "cannot certify Haiti as having fully cooperated with the United States on drug control, or as having taken adequate steps on its own, to meet the goals and objectives of the 1988 UN Drug Convention, to which Haiti is a party. However, U.S. vital national interests require that foreign assistance continue to be provided to Haiti."

In the case of Hong Kong, though it remains a major drug-transit center, the United States sees its role as a transshipment point for drugs to North America as having diminished. During 1999 Hong Kong introduced new legislation to strengthen its anti-money-laundering regime and the laws affecting drug profits. Its law enforcement agencies cooperated fully with those of the United States, and it continued to put in place new initiatives to increase the effectiveness of its anti-drugs efforts.

India is the world's largest producer of licit opium; it is also, unsurprisingly since it is located between Afghanistan and Myanmar, a major transit country for heroin destined for Europe. The Indian government takes active steps to prevent the illicit production of opium and had major success in reducing illicit poppy production between 1995 and 1999. In 1999 India had formal talks with Pakistan and Myanmar about cross-border counter-drug issues.

Jamaica is a major transit country for cocaine to the United States and Europe; it is the largest producer and exporter of marijuana in the Caribbean and a center of money laundering. In 1999 Jamaica attempted to update its anti-money-laundering regime to international standards, but faces complicated legal and political hurdles before its mechanisms are likely to be fully effective. The country suffers from high levels of corruption in the public sector and this is affected by the drugs business. Jamaica cooperates with the United States in anti-drugs activities and in 1999, for example, extradited four people to the United States. There is a need to increase security at Jamaica's ports. There was a substantial marijuana eradication program in 1999, financed by the United States, but Jamaica agreed to take over part of the costs of eradication teams' salaries from mid-2000.

Laos is the world's third-largest producer of illicit opium after Afghanistan and Myanmar and produced 140 tonnes (138 tons) in both 1998 and 1999. The government cooperates with both the United States and the United Nations in drug eradication programs and in May 1999 agreed to a program with the UNDCP to eradicate opium production over a six-year period up to 2005. Such a program will cost a minimum of $80 million. However, the highland farmers who grow the opium have no other source of income; even if they knew how to grow other crops and were supplied with the means to do so, there would remain the question of a market or markets for their new products. There is no quick or easy change of crop from opium to an alternative, and to be effective such a program requires years of careful planning and implementation. Seizures of heroin in 1999 fell while traffickers changed their routes and methods.

Mexico, despite substantial efforts by its government, remains one of the most important drug-trafficking and drug-producing countries in the world; it offers drug traffickers the huge advantage of proximity to the world's largest drug market, the United States, and a 2,000-mile (3,220-kilometer) border between the two countries that can reasonably be described as porous. Although a number of advances against the drug traffickers were recorded at the end of the 1990s, including substantial eradication of both marijuana and opium and more than 8,000 drug-related arrests in 1998, these efforts were undermined by massive drug-related corruption. The Mexican and U.S. governments cooperated closely in the war on drugs, but the 1996 decision to extradite offenders to the United States met with mixed support from the judiciary. The two governments are committed to high-level cooperation.

Myanmar, a country over which the United States exercises little influence, is the world's second-largest source of illicit opium and heroin (it used to be the first until this position was taken by Afghanistan), with 89,500 hectares (221,160 acres) under opium production in 1999. Although there is a policy of eradication and the level of opium production by the end of the last decade had fallen significantly, the government made few allocations of resources to reduce drug production and was either unwilling or unable to take on the most powerful drug-producing groups. In 1993 Myanmar passed a Narcotic Drugs and Psychotropic Substances Law, which conforms to the 1998 UN Drug Convention, but officials have been slow to implement the law. Money laundering in Myanmar is a significant factor in the country's economy, and there were no signs of any action to curtail the practice; indeed, the government encourages the drug groups to invest their profits in legitimate businesses. The U.S. view in 1999 was that Myanmar was not making efforts to curtail the drugs problem commensurate with the drug activities inside the country.

The dilemma posed by a policy of certification is aptly illustrated by the U.S. decision to give a certificate to Nigeria despite that country's failure to meet criteria for cooperation. As the U.S. government explained:

> Nigeria has failed to fully meet the criteria for cooperation with the United States on counter-drug matters and has not taken adequate steps on its own to meet the goals of the 1988 UN Drug Convention. U.S. vital national interests, however, require that Nigeria be certified so that the assistance that would otherwise be withheld remains available to support the continuing transition to democratic civilian rule and the increased efforts to improve cooperation on drug and other crime issues evident under the democratic government.[3]

This readiness to overlook Nigeria's failings in the drugs war may not be unconnected with the United States' need for Nigeria's oil. Nigeria is the principal drug-trafficking country in Africa and is assisted in its activities by the extensive Nigerian diaspora, especially in Britain and the United States. Nigerian crime mafias operate global networks, dominate the Sub-Saharan drug markets, and account for a large part of heroin imports into the United States while acting as a pivotal point in the transfer of cocaine from South America to Europe and elsewhere in Asia and Africa. Moreover, government counterdrug efforts are haphazard, obtain little material support, and are mainly targeted at lowly couriers. In addition, Nigerian money launderers are highly efficient and control global networks. The question of whether the new democratic government under ex-General Olusegun Obasanjo, who has denounced the drugs business, will prove more effective in tackling the drugs problem was still open at the beginning of the new century.

During 1999 the Anti-Narcotics Force of Pakistan made significant progress in reducing opium production and made record seizures of both heroin and opium. Pakistan has close working relations with the United States and the DEA, which provides assistance to its overall anti-drugs programs. Pakistan is willing to extradite its citizens to the United States, and four such defendants were extradited in 1999. However, the year did not witness any convictions of major drug traffickers.

Panama is a major transit country for cocaine from Colombia destined for the U.S. market. The drug is stockpiled in Panama prior to shipments to North America and Europe. It is also a center for money laundering. Panama implemented its own counterdrug program, the National Drug Strategy 1996–2001; it also has a comprehensive chemical control program.

Paraguay has two principal roles in the drugs business: as a transit country for Bolivian cocaine and as a money-laundering center. According to U.S. estimates, between 15 and 30 tonnes (14.8 to 29.5 tons) of cocaine transit Paraguay annually en route to Argentina, Brazil, the United States, and Europe. Little of this amount was seized in 1999. Paraguay also produces high-quality marijuana. There was scant evidence during 1999 of serious government efforts to curtail the country's drug-trafficking activities, yet the United States decided not to deny certification on the grounds that aid and military assistance to Paraguay were a U.S. national interest since they were designed to strengthen democratic institutions and promote modern civil–military relations.

Peru was one of the countries which, at the end of the decade, won high praise from the United States for its progress in eliminating illegal coca production; an estimated 24 percent of coca cultivation was eliminated in 1999. Peru had one of the best counterdrug alternative development programs, affecting 103 local governments, 700 communities, and 15,000 farmers. On the other hand, there was growing evidence that drug traffickers are establishing laboratories to process cocaine hydrochloride near the borders with Brazil, Colombia, and Bolivia. Despite its successes in eradicating illegal coca production, Peru is becoming a source of opium poppy cultivation. Higher prices for coca may tempt farmers who have abandoned its production to return to it.

Taiwan is an important transit country for drugs destined for the United States and a center for money laundering. Despite an aggressive anti-drugs policy, Taiwan recorded a 48.9 percent increase in new drugs cases in 1999. It cooperates closely with the United States.

Thailand, a member of the Golden Triangle, produced an estimated 1,000 tonnes (9,840 tons) of opium in 1999; it is also a major transit country for heroin destined for the United States. Thailand cooperates closely with the United States and has developed one of the most successful crop substitution and opium eradication programs in the world. The United States sees Thailand as an important ally in the war on drugs.

Venezuela is a major transit country for cocaine destined for the United States and Europe as well as a transit country for precursor chemicals used in the Andean cocaine-producing countries. Venezuelan law enforcement agencies, working closely with the DEA, achieved some considerable successes during 1999, closing exit routes at major ports and increasing the amount of drug seizures. A new criminal code was introduced in 1999; it has the potential to provide a more efficient, transparent system of justice and so reduce levels of corruption.

The government of Vietnam has made the fight against drugs a major priority. The country's proximity to the Golden Triangle ensures that Vietnam is a major transit point for opium and heroin; the government has strengthened its border patrols and in 1999 arrested 19,010 drug criminals, a 31 percent increase over 1998. Vietnam has increased its cooperation with China and several European Union countries to fight the drugs war and has worked closely with U.S. agencies. However, there is no U.S.–Vietnam counterdrug agreement. Opium poppy crops have not been eradicated, and in 1999 farmers in some high-poverty rural areas brought an additional 645 hectares (1,590 acres) under cultivation to increase the total to 2,100 hectares (5,190 acres).

The countries listed above are those whose drug production or anti-drugs programs (or lack of them) most affect the flow of drugs into the U.S. market. The list is far from comprehensive. The United States defends its certification process in terms of its openness or transparency; it makes each government publicly accountable for its actions. The policy may be faulted on two counts. The first is the so-called national interest of the United States that allows certification for a country, despite its failure to combat drug production or trafficking effectively, because, it is argued, there are other overriding reasons for giving aid, such as supporting the growth of democracy. Making such a distinction in one case but not in another is bound to create a sense of discrimination among the certificated countries that could well encourage others to abandon attempts to fight the war on drugs if, in the first place, they had been pressured into such measures by the United States. The second objection to the process is more general: Certification may be seen simply as a weapon of U.S. foreign policy designed to enable the United States to intervene in the affairs of vulnerable states whose policies it wishes to influence.

The Central Intelligence Agency (CIA) produces an annual *World Factbook* in which it lists every country and provides statistics about populations, governments, and economies, as well as other factual data; where appropriate, it gives an entry covering drugs. A typical entry in the *World Factbook* for 2000 was for Angola, which reads as follows: "illicit drugs—increasingly used as a transshipment point for cocaine and heroin destined for Western Europe and other African states."[4] Now, of the 274 countries listed by the CIA for the year 2000, 140 had no entry for illicit drug activity, while 134 were in some way involved. However, of the 140 countries that were apparently free of drug activities, a significant proportion consisted of remote islands—for example, in the Pacific—that were off the world's drug-trafficking routes, had tiny populations, or were uninhabited. A few countries—for example, the Central African Republic—were not mentioned as having any illicit drug connections and again, possibly, this was the result of remoteness. On the other hand, Somalia is passed over, although the consumption of qat in that country is more or less a national pastime. The 1993 *World Factbook* only lists 99 countries as being involved in drug trafficking —as producers, transit countries, consumers, or money launderers—so that over the seven years to 2000, according to the CIA, an additional 35 countries had become involved at some level in the illegal international drug-trafficking business. This figure, allowing for inaccuracies, must give pause for thought. The scope of the war on drugs was dramatically increased through the 1990s, especially by the United States, and yet the number of countries involved grew, according to CIA assessments, by a third. The figures suggest that involvement in drug trafficking, with all its ramifications, is growing at the rate of an additional five countries a year, despite all the efforts of the United Nations, the United States, and other countries to curtail the traffickers and the habit of consumption.

9

Colombia: Key to the Cocaine Trade

In the dry language of official UN documents, the annual report of the INCB for 1999[1] states: "In Colombia, the deterioration of public safety in general and the fact that substantial illicit coca leaf production and cocaine manufacture are taking place in areas beyond government control are hampering efforts by the government to fight illicit coca bush cultivation, coca leaf production, and cocaine manufacture and trafficking." Later, in the same section of the report (dealing with South America) it states: "The Board notes with concern that in Colombia the law on the confiscation of assets has not brought the expected results. Of the many thousands of pieces of property seized so far, none has been subsequently confiscated pursuant to the provisions of the law." These two statements alone suggest that the government of Colombia is either unable or unwilling to put its full force and authority into the fight against the production of illicit drugs. The report suggests that the area under coca bush cultivation in Colombia exceeded the areas under illicit cultivation in Bolivia and Peru combined. Finally, the report makes the following assessment:

> Colombia continues to be the world's leading cocaine producer. Efforts by Colombian law enforcement authorities have led to the discovery and destruction of several laboratories for illicit cocaine manufacture, one of which was capable of manufacturing up to 8 tons of cocaine per month. That is an indication of the technical and economic resources, as well as the manufacturing capacity, at the disposal of Colombian drug traffickers.

The preeminent position of Colombia as the principal source of cocaine is borne out by figures from the UN Office for Drug Control and Crime Prevention *World Drug Report 2000*[2] that show how in 1990, of a total coca leaf production of 319,200 tonnes (314,160 tons), Colombia then accounted for 14 percent (with Bolivia's 24 percent and Peru's 62 percent accounting for the remainder); but by 1999 of a total coca leaf production of 287,000 tonnes (282,470 tons), Colombia accounted for 68 percent, while Bolivia only accounted for 8 percent and Peru for 24 percent. The result is that, at the beginning of the new century, Colombia, in every sense, had become the lead country in the production, manufacture, and distribution of cocaine.

Levels of violence and lawlessness to be found in few other countries have characterized the public life of Colombia for more than three decades, and by the end of the twentieth century, this had resolved itself into two broad kinds: left-wing guerrilla violence against the state, which was met by military counterinsurgency campaigns as well as attracting right-wing death squad reprisals; and the war against the drug barons, which involves a wide range of highly organized drug traffickers opposed to the army, the police, and a growing U.S. commitment. As of mid-2001 there was no sign of any abatement in this ongoing violence.

The most notorious name associated with the Colombian drugs business is that of Pablo Escobar, who, before his death in 1993, had become one of the richest men in the world. It is worth looking briefly at his rise and fall since his life was intimately intertwined with the phenomenal growth of the drugs trade in Colombia. His story has been told in the book *Killing Pablo*.[3] Born in 1949, Pablo Emilio Escobar Gaviria was to become the richest, most ruthless and feared man in Colombia and, at the peak of his power, arguably the most feared terrorist in the world. In 1989 *Forbes* magazine rated him the world's seventh richest man. He was already a successful crook by the mid-1970s when the U.S. "pot" generation discovered cocaine, which became the fashionable new drug in North America. It was Escobar's control of the largest slice of the cocaine trade that enabled him to become one of the world's greatest criminals. By the end of the 1970s he, with a number of associates—the Ochoa brothers, Carlos Lehder Rivas, José Rodríguez Gacha—controlled over half the cocaine shipped to the United States, and together their fortunes could be measured in billions of dollars. The production of cocaine became Colombia's leading industry, and drug money was used to bankroll leading national and municipal politicians. By the mid-1980s Escobar owned properties all over Colombia and elsewhere in the world, controlled fleets of boats and planes, banks and other enterprises, and the city of Medellín that gave its name to his cartel enjoyed a boom fueled by drug money. The sheer scale of the drug money entering Colombia destroyed the rule of law, since officials from the highest to the lowest could be bribed or bankrolled. The key to Escobar's wealth and power was the ever-growing demand for cocaine in the United States. Over the five-year period 1976–1980, bank deposits in Colombia's four main cities more than doubled. The government of President Alfonso López Michelsen became complicit in this lucrative trade when it allowed a new practice, what the central bank called "opening a side window," whereby unlimited quantities of dollars, no questions asked, could be converted into Colombian pesos. In addition, the government permitted new speculative funds that, whatever their ostensible purpose, were invested in cocaine shipments. Colombia, and not just the criminal cartels, was getting rich on the proceeds of cocaine. Escobar, meanwhile, was gaining control of the drugs business outside

Colombia—in Bolivia, Panama, and Peru. At the same time, a growing threat to Escobar's position was developing as other drug barons, the Rodríguez Orejuela brothers—Jorge, Gilberto, and Miguel—were creating the rival Cali cartel. Escobar, meanwhile, had entered politics, becoming a Medellín substitute city council member in 1978, a year in which he underwrote the presidential campaign of Belisario Betancur Cuartas. Thus, by the beginning of the 1980s, Escobar was in politics and, moreover, had major political "friends," and had spread his wealth into a range of enterprises that effectively made him an independent power in Colombia.

In 1982 President Ronald Reagan established a task force to coordinate U.S. anti-drug-smuggling activities under the direction of Vice President George Bush. By the mid-1980s U.S. pressures had become sufficiently compelling that in 1985 Escobar offered to turn himself in to the government if it promised not to extradite him to the United States. (In 1979 Colombia had signed a treaty with the U.S. government that recognized the shipment of illegal drugs to be a crime against the United States, which called for drug traffickers to be extradited for trial in the United States, where they would be imprisoned if found guilty.) Escobar continued his rule of terror at home; judges who took cases against the drug barons were assassinated, and the government abandoned trial by jury because people were too frightened to serve on any jury in a case dealing with drug-trafficking offenses. For a time Colombia was treated to the extraordinary spectacle of Escobar spending some of his time in a special prison—built to his specifications with his money—from where he continued to direct his drugs empire.

However, in the United States cocaine had lost its cachet as the drug for professional or upper-class Americans and instead was traded on the streets as crack. More importantly, as far as U.S.–Colombian relations were concerned, President Reagan signed the National Security Decision Directive 221 in April 1986, which declared drug trafficking to be a threat to national security. This allowed the military to be used in the war on drugs, and attention was now turned, increasingly, to eliminating crops, laboratories, and traffickers in Central and South America. Colombia became the prime target for this new policy.

By 1987 high-level assassinations of his political opponents were carried out by Escobar's hit men, and by the end of that year, there were killings almost every day in Colombia's capital, Bogotá. However, Escobar's ruthless campaign of murders and his arrogance—he moved about the country with virtual impunity as though he was absolutely above the law—turned people against him and in 1990 he overstepped the mark. First, he had Luis Carlos Galán Sarmiento, the popular Liberal Party candidate for president who had vowed to rid Colombia of its drug traffickers, assassinated. Then, in an effort to kill Galán's successor candidate, César Gaviria Trujillo, who was equally opposed to the drug barons, he had his men plant a bomb on the

Avianca airliner on which Gaviria was to travel, killing 110 people, including two Americans. He had now become a world danger and not just Colombia's top criminal, and from this time on Escobar was on the run. By the end of 1992 Escobar's top aides were being killed by the new police detachment, called Search Bloc, that had been created solely to deal with the Medellín cartel and capture Escobar, and he was finally gunned down by the police in December 1993.

The story of Pablo Escobar is important for a number of reasons. It shows how those possessed of huge wealth can purchase almost anything (at least for a time), including government immunity from prosecution. It illustrates the extent to which governments can be corrupted at all levels and the fact that many Colombians were far more interested in obtaining a share of the vast drug-related wealth than they were in combating the trade. And finally, it should be remembered that throughout his career Escobar was only able to do what he did because the huge market for cocaine existed in the United States, where both the consumers and their criminal suppliers would go to almost any lengths to ensure that the supply did not dry up.

The scale of the war on drugs may be illustrated by one seizure operation that came to fruition in August 2000 when international law enforcement officers seized 27.9 tonnes (27.5 tons) of Colombian cocaine worth about $1 billion from a port on Venezuela's eastern Atlantic coast. It was described as one of the biggest drugs operations in history. Most of the shipment was bound for Europe. "Operation Journey" was a two-year investigation that involved a dozen countries sharing information and led to 43 arrests and the confiscation of five commercial freighters. The law officers claimed that the smugglers had already dispatched 69.1 tonnes (68 tons) of cocaine, mainly to Britain, France, Greece, Italy, Spain, Albania, Belgium, and the Netherlands in Europe, while Colombia, Panama, Venezuela, and the United States were involved in the Americas. Julio Mercado of the U.S. DEA praised the Venezuelans for locating a huge jungle storage facility in the Orinoco River delta. He said: "Today's drug gangs are too powerful for one nation to fight alone." This comment was especially interesting since, by that time, the Medellín and Cali cartels were virtually defunct; the drug traffickers had wasted no time in replacing them with other powerful organizations. Meanwhile, Colombia had been planting the more high-yielding Peruvian coca leaf to quadruple its harvests, while hundreds of U.S. military advisers were deployed, training anti-drugs battalions to find and seize the illegal crops that, in part, fund the left-wing insurgents of the Revolutionary Armed Forces of Colombia (FARC). It is instructive that, while Colombia permitted U.S. military advisers to train its anti-drugs battalions, Venezuela's President Hugo Chávez Frías refused permission for either Colombian or U.S. anti-drugs aircraft to chase smugglers inside his country's airspace. Although

Venezuela under Chávez is committed to fight the drug traffickers, the country is a major conduit for cocaine on its way to the Caribbean and a center for money laundering.[4]

1995

The story of Colombia's half-war against drugs from 1995 to the end of 2000 reveals a nation that cocaine wealth has rendered schizophrenic.[5] At the beginning of 1995, for example, there were 21 days of violent protest by the peasant farmers of the Amazon region of Putumayo at the government practice of fumigating coca fields from the air, and the protests only ended when the government promised not to fumigate plots of less than three hectares (7.4 acres). These would be destroyed manually. In February of that year, Liberal President Ernesto Samper Pizano pledged before the U.S. ambassador, Myles Frechette, to continue his government's fight against illegal drug plantations and to strengthen the level of prosecutions of drug offenders; an earlier report by the Colombian Justice Ministry appeared to support U.S. claims that Colombian judges showed excessive leniency in delivering sentences for drug-related offenses. The provision of further U.S. aid was tied to Samper's pledge. The year witnessed a determined attempt to break the power of the Cali cartel, which had replaced the Medellín cartel in importance since the death of Escobar in December 1993. The government announced the suspension of all gun licenses in the city of Cali and surrounding areas. On March 3 Jorge Elieser Rodríguez Orejuela, one of the Cali leaders, was arrested. Later in the year the government announced new plans to combat drug trafficking that included the possible expropriation of land used to grow drug crops, while $300 million was to be invested over two years (half from the federal budget and half from U.S. aid) to provide credits and land for peasant farmers willing to cultivate legal crops, while those refusing to cooperate would lose their land. In May a major offensive was mounted against the Cali cartel when 3,000 troops raided mansions owned by its drug barons, destroyed illegal crops of coca, marijuana, and poppies, and dropped hundreds of wanted posters for the two cartel leaders—the brothers Gilberto and Miguel Rodríguez Orejuela—and on June 9 Gilberto was arrested. This was seen as the biggest government success since the death of Escobar. On June 17 Henry Loaiza Ceballos, "The Scorpion," who was head of the Cali military wing, surrendered with his lawyer. Meanwhile, intensive government searches, raids, roadblocks, and seizures had crippled the Cali intelligence-gathering and money-laundering activities. The offer by the government of rewards for informers had paid off. Gilberto Rodríquez Orejuela promised to cooperate fully with the government and called on other Cali leaders to surrender; in return he sought a light sentence.

U.S. assistance had played a part in this successful crackdown on the Cali leadership, but the Colombian government ruled out the extradition of such traffickers to the United States. On June 7 President Samper stated that Colombia had a "sovereign and independent" anti-drugs policy. This statement was in response to a U.S. Congress measure that linked future aid to Colombia to the progress it made in eradicating illegal drug crops. Meanwhile, the U.S. authorities had charged 59 people, including a former senior Justice Department official, with having links to the Cali cartel and being involved in the importation of 200 tonnes (197 tons) of cocaine into the United States over a 10-year period. Early in July the Cali cartel's number three, José Santacruz Londoño, was arrested; the government offered sentence reductions in exchange for voluntary surrenders, confessions, and other forms of cooperation. On July 27 Santiago Medina, the treasurer of President Samper's 1994 election campaign, was arrested, accused of running a front company that had channeled money from the Cali cartel into Samper's campaign funds. The president ordered a congressional investigation. The U.S. "presence" in Colombia was always a factor in the anti-drugs war. The United States pressed for stiff sentences for drug offenders if better U.S.–Colombia relations were to be established, and the question was raised as to whether U.S. DEA agents were involved in searches for Cali personnel. The Colombian authorities insisted that these agents were only in the country as observers.

Another corruption scandal hit the government in August when the defense minister, Fernando Botero Zea, resigned following allegations that he had helped to channel millions of dollars from the Cali cartel into the campaign funds of Samper's 1994 election. Botero was arrested on August 15. At the time it was claimed that a total of $6.1 million out of $11.25 million in campaign funds had come from the Cali cartel. Following the arrest of Miguel Rodríguez Orejuela, the second brother in the Cali leadership, at the beginning of August, President Samper told Colombians to be ready for the Cali cartel's death throes. By September the campaign funds scandal had reached the president, who denied that he had had any knowledge of Cali funds being channeled into his election chest. The deputy prosecutor said that it had been fully determined that such funding had taken place but that it was for Congress to judge the president. Other political figures were implicated. Thirty-three deputies called on Samper to resign. Then the DEA became implicated in an assassination attempt of September 27 in Bogotá against President Samper's lawyer, Antonio José Cancinco. New allegations against the DEA followed in October when it was accused of trying to destabilize the Samper government. On October 4 an opposition deputy, Carlos Alonso Lucio, presented tapes to Congress of telephone conversations between DEA personnel and members of the Cali cartel. Lucio claimed that instability in

Colombia prevented the defeat of the drug cartels and benefited DEA officials, who gained financially from the continuation of drug trafficking. In response the DEA protested that the tapes were part of a "dirty tricks" campaign to divert attention from inquiries into charges about the use of drug money by the government.

1996

Throughout 1996 the Samper government was wracked by scandals relating to its ties with the Cali cartel. On January 30 an emergency session of Congress was convened to decide whether President Samper should resign to face prosecution on drug charges. The former defense minister, Fernando Botero Zea, who had been in detention since August 1995, claimed that Samper had knowingly accepted millions of U.S. dollars from the Cali cartel to assist his 1994 campaign. Samper, however, reaffirmed his innocence and called for a referendum on whether he should continue as president. This idea was rejected as unconstitutional. The crisis deepened, with opposition conservatives withdrawing officials from the government and seven foreign ambassadors resigning as well as an army general and Samper's personal lawyer. A Liberal Party senator, Maria Izquieredo, resigned on January 17 after admitting he had received $30,000 from the Cali cartel. He promised to cooperate with investigators. Business organizations called on Samper to resign and on January 26, a crowd of 4,000 students marched on the presidential palace in Bogotá to demand the same. The president continued to deny all the charges. A further embarrassment for the government followed the January 11 escape of Cali leader José Santacruz Londoño from a maximum-security prison in Bogotá. His escape was blamed on lax security measures and extensive corruption among the prison staff, some of whom were subsequently dismissed. Samper promised his recapture. He ruled out extraditing drug offenders to the United States. On February 27 both the upper and lower houses of Congress announced a new public investigation into the alleged cartel funding of Samper's 1994 election campaign. The corruption charges now affected half the members of the government.

On March 1 the United States removed Colombia from the list of countries that it deemed to be making progress against illegal drug trafficking. This move put additional pressure on President Samper, further strained U.S.–Colombian relations, and ended all U.S. aid (except for anti-drugs activities). Later in March, three cabinet members—the foreign minister, the interior minister, and the communications minister—were summoned to give evidence in the ongoing Samper investigation. The former defense minister, Fernando Botero Zea, again claimed that Samper had not only known about the funds from the Cali cartel, but also had masterminded the fund-raising operation. Others joined in the chorus of accusations against Samper, who, however, continued to deny the accusations, conceding only that drug money had entered his campaign funds. José Santacruz Londoño, who earlier had escaped from prison, was killed in a gun battle with the police. By April the scandal surrounding Samper had touched half the cabinet and was doing increasing damage to the entire Colombian political process, producing further resignations, accusations, and counteraccusations. Business leaders again called on the president to resign, but he refused. Then the Supreme Court asked the Senate to suspend the attorney general, Orlando Vasquez Velasquez, for 90 days so that he could face charges of obstructing justice. He had already fallen under suspicion of involvement with the Cali cartel. On May 3 he was arrested on charges of receiving large payments from the Cali cartel both before and after he had been sworn in as attorney general. On May 23 a congressional commission recommended to Congress by 10 votes to 3 that the charges against President Samper should be dropped. This recommendation had been widely expected since the Liberal Party dominated Congress. The commission argued that the evidence against the president was insufficient despite the submissions of two campaign officials and 3,200 files of evidence. On May 28 the lower house began to debate the issue.

Ironically, any U.S. interventions helped Samper, who was enabled to play on Colombian opposition to American interference in his country's affairs. For example, Samper dismissed criticism of the congressional commission's findings by Nicholas Burns, a U.S. official, as "inadmissible intervention" in Colombia's affairs. Charges against three cabinet ministers were also dropped, although lesser charges against them of covering up were sustained. On June 12 the Chamber of Deputies voted to exculpate President Samper of charges that he accepted drug money for his campaign. This vote—111 to 43—prevented impeachment proceedings. Many members of the chamber faced corruption charges themselves. The vote, however, did nothing to restore national confidence in the government. In the same month, Colombia turned down an official request from U.S. Attorney General Janet Reno for the extradition to the United States of four Cali cartel drug barons. The president of the Colombian Constitutional Court, Carlos Gaviria Díaz, said on June 27 that the 1991 Constitution laid down that native Colombians could not be extradited and that a 1979 extradition treaty with the United States, approved by a law of 1986, had been declared unconstitutional by the Supreme Court in 1987. In July the United States revoked Samper's visa under the terms of a law applying to individuals not cooperating in the fight against drug trafficking.

Also that month two Samper associates, Santiago Medina, who had been the treasurer of his election campaign, and Maria Izquierdo, a former senator, were sentenced for illegal enrichment from drug trafficking. Through August some 60,000 coca growers in the southern departments protested against the government's eradication program. They argued that their livelihoods depended on producing the drug crops and demanded a halt to aerial spraying and regional states of siege. They claimed that their case was quite different from that of the guerrillas or the drug traffickers. Government alternatives for these peasant drug producers included credits, subsidies for traditional crops, and payment for the voluntary destruction of coca crops equal to the prices they would receive for such crops. At the end of August, FARC, the left-wing guerrilla movement, launched a nationwide offensive against the government; it was a response to the government efforts to eradicate illegal coca and poppy crops. FARC obtains a large part of its finances from the drugs business. On August 20 Robert Gelbard, the U.S. assistant secretary for International Narcotics and Law Enforcement Affairs, accused the Samper government of lying. On September 1 the last important Cali leader, Helmer "Pacho" Herrera Buitrago, surrendered to the police after a 16-month manhunt; he was described by Samper as "the last of the cartel leaders." On September 23, when he addressed the UN General Assembly, Samper argued that the war on drugs was being lost and proposed a world agenda against drugs that would include an international judicial cooperation treaty with annexes permitting extradition. This proposal, which was well received by President Clinton, appeared to be an olive branch designed to soften the prevailing U.S. approach to Colombia. On September 29, however, the Colombian prosecutor general's office announced that 3.7 kilograms (8.2 pounds) of heroin had been found on the presidential jet on September 21 and that this indicated the existence of a drug-trafficking network at the Colombian air force base near Bogotá. Eleven members of the crew were charged with planting the heroin on the plane.

On October 23 a Senate committee approved a constitutional amendment that would reintroduce extradition for Colombian nationals wanted for trial in other countries. The move was both the result of U.S. pressure and a government effort to appease Washington. In November, commissions in both houses of Congress approved a draft bill to permit the authorities to seize assets of drug traffickers. The bill would be retrospective, to cover all assets obtained from past drug-trafficking. It also covered the illegal enrichment of public servants. The bill threatened the huge fortunes of the convicted Cali leaders. However, the reluctance of committee members and members of Congress, many of whom were implicated in the drugs business, to see the bill succeed made its future success problematic if not downright unlikely. Lawyers of Cali cartel members (who had been sentenced) mingled with the deputies during the debate. Nonetheless, the confiscation bill was seen to be essential in order to restore U.S. confidence in the government's commitment to fight the drug cartels and to persuade the United States to withdraw the threat of trade sanctions against Colombia. In December the Congress did approve the bill, the Senate unanimously and the House of Representatives by 103 to 4. The law was a landmark and embodied some of the harshest legislation ever enacted against the drug traffickers. But a revolt in the House of Representatives led to the defeat of the retroactive aspect of the bill.

1997

On January 17, 1997, lenient sentences of only 10 $\frac{1}{2}$ years and 9 years, respectively, were imposed on the two brothers, Gilberto and Miguel Rodríguez Orejuela, leaders of the Cali cartel, by a Cali judge. The prosecutor general, Alfonso Valdivieso, announced that he would appeal the sentences. During their 20-year reign over the Cali cartel, the brothers had been responsible for producing and smuggling thousands of tons of cocaine and heroin, murdering dozens of people, and engaging in high-level political corruption, including making the $6 million donation to the Samper election fund. The judge only fined them $12 million, though their fortunes were estimated at several billions. In March, following the decision of the Clinton administration to "decertify" Colombia for failing to cooperate fully in the fight against illegal drugs, the government suspended its drug crop eradication flights. The U.S. government accused the Colombian government of failing to reduce coca and poppy crop production, which, according to satellite data, had increased by 32 percent during 1996. Colombia, by then, had overtaken Bolivia as a leading grower of coca leaves. Nonetheless, the Colombian National Narcotics Council insisted that the eradication program should be carried out with U.S. equipment, training, and herbicides. Following Colombia's suspension of its spraying program, the U.S. State Department threatened further action against Colombia, but this only had the effect of hardening Colombian nationalist opinion against the United States. A protest rally held outside the U.S. embassy in Bogotá made the point that the United States had no moral authority to certify or decertify countries in Latin America. The interior minister, Horacio Serpa, stated that the possibility of reintroducing mechanisms that would allow extradition of drug traffickers to the United States had evaporated as a consequence of U.S. interference in Colombia's domestic anti-drugs efforts. For its part the United States linked its decertification with the high level of corruption in the Colombian administration as well as evidence that imprisoned drug barons were able to continue running their business from prison. On March 8 Serpa publicly described the U.S. ambassador, Myles Frechette,

as a "nasty gringo" after the latter had claimed that Cali leaders had offered him evidence connecting President Samper to the drugs trade. The
attorney general, meanwhile, had demanded that the U.S. authorities
should reveal evidence about corruption relating to Samper and Serpa.
However, Colombia drew back from this name-calling confrontation
when, in April, a new justice minister, Almabeatriz Rengifo López, presented a bill to Congress to reinstate the government's power to extradite
Colombian nationals (against the terms of the Constitution), a measure
for which the United States had been pressing. The government then outlined a new drugs strategy at a meeting of international drug experts held
at Cartagena. The government plan included extradition, the fostering of
crop substitution programs, improved prison security measures, the implementation of laws on the forfeiture of assets derived from drug trafficking, and called for improvements in the collection and analysis of
satellite data on drug crops. On June 19 the House of Representatives
agreed by 97 to 46 to a new debate on the issue of extradition; one version
of the bill would make extradition retroactive and so could lead to imprisoned drug traffickers being sent to the United States. An agreement was
reached on August 1 with the United States that would provide $70 mil-
lion in military aid to assist in the fight against drug trafficking. The
Colombian government committed itself to investigate, under U.S. super-
vision, reports of human rights violations and acknowledged that aid
would be suspended if it failed to act on any of the findings of the investigation. On August 9 a major Peruvian drugs baron, Waldo Simeón Vargas
Arias, was arrested in Bogotá. In September the Senate approved a bill
that made extradition nonretroactive. The decision was condemned in
both political and judicial circles since it would protect those involved in
criminal activities, especially drug trafficking. The bill passed the House
of Representatives. The former Senate president, Jorge Ramón Elias
Nader, was arrested in September on drug-related corruption charges. On
November 25 the House of Representatives approved by 119 to 38 a constitutional amendment to allow the nonretroactive extradition of
Colombian citizens on criminal charges. Since this measure only applied
to future crimes, it was seen as a virtual amnesty for past crimes and especially those associated with drugs. President Samper had argued that the
re-establishment of extradition "without condition" was essential in order
to improve Colombia's relations with the United States. In November the
government seized more than 300 properties that had been owned by the
late Cali cartel drug baron José Santacruz Londoño and imprisoned three
of his former allies. On December 16 President Samper and the presidents
of the Senate and House of Representatives signed into law the extradition legislation that had been approved in November.

1998

In February five leading prosecutors from the attorney general's office were suspended from their posts for 90 days by Attorney General Jaime Bernal Cuellar (a close associate of President Samper), accused of fabricating evidence against aides of the president. The suspensions were part of the ongoing scandal surrounding the 1994 election donations. The former defense minister, Fernando Botero Zea, was released on February 12 after serving one-third of a 90-month sentence for illicit enrichment and falsifying public documents. He had been accused of channeling millions of dollars from the Cali cartel into the 1994 Samper election campaign. On February 19 José Nelson Urrego Cárdenas, the last of the major figures linked with the Cali cartel, was captured by the police and charged with drug trafficking and grievous bodily harm. He was the leader of the Norte del Valle cartel and had an estimated personal fortune of $1.8 billion. At the end of February, the United States lifted sanctions against Colombia on the grounds that there had been improvements in its fight against drugs. However, Colombia was not included on the list of countries whose cooperation over drugs was certified as satisfactory. The Colombian government welcomed the decision but maintained its criticism of the certification process. Decertification had cost Colombia an estimated $800 million in aid and international finance. On March 5 Roger Eleazar Pombo (alias "El Placo") was arrested and became the first Colombian to be extradited to the United States following the approval of the extradition law of December 1997. Pombo was thought to be the second-in-command of the coastal cartel headed by Alberto Orlandez Gamboa ("El Caracol"). In May an appeals court added five years each to the prison sentences imposed on Gilberto and Miguel Rodríguez Orejuela, the former Cali cartel leaders, to bring their sentences up to 15 and 14 years, respectively. The anonymous judge who handed down this ruling ordered an investigation into the actions of a lower court judge accused of granting unwarranted sentence reductions. Also that month the police arrested Luis Reynaldo Marcia Sierra ("Martelo"), the head of the Bogotá cartel. Then in June, Alberto Orlandez Gamboa, the reputed head of the Cartel de la Costa, the Barranquilla-based drug gang, was captured. In September the U.S. House of Representatives threatened to withhold $200 million of anti-drugs aid to Colombia if the Colombian government halted its program of aerial spraying while it was negotiating with the FARC guerrillas. This U.S. aid was provided under its Western Hemisphere Drug Elimination Act, which called for $2.3 billion to be spent over three years on drug interdiction and eradication in Latin America. On October 1 the Colombian Constitutional Court upheld the extradition law of December 1997, which stipulated that extradition could not be applied retroactively to Colombian nationals. The result of the June presidential elections had been to bring the Social Conservative Party (PSC) candidate, Andrés Pastrana Arango, to power with

50.6 percent of the vote, to end 12 years of Liberal Party rule. Whether the change of party and president would make much difference to the war on drugs remained to be seen. Over October 28–30, President Pastrana visited the United States, an indication on both sides of a wish for better relations, he was the first Colombian president to visit in 23 years. He pledged his full commitment to the war on drugs and received aid to the value of $280 million for anti-drugs efforts and economic development. Little, however, appeared to have altered. On November 9 U.S. officials discovered approximately 745 kilograms (1,640 pounds) of cocaine on a Colombian air force plane at Fort Lauderdale Airport in Florida. The seizure led to the resignation of Colombia's air force chief, General José Manuel Sandoval, and six air force officers were later detained. Three air force noncommissioned officers (NCOs) were each sentenced to seven and a half years in prison for their attempt to smuggle 3.7 kilograms (8.2 pounds) of heroin into the United States on the presidential aircraft in September 1996. Two leading drug barons were murdered in prison during November. In December defense ministers of the Americas met in Cartagena, where the United States and Colombia signed an agreement that would lead to the creation of a specialized anti-drugs unit. The Colombian military would be provided with U.S. anti-drugs intelligence, training, and equipment, and instruction in human rights. The U.S. secretary of defense, William Cohen, reiterated that U.S. military aid was only intended for anti-drugs operations and not for counterinsurgency.

1999

Early in January 1999 it was revealed that U.S. State Department officials had met representatives of FARC in Costa Rica during the previous December to discuss the possible elimination of coca plantations in rebel-held areas. The secret meeting amounted to a sharp change in U.S. policy toward the insurgents. In mid-February the U.S. anti-drugs "czar," Barry McCaffrey, claimed that coca cultivation in Colombia had increased by 28 percent during 1998. Even so, he praised President Pastrana and said he had shown "political will to confront the problem and seek real solutions." In May the Colombian police claimed a major victory over paramilitary groups involved in drug trafficking. They had uncovered a cocaine factory operating under a jungle canopy in the central Magdalena Medio region, which produced over eight tonnes (7.9 tons) of cocaine a month. The raid marked a significant switch in the state approach to right-wing paramilitaries, a commitment President Pastrana is said to have made in order to advance peace negotiations with FARC. By September, however, there was mounting concern in both the United States and neighboring Latin American countries that the long-standing civil conflict in Colombia was beginning to destabilize the whole region. Refugees, drugs operations, and guerrilla warfare had already spread across Colombia's borders into Venezuela, Ecuador, Peru, Brazil, and Panama. On October 13 it was announced that the ringleaders of a drug-trafficking network, which, allegedly, had shipped up to 30 tonnes (29.5 tons) of cocaine a month to Europe and the United States, had been arrested. The arrests, it was claimed, were the result of a massive operation—"Millennium"—that had been carried out by Colombian security forces in collaboration with the United States, Ecuador, and Mexico. Thirty-one suspects were captured, mainly in Cali, Medellín, and Bogotá. These included Fabio Ochoa Vásquez, a former leader of the once powerful Medellín cartel. Others were captured outside Colombia. The arrests were made in connection with charges that the traffickers faced in the United States. Following the arrests the Colombian government said it was prepared to allow extradition, an announcement that raised controversy in the country. This new campaign was part of an effort by the Colombian government to persuade the U.S. Congress to approve a massive increase in funding for Colombia's anti-drugs policies (possibly as much as $2 billion over three years). The successful operation was described as the biggest blow dealt to the drug traffickers since the arrest in 1995 of the leaders of the Cali cartel. On November 11 a bomb exploded in Bogotá, killing eight and injuring 45 people; it was seen as an act of retaliation for the decision to resume extradition to the United States. It followed the Supreme Court's approval of the extradition to the United States of heroin trafficker Jaime Orlando Lara Nausa. Lara became the first Colombian to be sent to stand trial in the United States since 1991. On November 15 the authorities in Argentina arrested the widow and son of the former drug baron, Pablo Escobar, following the showing of a television program that revealed that they were being shadowed by the police as part of an anti-money-laundering operation. Several countries had denied asylum to Escobar's widow and children.

2000

A greatly increased U.S. involvement in Colombia was foreshadowed when, on January 11, President Bill Clinton announced the details of a two-year aid package for Colombia to cost $1.6 billion ("Plan Colombia"). Under the plan, two antinarcotics battalions would be created, trained, and equipped by the United States, which would also supply military hardware including 30 Black Hawk helicopters. The plan needed the approval of the U.S. Congress. A report on Colombia by the nongovernmental organization (NGO) Human Rights Watch in February linked military intelligence; paramilitary organizations; and hired assassins who acted together, threatened, and killed human rights workers and government investigators. The report claimed that half the country's 18 army brigades had links with paramilitaries. The charges were made at the time the U.S. government was trying to gain congressional approval for its aid package to assist Colombia to fight the drugs war. On March 30 the U.S. House of Representatives passed by 263 to 146 a bill to provide $1.7 billion in aid to Colombia; the increase over the original request was in order to bolster human rights and judicial reform. Colombia, however, had to demonstrate that it had a strategy to eliminate drug trafficking over five years. In April the anti-drugs police closed down what reportedly was Colombia's largest and most powerful heroin distribution and exporting operation. The police arrested 46 suspected traffickers, including a cousin of the late drug baron Escobar, and charged them with smuggling heroin worth more than $9 million a month into the United States. In June the police arrested Gladys Alvarez, known as "Doctor Claudin"; she was the widow of one of Colombia's most violent drug barons, the former Medellín cartel leader José Rodríguez Gacha, who had been cornered and killed in December 1989. She was charged with cocaine smuggling and money laundering. Meanwhile, the U.S. Congress approved a somewhat lower figure of $1.3 billion in aid for Colombia. Congressional opponents of the aid package warned that the Colombian army was heavily implicated in widespread human rights abuses and that the aid would draw the United States into involvement in the Colombian civil war. Supporters of the bill, on the other hand, claimed that human rights monitoring had been built into the bill and that there was a guarantee that U.S. personnel would not be drawn into the civil conflict. Finally, on August 3, President Clinton signed into law the bill to provide $1.3 billion in aid, mainly military, to assist the Colombian authorities in their war against the drug traffickers. This new, heavy U.S. involvement in Colombia was not welcomed by that country's neighbors, who believed it would simply lead to an escalation of the civil war and cause more drug traffickers and refugees to cross Colombia's borders. Brazil, in anticipation of such a development, moved 6,000 troops to its Amazon frontier with Colombia. There was outrage among human rights organizations because President Clinton had signed a waiver that allowed the aid to be used even though the U.S. State Department had reported that the Colombian armed forces had failed to satisfy most of the human rights conditions contained in the aid bill. These had been intended to break the links between the armed forces and the right-wing paramilitaries and to ensure that those accused of atrocities were tried in civilian rather than in military courts. In support of his bill, President Clinton made a brief visit to Cartagena at the end of August. A summit of 12 South American leaders met in Brasilía over August 31 to September 1 to discuss economic integration. However, the purpose of the meeting was overshadowed by concern about the new package of U.S. military aid to Colombia, which, it was believed, would only escalate the civil war and have an adverse impact on Colombia's neighbors.

The South American leaders expressed their support for the Colombian peace process but pointedly omitted an endorsement of the new U.S. plan. In September the police discovered a workshop in the mountains 30 kilometers (18.6 miles) from Bogotá and 300 kilometers (186 miles) from the sea in which drug traffickers had constructed part of a sophisticated submarine 36 meters (118 feet) long that was designed to transport 11 tonnes (10.8 tons) of cocaine. Technical documents in Russian suggested a link with the Russian mafia. In October a number of foreign workers on an oil installation across the border in Ecuador were kidnapped by FARC guerrillas, raising fears that Ecuador would be targeted by FARC because of the presence of a U.S. Air Force base at Manta in that country. A growing number of refugees were crossing into Ecuador to escape the fighting in Colombia. The army launched an offensive against FARC in order to lift the siege of Dabeiba in Antioquia state, 370 kilometers (230 miles) northwest of Bogotá on a major drug-smuggling route to Panama. Fighting in the southern state of Putumayo among security forces, FARC guerrillas, and right-wing paramilitaries led to a flood of refugees into Ecuador. Almost half the coca leaf produced in Colombia comes from Putumayo. This outbreak of fighting, the most severe in a decade, fueled fears that U.S. Plan Colombia to reduce the cultivation and trafficking in drugs would in fact lead to an intensification of the civil war and the displacement of large numbers of civilians. The European Union, in a markedly different approach to that of the United States, announced on October 18 that $320 million in aid, which it had promised for Colombia, would not be given to the government but instead would be distributed to NGOs operating in the country. The government expressed its disappointment. The two insurgent groups that had entered into talks with the government took different lines. The National Liberation Army (ELN) was prepared to discuss the possibility of eradicating coca production in those areas that it controlled. FARC, on the other hand, suspended the peace talks it had entered into with President Pastrana in protest at the implementation of the U.S.-sponsored Plan Colombia. Relations between Colombia and Venezuela became strained following the attendance in Caracas of a FARC delegation to discuss Plan Colombia at a Latin American Parliament.

In March 2001 aerial spraying of unlicensed coca crops was suspended (with tentative U.S. agreement) to see if voluntary agreements to switch to other crops would work. This change had been prompted by the fact that over 1999–2000, while spraying was in force, the areas planted with coca increased from 112,000 hectares to 130,000 hectares. At the same time, the powerful herbicides being used were blighting legitimate crops and polluting water supplies. On July 31, 2001, a judge ordered a halt to aerial spraying while an investigation of the impact on the environment was conducted, but on August 14 a circuit judge reversed his order on the grounds that the environmental impact of cocaine production was more harmful.

The fight against drugs in Colombia has always been complex. Thus, by September 2002 military operations against the guerrilla forces were accompanied by a significant increase in aerial spraying of coca crops with defoliant chemicals in such areas as Guamez valley in the southern state of Putumayo, and this despite significant questions concerning the efficacy and environmental impact of the use of such chemicals. Both leftist guerrillas and rightist paramilitaries raised money by offering "protection" to coca cultivators and distributors. Under U.S. pressure the Colombian government abandoned its two new policies: to induce small-scale farmers to diversify their crops and to restrict spraying to "industrial plantations" of three or more hectares.

Ecuador

By the end of the year 2000 there were increasing signs that Ecuador was being dragged into Colombia's drug war. A growing number of Colombian refugees were arriving in the border town of Lago Agrio in Ecuador, whose people and officials feared that more refugees, armed outlaws, and coca fields would spill across their northern border. By December 2000 the United Nations High Commissioner for Refugees estimated that more than 1,100 refugees had sought shelter in Ecuador since the previous September, when the paramilitary squads had become increasingly active in Putumayo state. Their arrival in the province had led FARC to retaliate by declaring an "armed strike," and this caused much destruction of property. Lago Agrio, meanwhile, prepared to receive many more refugees as the Colombian government made a determined bid to gain control of Putumayo, now bolstered by the new U.S. aid program. With U.S. troops training elite antinarcotics units to carry out jungle strikes and equipping them with powerful Black Hawk helicopters, all the signs pointed to an escalation of violence. The U.S.–Colombian objective was to capture the coca plantations and cocaine laboratories from the rebels. The local people feared that, should the coca fields be destroyed, they will lose their occupation and become jobless. Without alternative crops the local economy will collapse. The more successful the U.S.-inspired anti-drugs drive in Putumayo, the greater the likelihood that both the FARC rebels and the drug traffickers will move across the border into Ecuador.

Early in February 2001 President Andrés Pastrana went into the heart of FARC-held territory for talks with the guerrilla leader, Manuel Marulanda Vélez, in the hope of ending a conflict that had cost 35,000 lives over the previous 10 years. The meeting took place in the tiny village of San Vicente, the center of the demilitarized zone (the size of Switzerland) that the president had ceded to FARC in 1998; the zone is known as "Farclandia." The meeting followed weeks of negotiations. The president, who came to power on a peace manifesto, was coming under increasing pressure from the right as a result of his concessions to the rebels. A starting point for negotiations was the possibility of exchanging prisoners: FARC held some 500 military prisoners. A previous attempt at negotiations in November 2000 had broken down because FARC accused the government of tolerating the ultraright paramilitary death squads. Such squads, led by Carlos Castaño, massacred rebel sympathizers in the villages. Castaño wrote a letter to the president in which he attacked Pastrana's negotiations with the rebels and ended: "With your tolerance, the FARC rebels have strengthened themselves militarily and strategically." The president was also under pressure because of his promise to grant a second safe zone in the north of the country to the 6,000-strong ELN. FARC's principal concern was with the growing U.S. involvement in Colombia's drugs war. U.S. officials had denounced the FARC guerrillas as "narco-guerrillas" who purchase their arms with the money from cocaine, which the traffickers pay for protection. At the time of the February meeting, President Pastrana had failed to produce any results from his negotiations and, in consequence, had lost a great deal of political support.[6]

Growing Desolation

An article in the British Sunday newspaper *The Observer* in June 2001[7] paints a devastating picture of the damage done by the aerial spraying that is only supposed to eradicate the coca leaf. Roundup Ultra, which is sprayed on crops from the air, contains the weed killer Cosmoflux 411F in concentrations 100 times stronger than is permitted in the United States. Staples such as pineapples, bananas, and maize are all being destroyed by the spraying program; babies and children are falling ill, and people who in any case are among the poorest in Latin America are being reduced to still worse poverty and misery. Plan Colombia, which was conceived by President Clinton and embraced by his successor President George W. Bush, is designed to eliminate cocaine production in Colombia; a major aspect of the plan is aerial spraying of the coca bushes with a highly concentrated chemical toxin. However, all the preliminary evidence suggests that the spray inflicts far wider damage than simply destroying the coca harvests that are the target. Indeed, it appears that the coca bushes survive, while the human beings who live in the region and the environment are the principal sufferers. *The Observer* accuses both the Colombian and U.S. governments of trying to keep secret the damage that results from the spraying, for, despite growing evidence to the contrary, their spokesmen claimed in May 2001 that "the aerial spraying did not cause any injury or significant damage to the environment." In fact, the coca bushes have not been killed but are producing fresh crops of leaves. A teacher at the school in El Placer, one of the affected areas, claimed that "about 230 of the 450 pupils at our school have gone down with diarrhea, and respiratory and constantly recurring skin infections." Rather than destroying the coca crops, Plan Colombia is leading to a general deterioration of life in the region and extensive pollution of the Amazonian forest. Another aspect of the plan has been to provide the armed forces with U.S. weapons, although, as opponents of the plan point out, these are the same troops that for years have waged battles against unarmed civilians and committed atrocities against them. Meanwhile, thousands of Colombians have fled from Putumayo state into Ecuador. As of 2001 there were an estimated 2.1 million Colombians displaced by the civil war. The other accusation leveled at the United States is that it does nothing to halt the drugs trade in the United States itself where the bulk of the profits are made and where, all too often, the leading racketeers go free while a disproportionate number of minor figures, usually from ethnic minorities, fill the prisons.

The chemical used in the spraying of coca crops is based on the compound glyphosate. Glyphosate is manufactured by the Monsanto Corporation, using British-produced ingredients—hexitan esters—supplied by ICI Speciality Chemicals, and liquid isoparafins manufactured by Exxon. Glyphosate damages the human digestive system, the central nervous system, the lungs, and the blood's red corpuscles. A Colombian agronomist, Elsa Nivia, who works with the Pesticide Action Network, attacks the U.S. government's claim that Roundup Ultra is safe. She has written that in the first two months of 2001 local authorities in Colombia reported 4,289 people suffering skin or gastric disorders, while 178,377 animals were killed by the spraying, including cattle, horses, pigs, dogs, ducks, hens, and fish. Just two weeks after the appearance of the *Observer* article, ICI ended its controversial involvement in the Colombian spraying operation. The company decided it did not want to be involved in the program, especially after seeing reports of children falling ill after inhaling the chemicals.[8]

Meanwhile, the Colombian drug barons, who are always seeking new outlets, shifted their focus from the United States to Europe, where cocaine has become the prestige drug, prices are higher, and the removal of border controls in the European Union has made drug trafficking that much easier. According to a report drawn up in 2001 by Donnie Marshall, the outgoing chief of the DEA, the supply of cocaine to the United States was, perhaps, outstripping the demand since prices were stable. As a result the traffickers were turning to the European and Russian markets. As his report stated: "In Europe, cocaine seems to have the prestige and allure of danger, thrills, and enhanced endurance that attracted American athletes, media stars, and Wall Street traders to the drug in the 1980s."[9] American youths, on the other hand, appeared increasingly to be turning to ecstasy. Even so, the U.S. coke habit still required an annual supply of at least 300 tonnes (295 tons). Mr. Marshall believed that the drug syndicates were not seeking to increase their markets in the United States; instead, they were looking to Europe and the former Soviet Union countries. Despite Plan Colombia and the efforts to eradicate the coca leaf, the going rate for a kilo of cocaine in the United States remained steady at about $36,000. Over the previous five years, Colombia's annual production of cocaine had doubled and in 2001 was estimated at 580 tonnes (571 tons). However, according to a UN report, the DEA was underestimating the Colombian cocaine output, which the UN believed was over 800 tonnes (787 tons) a year. European cocaine demand, at less than a third that of the United States, leaves room for a massive expansion in consumption, especially as the target population, including Eastern Europe, is double that of the United States. It was also suggested that the bigger and more frequent seizures of drugs were more a sign that the flow of drugs from Latin America was unstoppable than that the anti-drugs war was being won.

The Role of the United States

The U.S. role in Colombia has become the key to what develops over the next few years. The injection of more than $1 billion of U.S. aid, mainly destined for the police or military, under President Clinton's Plan Colombia at the beginning of the century added a new dimension to a level of ongoing violence that is the worst in the Americas and possibly the worst in the world. Colombia has now suffered a civil war for more than 30 years, and there is no resolution in sight. The principal groups involved in confrontation and fighting are the two insurgent groups—the ELN and FARC; the army and the police; the right-wing death squads, often working closely with the army; and the drug traffickers. There are other subsidiary groups involved in the violence as well. And as usual, as in any such violent situation, the majority of the country's peasants keep their heads down and try to survive. They do so by growing the coca leaf to sell to the drug cartels. The shopkeepers pay weekly protection money to the insurgents, and the insurgents fund their campaigns with the proceeds of cocaine. In Barrancabermeja, 322 kilometers (200 miles) north of Bogotá, which is in the center of a region where the rebels are fighting for control, there are on average three violent deaths a day. Many of the people are too frightened to do anything; they are afraid of being taken either for sympathizers with the rebels, in which case they are liable to be targets of the police, the army, or the death squads; or of being taken for informers, in which case they become targets for the rebels. Barrancabermeja lies on the edge of the area occupied by the ELN, which President Pastrana has promised to make a no-go zone. The refinery in Barrancabermeja produces 70 percent of the country's petrol and though the promised no-go zone is only a tenth the size of the FARC no-go zone, it is densely populated and rich in resources. Much of the region is under paramilitary control and the 7,000-strong right-wing militia, led by Carlos Castaño, see themselves as peacekeepers and expect to play a part in any negotiations. The head of the police in the area, Jaime Martinez Santa Maria, claimed in 2000: "Any ideology is long lost. The revolution is dead, and it is all economics. It is about who controls the black market gasoline concession and all the cocaine."[10]

The United States, which in any case has been exerting increasing pressures on Colombia for two decades, decided at the end of Clinton's presidency to increase its involvement in Colombia. That decision, the launch of Plan Colombia, may well come to be seen in retrospect as comparable to President Kennedy's decision to increase the U.S. military presence in Vietnam in the form of military advisers. There is little doubt that Plan Colombia and the implication of much greater U.S. involvement on the ground in the anti-drugs war have raised many doubts and fears about the ultimate impact on Colombia and its neighbors. Supporters of Plan Colombia argue that the additional U.S. backing will enable President Pastrana to force through his peace proposals with the ELN and FARC, since the destruction of the coca fields will deprive the rebels of their principal source of income, which is derived from taxing the drug cultivators. This is an optimistic view and must be tempered by evidence from other jungle wars. Neither the drug barons nor the rebels are going to be defeated easily; they have existed in parallel harness—the rebels to change the political system, the drug cartels to make fortunes—for more than 30 years. Experience from Vietnam and, more recently, from disintegrating Yugoslavia would suggest that the U.S. involvement will have to be much greater than that envisaged under Plan Colombia if success in the drugs war is to be achieved. Opponents of Plan Colombia first attack the waiving of human rights conditions that the U.S. Congress initially attached to the plan for the Colombian security forces, whose record in this respect has been abysmal. More importantly, they believe that U.S. military advisers will simply become mired in an unwinnable war, although their presence and the arms and other equipment that will come with them will no doubt escalate the violence and spread it across Colombia's borders. Suggested parallels with Vietnam have been discounted by U.S. National Security Adviser Sandy Berger; he insisted (in August 2000) that the U.S. presence will be restricted to 500 soldiers and 300 contracted employees at any given time and that U.S. personnel must not become involved in combat. Furthermore, the destruction of coca and poppy crops and the seizure of cocaine or heroin will be left—largely—to the Colombians. Colombia's neighbors—Brazil, Ecuador, Panama, Peru, and Venezuela—have each expressed concern at the growing U.S. presence in Colombia and believe that it will simply force refugees and drug traffickers across the borders into their countries. Environmentalists fear that the defoliants being used to spray the coca crops will blight the rain forest and, despite Sandy Berger's denial of any comparison, many U.S. legislators warn of another Vietnam. Alfonso Cano of FARC said of Plan Colombia: "The United States needs an excuse to continue to play the role of the world's policeman and now that excuse is drug trafficking."[11] He went on to deride the new U.S.-backed drug offensive, which he described as a disguised counterinsurgency effort. When he visited Cartagena at the end of August 2000, President Clinton said, "We will not get involved in the internal conflict of Colombia, nor is this about Yankee imperialism," but his remarks did not convince his South American audience. At the Brazil summit, which was being held at that time and was attended by the presidents of Bolivia, Colombia, Ecuador, Peru, Argentina, and Chile, plans for a multinational military force that would intervene in the Colombian conflict were rejected. Brazilian Foreign Minister Luiz Felipe Lampreia spoke for the region when he said: "Brazil will not participate in any such international force. What's more, Brazil stands firmly against the idea of any foreign military force in Colombia." The message to the United States was clear enough. Its urgency was enhanced when Vladimiro Montesinos Torres, the right-hand aide of President Alberto Fujimori of Peru, revealed that the United States had drawn up plans for a "multilateral invasion force to help the struggle against subversion." The increased U.S. concern about Colombia appeared to date from a January 1998 article in the *Washington Post,* which quoted State Department officials who had suggested that the left-wing rebels could seize power in Colombia within five years. The multilateral force envisaged by the United States for intervention in Colombia was concerned with "subversion" rather than drugs.

Any examination of the events in Colombia during the 1990s suggests a country that is virtually uncontrollable and close to disintegration. Despite the fact that it is the world's largest source of cocaine, drugs are only a part of Colombia's problem; the civil war had been continuing for more than a decade when the huge escalation in demand for drugs from the United States led to a rapid growth of cocaine production in the mid-1970s. A massively increased U.S. involvement in Colombia, whether to assist in fighting the drugs war or in reality to prevent left-wing insurgents taking control of the country, is less likely to resolve Colombia's many problems than to exacerbate them. Indeed, the war on drugs exacerbates the very instability that acts as the breeding ground for drug-trafficking groups.

10
Colombia's Neighbors

Colombia may be the center of the cocaine trade, but the rest of South America is involved, more or less willingly, in most other aspects of drug trafficking whether as coca producers (Bolivia and Peru), transit countries (Brazil and Venezuela), or money launderers (Argentina). Once the traffickers have moved into a country the transit routes are opened, the money and corruption follow, and new vested interests with growing stakes in the trade emerge (see Figure 10.1). The pervasive way the illicit drugs trade spreads

Figure 10.1 Colombia and neighboring countries. (Cartography by Map Creation, Ltd., Maidenhead, Berkshire, U.K.)

was highlighted at the sixth Ibero–American Summit, which was held in Santiago, Chile, in November 1996. President Eduardo Frei Ruíz-Tagle of Chile emphasized the threat to democracy that was posed by official corruption, which was linked to the drugs trade. No country was free of the danger. The conference pledged to coordinate the efforts of its members against drug trafficking and to seek further assistance from countries that were markets for illegal drugs, principally the United States. The following year, in May 1997, the presidents of Costa Rica, the Dominican Republic, El Salvador, Guatemala, Honduras, Nicaragua, and the United States, and the prime minister of Belize, met in San José, Costa Rica, where they agreed to cooperate more closely in an effort to combat drug trafficking in the region. Although Latin American leaders are sincere in their determination to fight the drugs trade, it is the United States, with its open purse and determination to bring the fight against drugs into the source countries that provides the driving force in this endless and shifting battle.

Bolivia

In the second half of the 1990s Bolivia, under pressure from the United States, made determined efforts to fight drug trafficking. In September 1995 the Special Force against Drug Trafficking (FELCN) confirmed that four of its senior officials had been dismissed and, with 10 civilians and 13 members of the police, had been implicated in the shipment of 4.1 tonnes (4 tons) of cocaine that had been seized in Lima, Peru. According to the Bolivian Workers Central (COB), the main trade union confederation, the seizure was connected with the arrival of a Panama-based U.S. Galaxy transport aircraft carrying military personnel. COB warned of possible U.S. military intervention under the pretext of fighting drug trafficking. Whether there was any truth in this suggestion, the possibility of U.S. intervention surfaces very quickly and is undoubtedly a factor in any political calculation relating to the drugs trade. Meanwhile, Bolivia's foreign affairs minister, Antonio Aranibar Quiroga, returned from a visit to Washington where he claimed the U.S. government had promised to increase its anti-drugs aid. Also that September, 1,000 anti-drugs force police, supported by DEA helicopters, made a sweep of the eastern Chapare region and forcibly occupied five villages in their drive to eradicate coca production. The president of the eastern Chapare region coca growers' association, Evo Morales, said that the coca eradication took place without discrimination between new and traditional coca plantations and despite an earlier agreement between the government and the coca growers on the voluntary eradication of new coca plantings. The fact that such an argument could arise demonstrates the complexity of the problem: The traditional coca growers mean to retain the source of their livelihood. Talks between the government and coca growers broke down in November of that year when the government announced that it intended to meet its target of eradicating 5,400 hectares (13,340 acres) of coca plantations before December 31, the deadline being a condition for receiving more U.S. aid. Evo Morales responded that local self-defense groups would resist any forcible eradication.

The contradictions in the policy became clear during November 1995. On the one hand some 3,000 hectares (7,410 acres) of coca had been destroyed under a voluntary scheme that included compensation. But then, on November 15, some 2,000 antiriot police were deployed in Sinahota village against 5,000 coca producers. At the same time that this violent action was taking place, 100 members of FELCN were arrested for themselves engaging in drug trafficking. The investigating commission reported that FELCN was underfunded, corrupt, negligent, and inefficient. Despite these contradictory developments, on December 21 the government announced that it had regained international credibility because it had surpassed the U.S. eradication target of 5,400 hectares (13,340 acres) for the year, having eradicated 5,520 hectares (13,640 acres), and so could ask for more U.S. aid.

Peasant coca growers' opposition to forced crop eradication led to a new confrontation with the government at the beginning of 1996. In mid-January 50 women coca growers went on a hunger strike after the government refused to discuss their demands, which included improved guarantees of human rights and an end to the forced eradication of coca crops. Other coca growers established roadblocks in the eastern Chapare region as a gesture of solidarity with the women who were on the hunger strike. The women ended their hunger strike on February 3 after the government had signed an agreement with COB. In return for the coca growers ending their protest actions, the government agreed, in its turn, to end the program of forced crop eradication, to free imprisoned coca growers, and to guarantee respect for human rights in the Chapare region.

On January 9, 1996, the U.S. government refused a visa to former President Jaime Paz Zamora (1989–1993) of the Movement of the Revolutionary Left (MIR), his sister, and the former party president, Oscar Eid Franco. The U.S. action led to cross-party protests in Bolivia, which were seen as boosting Zamora's chances of making a political comeback in the 1997 elections. The U.S. action was taken on the grounds that the three had links with drug trafficker Isaac "Oso" Chavarria. Zamora had denied receiving drug money for his presidential campaign, although in 1994 he had retired, apparently "permanently" from politics, following allegations about his involvement in drugs. In November both chambers of the Bolivian Congress approved an extradition treaty with the United States; both countries ratified the treaty on November 21. It was immediately likely to affect 20 Bolivians then linked to the drugs trade. During 1997 the Bolivian government tried to implement a U.S.-backed program to prevent the manufacture of and trafficking in cocaine. This program, however, would run into serious difficulties during 1998.

In February 1998 the coca producers of Cochabamba department declared a state of emergency and rejected the government's "For Dignity" anti-drugs plan. They claimed that the government had not carried out an agreement it had signed with them in October 1997 that provided for an alternative development program. Moreover, the coca producers insisted that they had fulfilled their promise to eliminate 7,200 hectares (17,790 acres) of coca crops during 1997, and by doing so had prevented Bolivia being "decertified" by the United States. The growers therefore reactivated the self-defense committees, which had been inactive since July 1997, to guard their crops. In March Spain agreed to make two concessionary loans worth $130 million to Bolivia to assist its fight against poverty and drugs. In April the Bolivian government, which had decided to use force in support of its eradication program, mounted a combined army and police operation against the Cochabamba and Chapare coca producers. By the end of the month, 10 people had been killed and 40 injured in clashes between the two sides. In June the government announced that compensation paid to farmers who stopped growing coca was to be reduced from $1,650 to $800 from July 1.

On September 2, 1998, more than 1,000 coca growers marched in La Paz to demand a government review of its plans to eradicate all illegal coca plantations by 2002. Most of the demonstrators came from the Chapare region, where 95 percent of the coca grown is turned into cocaine. The government, however, would not respond to the demands of the marchers and said instead that it would proceed with its plans to eradicate more than 9,000 hectares (22,240 acres) of illegal coca plantations in the Chapare region before the end of the year. The marchers then announced a hunger strike; later, their peaceful demonstrations turned to violence. In March 1999, as a result of the government's hard line, the United States endorsed Bolivia with certification for cooperating fully with the United States in the fight against drugs.

Relations between Bolivia and the United States suffered a number of setbacks during 2000. In March the U.S. ambassador to Bolivia, Donna Hrinak, accused the Bolivian information minister, Jorge Landivar, of securing the acquittal of a leading drugs suspect, Marino Diodato, who was married to a niece of President Hugo Bánzar Suárez. (As in Colombia, the political system of Bolivia appeared to be touched at many levels by the drugs business.) Landivar resigned and was replaced by Ronald MacLean Abaroa, a former foreign minister. However, the U.S. ambassador's remarks were described as offensive by Oscar Hassenteufel, the president of the Supreme Court, while the interior minister, Walter Guiteras Dennis, said, "We don't accept American interference."

In October, following a series of strikes, an agreement was reached between the government and workers, which covered a number of worker grievances. The government promised to invest $80 million in the Chapare region and Cochabamba department so as to diversify the local economies away from coca production. The government, however, did not agree to halt coca eradication operations that were then being carried out by the military and included burning and spraying fields in those areas where planting had exceeded agreed limits for "traditional" production, or where there was no agreement for even limited production. The government regarded the coca eradication program as "non-negotiable"; it had been warned by the U.S. ambassador, Michael Rocha, that Bolivia would be subjected to U.S. sanctions if it failed to meet coca eradication targets. In an interview that month (published October 23), President Hugo Bánzar conceded that the eradication of coca in Bolivia had deprived communities of about $500 million of income, equivalent to 6 percent of the GDP. Nonetheless, "For Dignity," which had been launched at the end of 1997 and aimed to eliminate all illegal coca plantations by 2002, was to continue.

In its annual review of the worldwide fight against the drugs trade for 2000, the U.S. government praised Bolivia for having exceeded the targets for eradication that it had set itself; in 1999 the Bánzar government had eradicated an unprecedented 16,999 hectares (42,010 acres) of coca, equivalent to a reduction of the total crop by 43 percent. The review also pointed out that although Bolivia remained the world's third-largest producer of cocaine, with an annual capacity of 70 tonnes (68.9 tons), its cocaine had become harder to market because of successful law enforcement efforts aimed at preventing precursor chemicals being smuggled into the country. As a result, cocaine producers were obliged to use less efficient means of processing the drug with substitute or recycled chemicals. The purity of finished Bolivian cocaine hydrochloride (HCI) had dropped as low as 47 percent with the result that Brazilian and other traffickers only bought Bolivian cocaine base and then finished the processing in Brazil. Meanwhile, the export volumes of alternative development crops had increased. A cautious assessment of Bolivia's involvement in drug trafficking at the end of the century indicated some real advances in reducing overall coca production, though there was little indication that this had reduced the amount of cocaine offered to the principal markets in North America and Europe. Furthermore, there were signs that reduced production in Bolivia merely encouraged increased production in Brazil—a consideration that must apply to any successful curtailing of production.

Popular pressure in April 2001 persuaded the government to agree at the end of June to suspend the coca eradication program in Yungas, following clashes between peasants and troops. Protests continued through July, and it was admitted that the virtual eradication of coca production in Chapare, which had been claimed, was not true. In November the eradication program in Chapare was temporarily suspended after four farmers had been killed in further clashes. The government, meanwhile, had been warned by Washington that it would cut off aid if eradication targets that had been set under "Plan Dignity" were not met.

Government–peasant clashes continued in 2002. Coca farmers were angry at being deprived of their livelihoods by U.S. policy. When farmers in the department of Cochamba attempted to reopen a coca leaf market that had been closed by presidential decree, seven people were killed in the subsequent violence. Congress then voted to strip Evo Morales, president of the coca growers association, of his parliamentary immunity from prosecution for his alleged incitement of his followers to violence. However, following mediation by the Roman Catholic Church in February, the government suspended its decree closing the coca leaf market to allow limited dealings.

In January 2003, the government agreed to withdraw troops from coca eradication operations while a study was undertaken as to whether the quota for coca grown for "traditional purposes" such as chewing or tea production should be increased. It was clear that the battle to keep producing coca leaves would continue indefinitely.

Peru

The fight against coca production followed a similar path in Peru as in Bolivia, and Peru came under comparable pressures from the United States. In November 1995, for example, arrest warrants for 11 army officers were issued for drug-trafficking offenses; among the officers were two generals. However, the military authorities handed over only five of the accused to the civil authorities, claiming there was insufficient evidence against the others. The charges arose out of information supplied to the government by drug baron Abelardo Cachique Rivera, who had been arrested the previous June and was then serving a 30-year prison sentence. He claimed the army officers had received money to allow the transport and manufacture of cocaine in areas under their control. On July 23, 1996, Peru signed an anti-drugs pact with the United States; this replaced the one agreed upon in 1991. The agreement came in the wake of a number of substantial drug hauls by Peruvian air force planes and ships. During September 1996 various ministers in Congress denied that Vladimiro Montesinos Torres, the head of the National Intelligence Service, had used his influence to protect drug traffickers, although in court a self-confessed drug baron, Demetrio Chávez Peñaherrera, claimed to have paid Montesinos $50,000 to protect his illicit airstrip in the Huallaga Valley; the northern Huallaga Valley is the center of Peru's drug operations. Following close cooperation between the intelligence and police services of Ecuador and Peru, the most wanted Peruvian drug baron, Willem Alvarado Linares, was arrested in Quito, Ecuador.

During the balance of the 1990s Peru maintained its anti-drugs program, although the disturbed politics of President Alberto Keinya Fujimori's last years in office overshadowed most other developments. In February 1999 the army chief of staff, General Tomás Marky, was arrested and charged with drug-related offenses. His arrest came just when the U.S. government had fully certified Peru for its efforts to combat the drugs trade and had announced an increase in its antinarcotics aid. The U.S. report on Peru for 2000 praised the government for having made excellent progress in eliminating illegal coca production—an additional 24 percent during the year, making a total reduction of 66 percent over the four years up to and including 1999. More significant than the area of 15,000 hectares (37,070 acres) of coca cultivation that had been eliminated were the alternative programs that had been introduced. According to the U.S. report, Peru's counterdrug alternative development program, "working through 103 local governments, almost 700 communities, and more than 15,000 farmers, significantly strengthened social and economic infrastructure in these areas and helped shift the economic balance in favor of licit activities." These figures certainly appear impressive. They were counterbalanced, however, by growing evidence that traffickers were producing cocaine within the country's borders and setting up laboratories along the borders with Brazil, Colombia, and Bolivia so that they could leave the country swiftly without risk of interception. In addition, there was a new development: There was evidence that opium poppy cultivation was on the increase. Nonetheless, Peru had achieved a significant reduction in coca cultivation and the strong anti-drugs policy appeared to be obtaining positive results.

In June 2000, following Peru's much-criticized elections of April and May, an OAS mission visited Peru to present various reform proposals. The United States suggested that the reforms should be enforced, declared that its future attitude would depend on the extent to which Peru acted on the OAS recommendations, and hinted that it might take unilateral action. Moreover, in mid-July President Clinton excluded $42 million of emergency antinarcotics aid for Peru from the $1.3 billion aid package (mainly for Colombia) that he had announced at the beginning of the year.[1] This exclusion heightened South American suspicions that U.S. pressures for action to curtail drug production could be used to obtain other political results as well. In December 2000 President Valentín Paniagua Corazao announced that José Carlos Ugaz, a special prosecutor, had extended his investigation to review allegations that former President Fujimori had received illegal campaign contributions in 1990 from the Colombian cocaine cartels. Ugaz's original task had been to investigate allegations that the disgraced former head of the National Intelligence Service, Vladimiro Montesinos, had managed a network of secret bank accounts in order to launder the proceeds of illegal arms deals and drug transactions. The fact that the highest political figures in the land were tainted with corruption in relation to the drugs trade was bound to cast doubt on the long-term success of any anti-drugs program.

In March 2003, after weeks of highway blockades by coca growers, the government, while refusing to halt its coca eradication program, promised to allocate U.S. $11 million for reforestation projects in the Amazonian coca-producing areas. However, continuing pressure led President Alejandro Toledo to sign a decree on April 23 to conduct the program of destruction of coca leaves at a "gradual" pace and "coordinated" with the farmers. The agreement was reached after several thousand coca growers had marched from the country's 14 recognized coca-producing areas to the capital. The government also promised that aid to encourage crop diversification should be paid directly to the farmers rather than being processed through NGOs. Nonetheless, the government was committed to eradicate 8,000 hectares of coca crops during 2003; that is, 12 percent above the eradication figure for 2002. Peasant opposition to the program showed no signs of abating.

Brazil

Though it is not (as yet) a major drug producer, Brazil is deeply involved in the illicit drugs business as a consumer, transit country, and center for money laundering. In May 1995 Rio de Janeiro suffered weeks of drug-related violence that included 60 murders. On May 8, 14 drug traffickers were shot dead in a gun battle as police moved into a shanty town where gangs had been fighting each other for control of prime drug sales positions. Brazil faces the same problem as in Colombia, Bolivia, and Peru: how to tackle the illegal drugs trade effectively when politicians and other leading officials in the judiciary or military/police services have been drawn into a nationwide web of corruption by drug money. On September 3, 1999, for example, Judge Leopoldo Marques do Amaral was murdered in the state of Mato Grosso because, it was believed, he possessed documents that revealed the involvement of the state judiciary with drug traffickers. He had evidence that he had recently presented to the Senate relating to a case in 1996 when the condemned trafficker, Valdenor Alves Marchezan, was freed because he bribed two judges who returned to him an aircraft, which he had used to fly cocaine into Brazil. The judge's assassination led to calls for a reform of the judiciary. In November 1999 the government set up a federal task force—nucleo de combate a impunidade—to investigate organized crime, especially drug trafficking, and its influence over certain areas of the country's political life. The following month the defense minister dismissed Brigadier Werner Walter Brauer, the air force chief of staff, who had criticized the minister, Elcio Alvares, for employing an adviser suspected of links with drug barons. In this case there were other reasons for the antagonism between the two men, but, as so often appeared to be the case, there seemed to be little difficulty introducing a drugs angle into a high-profile political row.

At the end of the twentieth century, Brazil was both a major transit country for drugs destined for the U.S. market and an important producer of precursor chemicals and synthetic drugs. In addition, it suffered from significant drug abuse problems of its own, while its drug barons formed a powerful criminal elite. The government of President Fernando Henrique Cardoso, who took office in 1995, had made determined efforts to reduce the country's role as a transit route and to combat the domestic and international drug syndicates that operated in and through Brazil. Some important advances were made in 1999 against drug-related corruption and money laundering. An important initiative was the creation in April 1999 of the Congressional Panel of Inquiry (CPI) on drug trafficking. Its task was to assess the extent of collusion in drug trafficking and money laundering by Brazilians in positions of power and authority in both the public and private sectors. The panel's first investigations into the country's drug networks led to 115 arrests, including those of government officials. In its first year of operation, the CPI was able to demonstrate the extent to which the drugs trade had corrupted public institutions and individuals. Seizures of both cocaine and cannabis were greater in 1999 than in the previous year; no evidence was found of either opium or cocaine production. Brazil has a highly developed banking sector and this has long been a conduit for drug money. In November 2000 federal police and officials from financial regulatory authorities launched an investigation into a huge money-laundering network that was believed to have processed Real 60 billion during the 1990s from drugs and armaments. The following month, on December 8, the CPI published a 1,200-page report (after an 18-month investigation) in which it named 827 individuals in national and local government, Congress, the judiciary, banking, the police, and armed forces who were linked in one way or another to the production or distribution of drugs or to money laundering. The report revealed levels of complicity in the drugs trade that extended widely through official society. It also claimed that $50 billion, a figure equivalent to 10 percent of the worldwide drugs trade, was laundered annually through the financial system. The CPI report called for increased supervision of the banking system and the establishment of a permanent commission to investigate the drugs trade.

Venezuela

Venezuela acts as a major transit country for Colombian cocaine en route to the United States and Europe, with an estimated 100 tonnes (984 tons) of cocaine passing through the country annually. It is also a transit route for precursor chemicals used in Colombia, Bolivia, and Peru, while its banking system plays an important role laundering money from the Colombian cartels. As with its neighbors, Venezuela is affected by the all-pervasive corruption that drug trafficking always leaves in its wake. In 1998, for example, the president of the national counternarcotics commission, Carlos Tablante, presented charges to the Council of the Judiciary against 10 judges for allegedly accepting bribes in exchange for rulings in favor of drug traffickers. There was an increase in drug seizures during 1999, which in part resulted from close cooperation between the Venezuelan and U.S. drug enforcement agencies; however, it was also in part an indication of the increase in drug transshipments through the country. There were also increased seizures of chemical precursors, with more than 112 tonnes (110 tons) of potassium permanganate, a major chemical needed in the production of cocaine, being seized. Corruption remained a major obstacle to a more effective anti-drugs policy, and for this reason the government implemented a new criminal code in 1999 with the potential to provide a more transparent system of justice.

Venezuela's anti-drugs efforts were rewarded with a major success in August 2000 when international law enforcement officers seized 25 tonnes (24.6 tons) of cocaine worth approximately $1 billion from a port on the country's eastern Atlantic coast. It was one of the biggest antinarcotics operations in the history of the drugs war. "Operation Journey," as it was called, followed two years of investigations in which 12 countries—including Britain, Belgium, the Netherlands, and Albania from Europe—had shared information with U.S. and South American authorities. A total of 43 arrests were made, as well as the confiscation of five commercial freighters. The alleged leader of the smuggling ring, Ivan de la Vega, and four others were sent to face drug-smuggling charges in Florida. The smuggling operation was geared to transport drugs from Colombia through the Venezuelan jungle to Europe and used up to 10 commercial freighters for the purpose. Announcing the completion of the successful operation on August 26, the U.S. commissioner of customs service, Raymond Kelly, said "Operation Journey" had provided a "powerful new blueprint for fighting the international drug trade." There was also high praise for the Venezuelan authorities that had seized nearly 10 tonnes (9.8 tons) of cocaine the previous week in the Orinoco River delta. The success of "Operation Journey," which had been partially funded by the DEA, was expected to help ease tensions between Venezuela and the United States that had followed Venezuela's refusal in 1999 to allow U.S. anti-drugs air surveillance over its territory.

Ecuador

Wedged between its two much larger neighbors, Colombia and Peru, Ecuador has little chance of escaping involvement in the drug trafficking of the region, and by the end of the twentieth century, as pressures mounted against coca producers in the south of Colombia, there were growing fears in Quito that the country's northern border region would see an influx of refugees and drug traffickers from that country. During 1999 Ecuador, although suffering major economic troubles, nevertheless cooperated closely with the United States in counterdrug activities. The country's geographical position ensures that it serves as a major transit route for cocaine destined for the United States, as well as for precursor chemicals en route to drug laboratories in Colombia and Peru. During 1999 the Ecuadorean National Police (ENP) seized 10 tonnes (9.8 tons) of cocaine and coca base, more than twice as much as the seizures for 1998 (which only came to 3.9 tonnes [3.8 tons]). There were also increased seizures of heroin and record seizures of methyl ethyl ketone (MEK) and other precursor chemicals. Various reforms were instituted covering the judicial system, law enforcement agencies, and the customs service, and a unified anti-drugs division was established within the ENP. The government published a five-year counterdrug strategy that set out the roles and responsibilities of the different agencies that were involved in the anti-drugs war. Finally, in a move that allowed greater direct U.S. involvement in Ecuador, the government entered into a 10-year agreement that allowed U.S. regional counterdrug detection and monitoring missions to operate from the Ecuadorean air force base at Manta. In contrast to all these developments, in March 1998 the National Congress had approved a bill proposed by the attorney general's office to decriminalize drug consumption.

Paraguay

The government of Paraguay has often declared its determination to reduce drug-trafficking operations in the country, but this is probably more for external reasons—to appease Washington—than because there is much political will or, perhaps, government ability to stop the trade. Paraguay is not a major drug-producing country, although it is the source of high-quality marijuana; in 1999 the government seized large amounts of marijuana and eradicated 900 hectares (2,220 acres) of an estimated 2,500 hectares (6,180 acres) of marijuana fields. Paraguay, however, is a major drug-transit country, principally for Bolivian cocaine, and is also an important money-laundering center. U.S. experts believe that between 15 and 30 tonnes (14.8 to 29.5 tons) of cocaine pass through Paraguay each year en route for Argentina, Brazil, the United States, and Europe, yet in 1999 only 95 kilograms (209 pounds) of cocaine were seized and only 211 arrests of low-level cocaine and marijuana traffickers were made. The United States did not consider that the government of Paraguay accomplished its counterdrug goals in 1999 in such a way as to earn full U.S. certification; for example, the government did not investigate, arrest, or prosecute any major drug traffickers, nor did it take serious action against corruption, whether in general or specifically related to drug-trafficking activities. Furthermore, the government failed to implement its 1996 law against money laundering by arresting or prosecuting violators and did not provide adequate funds for its anti-money-laundering secretariat. There were other charges leveled at the government by the United States and the "balance sheet," if it could be expressed in such terms, clearly indicated that Paraguay was not serious in its anti-drugs activities and should not, therefore, be certified. And this is where the certification system runs into problems. The U.S. International Narcotics Control Strategy Report (INCSR) for 2000 is worth quoting at length:

> Denial of certification would, however, cut off civilian and military assistance programs designed to strengthen Paraguay's democratic institutions and promote modern civil-military relations. Strengthening democracy in Paraguay is a U.S. vital national interest, and failure in this effort would affect negatively all other U.S. interests, including cooperation with respect to illicit drugs, terrorism, intellectual-property piracy, and environmental preservation. The events of 1999—which included defiance by then-President Cubas of the Supreme Court, the assassination of Vice President Argana, the killing of student demonstrators, the impeachment and resignation of Cubas, drought, rural unrest, and the reported presence of fugitive former general and coup plotter Lino Oviedo—demonstrate the many challenges facing Paraguayan democracy. They also contributed to the GOP's unsatisfactory counter-drug performance. Denial of certification would undermine the U.S. ability to strengthen Paraguay's democratic institutions and would put at risk all other U.S. vital national interests.[2]

This long list of U.S. concerns suggests that the certification process in relation to drugs is less important than a U.S. ability to be involved in Paraguay's affairs as a whole, and the same U.S. attitude may well be made in relation to other countries that are given or denied certification.

Argentina and Chile

Argentina and Chile are not mainstream drug-trafficking nations in South America, though both have their share of drug-related problems. Argentina, however, is especially associated with money-laundering activities. On September 1, 1999, the Chamber of Deputies approved a bill that penalized money laundering as the result of illegal activities, including drug trafficking. The chamber was responding to U.S. pressures to pass such legislation.

In February 2001 Pedro Pou, the president of Argentina's central bank, faced criticisms that he had turned a blind eye to money laundering. The accusations came in the wake of the publication of a report by Democratic members of the U.S. Senate that such money laundering involved both U.S. and Argentine banks. As a result, the Argentine government established a congressional commission to investigate the charges against Pou. The commission reported in April, and Pou was dismissed.

The British Sunday newspaper *The Observer* reported in December 2000 that the Chilean army and secret police had spent almost two decades secretly flooding Europe and the United States with massive shipments of cocaine. This trafficking had begun during the dictatorship of General Augusto Pinochet Ugarte. In 1986 and 1987, for example, 12.2 tonnes (12 tons) of cocaine with a street value of several billion pounds was sent to European destinations through Spain. The distribution in Europe was controlled by Chilean secret police stationed at the Chilean embassies in Madrid and Stockholm. According to *The Observer*, Pinochet was a party to these trafficking operations. As he had said in October 1981: "Not a leaf moves in Chile if I don't move it—let that be clear." Moreover, the former head of the Chilean secret police, who was implicated in these drug-trafficking operations, told the Chilean Supreme Court in 1998 that he undertook nothing without General Pinochet's express permission. Evidence of Pinochet's collaboration with Colombian drug dealers was revealed in *La delgada línea blanca* [The Thin White Line], a book by Rodrigo de Castro (a former international civil servant in Chile) and Juan Gasparini, an Argentine journalist.[3] The complexities of U.S. involvement in drug activities are exposed in the story of a former U.S. marine, Frankell Ivan Baramdyka, who was extradited from Chile in 1993 and convicted in Southern California of drug offenses. In the early 1980s he had worked for U.S. intelligence when he was encouraged to traffic in drugs, provided he channeled some of the profits of his operations to the Contra terrorists then opposing the Sandinista government in Nicaragua when it was U.S. policy to support them. Baramdyka revealed how he first made contact with the Chileans in 1984 when he delivered $2 million to the Chilean consulate-general in Los Angeles on behalf of Colombian cocaine producers; it was payment for chemicals that had been supplied by the Chilean army. Marco Antonio, Pinochet's younger son, was then on the consulate-general's staff. Later, Baramdyka set up trafficking operations for the Chileans in Santiago and ended up overseeing the army's drug export activities.[4]

Uruguay

In an interview of December 5, 2000, in Mexico City, President Jorge Batlle Ibáñez of Uruguay called for the legalization of cocaine by the authorities in the United States so as to deprive drug traffickers in South and Central America of their principal market. The president drew an analogy with the end of prohibition of alcohol in the United States in the early 1930s and argued that such a course would encourage legitimate suppliers to enter the market and so undercut the criminal gangs.

11

Central America, the Caribbean, and Mexico

When George W. Bush took over as U.S. president at the beginning of 2001, the United States had just embarked on its massive $1.3 billion, much-criticized "Plan Colombia" aimed at stopping the production of marijuana, cocaine, and heroin in that country. Already, there were 500 U.S. troops in Colombia in support of an army that itself deals in drugs and has one of the worst human rights records in the world, including providing regular support for right-wing civilian death squads. As the year commenced there were an estimated two million Colombian refugees, while both the former U.S. Secretary of State George Shultz and the economist Milton Friedman had joined the swelling ranks of those who argue that the war on drugs is causing more harm than drug abuse itself. Another eminent American, William Ratliff of the Hoover Institution at Stanford University, argued at the end of 2000 that Plan Colombia was heading for crisis. Adding to the growing sense of confrontation in Colombia, where a long-standing civil war between left and right shows no sign of abating, the Revolutionary Armed Forces of Colombia (FARC) issued a New Year's message in which it threatened "to defeat the evil war plans of the governments of the United States and Colombia." And to drive home the contradictions inherent in U.S. policy, José Vicente Rangel, the foreign minister of neighboring Venezuela, challenged Washington to explain why $4 billion worth of marijuana is grown in the United States.[1]

The Central American Countries

Guatemala, which it is hoped has just emerged from a third of a century of internal conflict, has now joined the ranks of other Latin American countries that are "cooperating" with the United States in combating drug trafficking. It seems unlikely that the Guatemalan government will be very effective in this regard, even if the will is there. The country's geographic location alone makes it an ideal halfway house for the transit of drugs from Colombia to Mexico and on to the United States, while its scarce law enforcement resources and poverty make it open to the pervasive corruption that comes in the wake of all drug trafficking. In 1999, however, the U.S.-trained Department of Anti-Narcotics Police (DOAN) seized 10 tonnes (9.8 tons) of cocaine. In 2000, although there were some major convictions for drug offenses, in some cases judges released suspected drug traffickers on questionable grounds, giving rise to the usual suspicion of corruption in the ranks of the judiciary. U.S. money, training, and pressures may elicit all the correct responses from the Guatemalan government, but it is doubtful that they will achieve a great deal more.

Anti-drugs activities in other Central American countries varied in both intensity and commitment. In March 1999 Alvaro Jimenez, a senior judge in San José, Costa Rica, was detained on charges of belonging to an international drug-trafficking gang. In July 2000 the legislature of El Salvador voted to allow the United States to establish an antinarcotics base at Comalapa international airport. This represented the first permanent deployment of U.S. military personnel in the country since the end of its civil war, and the move was fiercely resisted and denounced by former left-wing guerrillas who had fought the U.S.-backed army for 13 years up to the 1992 peace agreement. The Farabundo Marti National Liberation Front (FMLN) claimed that the agreement violated the country's sovereignty and that it would refer the matter to the Supreme Court. Nonetheless, the measure was passed by 49 to 35 votes. In addition, the legislature passed a constitutional amendment to enable El Salvador to negotiate an extradition treaty with the United States. In 1998 the National Assembly of Nicaragua passed a law under which alleged drug traffickers would have to stand trial before a judge rather than a jury and would be restricted in the matter of posting bail. Those convicted would not be eligible for pardon or amnesty. The law also provided for the creation of a Financial Commission for Banking Operations Control in order to prevent money laundering. These three countries—Costa Rica, El Salvador, and Nicaragua—appeared to be falling in with U.S. arguments about what to do to combat drug trafficking, though their ability to be effective is questionable and in the case of El Salvador, close liaison with the United States seems more likely to stir up former left–right antagonisms than to combat drug trafficking.

The U.S. invasion of Panama in December 1989 in order to end the rule of Manuel Noriega was a foretaste of what was to come in the anti-drugs war. Noriega was deeply corrupt, heavily involved in drug trafficking, and is now serving a long prison sentence in the United States where, no doubt, he will die. He was also a stooge of U.S. policies and the CIA who got out of hand and would no longer do what Washington wanted, which was why his political career had to be brought to an end. Corruption is always a two-way street.

In 1996 an investigation was launched in Panama to discover how money from drug cartels entered the 1994 election campaign funds of President

Ernesto Pérez Balladares. Reports had persisted since 1994 that the Balladares government was tainted with Colombian drug money, and on June 21, 1996, the president admitted he had unwittingly received two checks for $51,000 from a company headed by José Castrillon Henao, a Colombian arrested in Panama the previous April on charges of heading the Cali cartel sea-going cocaine export operation to the United States. It was an all-too-familiar story.

On May 5, 1999, the United States was obliged to close its Howard Air Force Base anti-drug-trafficking mission in Panama in accordance with the Panama Canal Treaties, which it had signed in 1977. U.S. officials claimed that the move would reduce the effectiveness of the fight against drug trafficking in Latin America and the Caribbean. The main operations for the anti-drugs task force were transferred to Florida. Meanwhile, agreements had been reached to fly missions out of Ecuador, Curaçao (Netherlands Antilles), and Aruba. In late January 2000 Panama negotiated an anti-drugs agreement with the United States that, it hoped, would lead to greater financing and training for its security forces. According to Justice Minister Winston Spadafora, Panama sought $30 million worth of aircraft, equipment such as patrol boats and radar, and training. The minister suggested that the money might come from the $1.6 billion then being sought by the U.S. government from Congress for its projected program in Colombia. No doubt the Panama government believed that if the United States could find such a huge sum for its operations in Colombia, a mere $30 million for Panama would hardly be noticed. The government rejected Democratic Revolutionary Party (PRD) accusations that the accord infringed upon national sovereignty. The previous administration had broken off negotiations for a multinational anti-drugs center in Panama.

There is a depressing sameness about U.S. relations with the countries of Latin America. Anti-drugs programs, largely dictated by Washington, are put in place; their observance is usually if not always half-hearted and when they do appear to be achieving results, the drug barons work overtime to corrupt the necessary politicians and officials (if these have not already been corrupted by drug money) to make the programs less effective. Then the government asks for more U.S. aid. Panama remains a major transshipment point for drugs destined for either the United States or Europe, and cocaine from Colombia is stored there before being repackaged for its onward journeys. As the annual U.S. International Narcotics Control Strategy Report for 2000 points out: "Panama's location, largely unpatrolled coastlines, advanced infrastructure, underdeveloped judicial system, and well-developed financial services sector make it a crossroads for transnational crime, such as drug trafficking, money laundering, illicit arms sales and alien smuggling."[2] The report might have added that these lucrative occupations were unlikely to be curtailed easily.

The Caribbean

During the 1990s the drug cartels spread their operations into the islands of the eastern Caribbean (Figure 11.1). In response to tightened security along their established transit routes, the drug traffickers began to exploit the eastern Caribbean's lack of familiarity with drug-smuggling operations and sent increasing amounts of drugs destined for the European market through these islands. Thus, the UNDCP, funded by the European Commission and based in Barbados, found that 180 tonnes (177 tons) of cocaine was smuggled from South America through the eastern Caribbean into Europe, with about 60 percent of it arriving in Europe via Britain during 1996. This amounted to 50 kilograms (110 pounds) a day being carried either on cargo ships or passenger flights, and there was growing evidence that British tourists would act as "mules" or carriers when they returned home. The director of the UN program in Barbados, Dr. Sandro Calvani, said that the trade could only be curtailed if all the islands worked together.[3] Barbados, meanwhile, had become a prime target for traffickers since it was the Caribbean's most easterly outpost with the best air and sea freight facilities in the region and close trade links with Britain. Although Barbados has some of the toughest anti-drug laws and penalties in the Caribbean, statistics for 1995 and 1996 showed that in the former year there were 745 drug cases brought to court, while in 1996, there were 827 cases recorded up to the end of October. The other islands of the Leeward and Windward chain were being dragged into the narcotics trade, and an Internet advertisement promoted money laundering in Antigua with the statement that "We handle cash derived from ANY activity." A European Union report highlighted the vulnerability of these small islands: Weak economies, underpaid and demoralized officials, and low counternarcotics spending laid the eastern Caribbean open to the drug traffickers. The report suggested and pointed out that, "At street value, 1 kilogram of cocaine is often worth more than the average salary of a judge in the Caribbean and a customs officer could house, feed, and educate his family for three years for just not searching one suitcase." Dr. Calvani suggested that the drug barons might also attempt to infiltrate the political arena in the eastern Caribbean; he believed they were becoming eager to achieve political power as well.

By 1999 the British Foreign and Commonwealth Office was threatening to take tough action against its remaining island colonies in the region (13 in all), unless they halted their participation in drug money laundering. The targeting of tiny, vulnerable economies for money-laundering activities emphasized the futility, or perhaps dishonesty, in the way the war on drugs is waged by the United States and Britain. The same governments realize that their chances of preventing either drug taking or money laundering through their own banks and by their own populations are derisory, but it is necessary

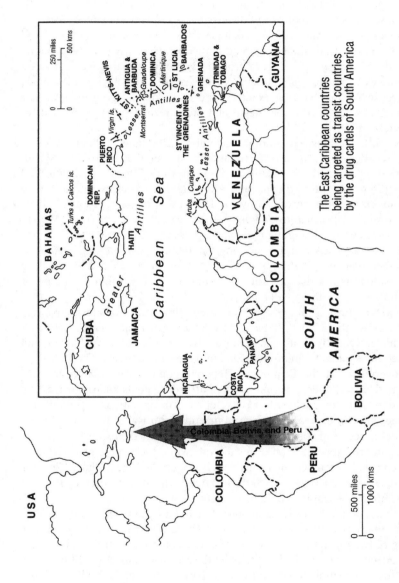

Figure 11.1 The eastern Caribbean. (Cartography by Map Creation, Ltd., Maidenhead, Berkshire, U.K.)

to demonstrate that some action is being taken somewhere. As always, the small and weak are the most vulnerable, the easiest to target, and the most likely to be made scapegoats. It should be recalled that in the 1960s Britain encouraged the small islands of the Caribbean to move into the field of financial services since there was little else they could do anyway. Assisted by financiers from the major money centers such as Amsterdam, New York, and London, these islands did build up offshore operations where taxes could be avoided and money moved from around the world, and this was seen as a laudable way of boosting what otherwise were minuscule economies. Now, however, when this banking expertise is used to launder drug money, their operations are deemed to be illegal and pressure is exerted to make them stop such activities.

The U.S. Caribbean anti-drugs "Operation Libertador," which ended in 2000, resulted in 2,876 arrests (including that of the narco-king Martin Paulino Castro), and the seizure of 20 tonnes (19.7 tons) of cocaine, 29 tonnes (28.5 tons) of marijuana, and 82,000 tablets of ecstasy in the course of a month, and was described by the DEA as "a major takedown" of the drugs business. But a former Jamaican police colonel, Trevor McMillan, who was fired after inaugurating a cleanup of Jamaica's police in 1996, responded to this DEA claim by arguing that the U.S. war on drugs had done little other than assist in the spread of corruption. As he said: "What the drug war has done is to drive the price of drugs up. Until we remove the profit from trafficking, nothing will change."[4]

The Dominican Republic and Haiti are both significant transit countries for drugs to the United States from South America. Drugs reach the Dominican Republic by air and sea or across the land border with Haiti, and are then transported to Puerto Rico and into the United States. Through 1999 the government of the Dominican Republic continued to cooperate fully with the United States government on counterdrug goals and objectives. Its anti-drugs activities included the development of an anticorruption bill for submission to Congress; a ministerial meeting with Haiti that reached what were described as historic border control accords; and the extension of overflight authority for U.S. anti-drugs aircraft while the Dominican navy and army engaged in joint counterdrug exercises with the U.S. military. None of these decisions or actions carried the conviction that drug trafficking through the Dominican Republic would be brought to an end.

A similar appraisal of Haiti suggests much the same scenario. As the U.S. annual report on certification points out: "The U.S.G. cannot certify Haiti as having fully cooperated with the United States on drug control, or as having taken adequate steps on its own, to meet the goals and objectives of the 1988 UN Drug Convention, to which Haiti is a party. However, U.S. vital national interests require that foreign assistance continue to be provided to Haiti." The same arguments applied elsewhere in the Americas are given to explain

Haiti's inadequate performance: It has an underdeveloped judicial system, limited police capabilities, an inexperienced anti-drugs unit, and no ability to intercept drug airdrops. As a result, the seizure of cocaine in 1999 was only one-third that of 1998, while the flow of cocaine was estimated to have increased by one-fourth. The root problem for Haiti is simply poverty and a consequent sense of hopelessness. Why should the poorest territory in the Western hemisphere bother about fighting drug trafficking when its people are so miserably poverty-stricken?

Jamaica

Jamaica, which has become a major transit country for cocaine from South America en route to either the United States or Europe, is also the Caribbean's largest producer and exporter of marijuana. In May 1997 Jamaica entered into a maritime drug-trafficking agreement with the United States that permits U.S. drug enforcement agents, in cooperation with their Jamaican counterparts, to enter the island's airspace and territorial waters in pursuit of suspected drug traffickers. As with most other Latin American countries, Jamaica is prepared to participate in joint U.S.–Jamaican operations against drug traffickers. And, like most other affected countries, Jamaica suffers from serious problems of corruption, and these are exacerbated by the extent of the drug trafficking operations centered upon the island. Jamaica is prepared to extradite drug offenders to the United States; four people accused of drug offenses were sent to the United States in 1999 while another 16 were awaiting the results of extradition requests. Although 6,718 drug offenders were arrested in 1999, no major drug traffickers were among those arrested, and they continued to operate with apparent impunity. Jamaica has a marijuana eradication program, although this does not appear to curtail either the production or the export of the drug.

By the new century the impact of Jamaican drug trafficking was probably considerably greater in Britain than in the United States. In part this reflected the strong ties between the traffickers in Jamaica and the "yardie" gangs in London and other big cities in Britain. In major articles in the London *Evening Standard* of September 2001, the crime correspondent Justin Davenport said: "More people are getting involved in the drugs trade because they can see the profits to be made. More people are becoming desperate for money and more people are trying to find an easy way to survive." In his article Davenport told of the increasing number of British women prepared to act as "mules" and smuggle either cannabis or cocaine from Jamaica to London.[5] At the time of this writing there were more than 110 Britons serving sentences in Jamaican jails, 60 of them women, and almost all of them caught trying to smuggle drugs out of the country. In Britain, at the same time, there were more than 1,000 Jamaicans, including 400 women, in prison for trying to bring drugs into the country. Statistics in relation to this one Caribbean island demonstrate the sheer volume of the trade that is intercepted and raise the obvious question: how much gets through? On one British Airways flight from Montego Bay, eight passengers were caught with cocaine. And on another Britain-bound flight, six "mules" were arrested by customs officials in Jamaica and another five at Gatwick airport in Britain. The "mules," despite the risks they take, only receive about £1,000 for the job. By 2001 there was a huge differential in the profits to be made from cocaine reaching the U.S. market and the British market. A kilogram of cocaine reaching the U.S. market had a value of around £20,000, while a kilogram reaching Britain was worth £125,000. As Deputy Superintendant James Forbes of the Jamaican Constabulary said: "The market in the U.K. is highly lucrative. The amount of profit to be made is awesome compared to the U.S. I think more people are getting involved in the drugs trade because they can see the profits to be made." He continued: "At the same time there has been a significant increase in the flow of drugs into Jamaica from countries such as Colombia and Venezuela." High-powered speedboats, known as "go-fasts," can make the journey from Colombia to Jamaica in four hours, and the Jamaican police do not possess the means to catch them. Alternately, cocaine is smuggled by air: The planes either land at remote strips or drop their consignments into the sea with a timing device attached so that they can be traced and picked up by fishermen. As far as the couriers are concerned, the driving motivation is poverty.

Drug smuggling makes good newspaper copy, and the British press through 2001 had a range of articles on the subject. One article in *The Observer* in September described how a British naval vessel, HMS *Coventry*, and its Lynx helicopter were involved in a sea chase in the Caribbean. HMS *Coventry* was part of the Royal Navy's Atlantic Patrol Task (north), and for 10 years this or other naval vessels have been used to intercept and seize drugs as they cross the Caribbean on their way to Europe or America. The helicopter chased a go-fast speedboat capable of up to 240 kilometers (150 miles) an hour and was in contact with three speedboats full of Belizean soldiers closing in on the smugglers. In this particular case the smugglers headed into an inlet on the coast of Belize where they abandoned their boat and fled into the jungle. The boat contained a tonne of cocaine with a street value of £60 million. It made a good newspaper story but as the author, Jason Burke, said, the seizure would make little difference to the traffickers—even though similar hauls are made every few months—because the cocaine trade is worth billions a year and the big Colombian gangs, who produce up to 800 tonnes (787 tons) of cocaine a year, can easily stand the loss. As Brigadier General Alan Usher of the Belize Ministry of National Security said: "They [the traffickers] have the advantage because of the sheer volume they are moving. If they need to get one shipment through they can send 10. Just one that is successful will make them a huge amount of money."[6]

Mexico

Mexico, which shares a 3,326-kilometer (2,070-mile) border with its northern neighbor, is the obvious first route for drugs entering the United States, but as the United States has discovered in another connection—illegal immigrants seeking work—the border is exceptionally porous and difficult to police. Moreover, there is a massive two-way movement of legitimate trade and tourists that has grown substantially since 1993 when Mexico and Canada entered into the North American Free Trade Agreement (NAFTA) with the United States. This has produced a conflict of interest: on the one hand, the United States may wish to exert greater pressure on Mexico over its handling of drug trafficking; on the other hand, it does not wish to upset its neighbor whose adherence to NAFTA may be seen as a "vital American interest." In any case, with its size, resources, large population (estimated at 100 million in mid-2000), and its rapid if uneven economic development that offers major opportunities for U.S. investment and trade, Mexico represents a very different proposition to most other drug-trafficking countries in the region, with the result that Washington is more wary in its dealings with Mexico than with other Latin American countries.

These considerations aside, Mexico is now a major source of drugs as well as a conduit for them passing northward into the United States. An examination of developments since the mid-1990s shows much the same pattern as elsewhere in Latin America. Two arrests in 1995 tell the story. In June Héctor Luis Palma Salazar, one of the country's most powerful drug barons, was arrested. And in November the Swiss authorities arrested Paulina Castañon, the sister-in-law of former President Carlos Salinas de Gortari (1988–1994), as part of a drug-trafficking investigation. She had attempted to withdraw $84 million from a Swiss bank account, using false documents that belonged to her husband, Raúl Salinas de Gortari, who had been in prison since the previous February. He had amassed the money while holding government office from 1982, and on November 26, 1995, he was charged with forgery and illicit enrichment. On January 14, 1996, Juan García Abrego, the leader of the Gulf cartel and one of the world's most wanted drug traffickers at the time, was arrested in Monterey and subsequently deported to the United States to stand trial. He was thought to have strong links with Colombian drug cartels and to control one-third of cocaine shipments into the United States. The arrest was hailed as a triumph for Mexico's Attorney General Antonio Lozano (the only opposition member in the cabinet), who had earned widespread respect for tackling drug-related corruption in the police and the anti-drugs forces. In October 1996 Abrego was convicted in a U.S. court of shipping cocaine into the United States and laundering $10.5 million of drug profits.[7]

There were many developments in the anti-drugs war during 1997, though few showed Mexico in a good light. In February, General Jesús Gutiérrez Rebollo, the head of the national drug agency, was arrested on charges of being in the pay of Amado Carrillo Fuentes, the country's most powerful drug baron, and for aiding and abetting the trafficking of cocaine. In the aftermath of his arrest, the Mexican media suggested that the influence of the drug cartels was far greater than had been realized and that this influence permeated the government, judiciary, military, and police. The Rebollo case seriously affected U.S.–Mexican anti-drugs operations since he was the highest ranking military officer ever linked to the drugs trade and had had access to top information. He knew, for example, about DEA plans to eradicate drug trafficking along the U.S.–Mexican border. On February 25, the Attorney General Jorge Madrazo Cuellar announced a major reform of his office to address the crisis in the government's handling of the anti-drugs war. Leaked U.S. prosecution evidence linked the family of former President Carlos Salinas de Gortari with the drugs trade, while other evidence uncovered by the *New York Times* accused the governors of Sonora and Morales states of links with the drug cartels. However, what was seen as a breakthrough came with the arrest on February 26 of Oscar Malherbe de Leon, the operational head of the Gulf cartel, which had links to the Colombian Cali cartel. In March a U.S. civil court confiscated all but $1.1 million of $9 million that had been deposited by a Mexican official in a Texas bank over the period 1993–1994 on behalf of the former Mexican Deputy Attorney General Mario Ruíz Massieu. He had received the money as bribes from members of the drug cartels. Also that month a new head of the National Institute for Drug Combat (INCD), Mariano Herran Salvatti, replaced General Gutierrez, who had been arrested in February on drugs charges. Another army general was arrested on March 17 on suspicion of offering $1 million a month to a general to act as a cocaine courier to the United States.

The Mexican government introduced new banking regulations to come into effect in 1998. These laid down that banks, brokerage houses, and large foreign exchange houses must report all cash transactions above $10,000 and inform the bank regulators of suspicious transactions. The banks would be made criminally liable for aiding and abetting money launderers. Relations with the United States plummeted during March despite President Clinton "certifying" Mexico as an ally in good standing in the international fight against drugs. The U.S. State Department, on the other hand, had reported "endemic corruption" in Mexico, making it a prime international haven for the laundering of drug-related funds. And the U.S. House of

Representatives voted to set a 90-day deadline for Mexico to demonstrate that it merited its status as a full ally of the United States in the fight against drugs. A new anti-drugs force was announced at the end of April to replace the discredited INCD. The new force was to be headed by Attorney General Jorge Madrazo Cuellar. It was the first of a series of reforms ordered by President Ernesto Zedillo Ponce de Léon to restore confidence in the criminal justice system. New agents would undergo special training and be subject to stringent checks, including lie detector tests; they would also be better paid. The Swiss prosecutors investigating the frozen funds of Raúl Salinas de Gortari, brother of former President Carlos Salinas de Gortari, linked him to the smuggling of between 46 and 50 tons of cocaine to the United States. He was accused of receiving large sums of money from the Gulf drugs cartel. In September the entire staff of the air interdiction branch of the attorney general's anti-drugs office were arrested on charges of using one of the department's own aircraft to smuggle 60 kilograms (132 pounds) of cocaine from Guatemala to an airport in Mexico City.

On May 18, 1998, the United States announced the indictment by a U.S. district court in Los Angeles of three Mexican banks and the arrest of more than 160 people including 26 banking officials from 12 of Mexico's largest financial institutions. Two Spanish banks operating in Mexico were also included in the indictment and charged with laundering the profits from cocaine cartels. Five Venezuelan bankers were arrested; $35 million was seized as well as two tons of cocaine. It was expected that $122 million would be recovered from 100 bank accounts that had been frozen in the United States and Europe. These arrests and seizures were the result of a three-year undercover operation. The investigation revealed links between banks and drug-smuggling cartels in Colombia and Mexico. It was trumpeted as the "largest, most comprehensive drug money laundering case in the history of U.S. law enforcement." At the time it was estimated that $8 billion a year was laundered through the Mexican financial system. The Mexican banks involved—Bancomer, Serfin, and Confin—agreed to cooperate with the investigations. The U.S. Federal Reserve Board issued temporary "cease and desist" orders suspending the American operations of two of the three banks. However, Mexico protested to the U.S. government for activities carried out on Mexican soil under the U.S. "Operation Casablanca" and because of U.S. lack of compliance with bilateral agreements on drug-trafficking cooperation. The Mexican government said it would prosecute U.S. agents who had violated its national sovereignty. Members of the opposition in the Mexican Congress expressed their outrage and humiliation at the U.S. operation and demanded the resignation of Guillermo Ortíz, the central bank governor, and other bank regulators for negligence. The operation also had the effect of reducing confidence in Mexican banks, whose shares collectively fell in value by 4 percent. The *Wall Street Journal* and the

Miami Herald questioned the operation on the grounds that it had not also investigated U.S. institutions.

In February 1999 the U.S. government recommended to Congress that it should again certify Mexico for its anti-drugs program. And this was done at the end of the month. On February 27 the police chief of the northern town of Tijuana, Alfredo de la Torre Marquez, was murdered by unidentified gunmen; the murder came two days after President Zedillo, on a visit to a nearby town, had announced a crack-down on organized crime and drug trafficking in the region, which borders the United States. During a major narcotics case in April the attorney general's office ordered the arrest of the former state governor of Quintana Roo, Mario Villanueva Madrid, and 100 other people on charges of organized crime. Villanueva was accused of drug trafficking and involvement in the Juárez drug cartel. He was arrested just 24 hours after his term as governor ended. Meanwhile, two of the banks accused of malpractices as a result of "Operation Casablanca," Bancomer and Serfin, pleaded guilty to charges of money laundering at a Los Angeles court on March 29. They had been indicted in May 1998 following a "sting" operation. In September Mario Ruíz Massieu, the former deputy attorney general in charge of anti-drug law enforcement, who had been arrested in 1995 in the United States and was awaiting trial on drug money-laundering charges, committed suicide. On November 10 the governments of the United States and Mexico ended all military cooperation in fighting drug trafficking following sharp differences between officials of the two countries about how the war on drugs should be waged. Mexico also refused to take part in joint naval exercises to detect, pursue, and stop vessels carrying narcotics.

The Juárez cartel suffered a major setback when Juan José Quintero Payán was arrested on November 29; he was the number two in the cartel structure of which he was a founding member. Also at the end of November a mass grave was uncovered near Ciudad Juárez close to the U.S. border. A large number of police and troops as well as U.S. FBI agents had taken part in the search that revealed the grave. Two of the bodies were those of FBI agents and all of them were thought to be the victims of the Juárez cartel, which used Ciudad Juárez as a base from which to move cocaine across the border into the United States. The investigators expected to find up to 100 bodies. Human rights groups believed that some of the killings might have been carried out with the acquiescence of Mexican security forces in the pay of the drug cartels.

Mexican efforts to eliminate, or at any rate reduce, drug trafficking were constantly thwarted by corruption and judicial obstacles to the extradition of fugitives to the United States, although there was no obvious reason why those accused of drug trafficking should not be tried and dealt with inside Mexico. Various steps were taken by Mexico during 1999 to upgrade the efficiency of its law enforcement agencies. These included acquiring new technology such as aerial radar platforms; improving telecommunications; and redistributing land, air, and maritime assets to increase coverage of priority areas. The eradication program made substantial progress during 1999, with marijuana eradication up 39 percent over 1998 so that net production was down 19 percent; opium poppy eradication was down 10 percent from the 1998 figure, although there was a 25 percent drop in net opium gum production. Whether this rate of reduction was permanent remained to be seen. A new law was passed to codify the use of seized or forfeited assets. The major bar to greater success for Mexico's anti-drugs war was the high level of drug-related corruption, and though President Zedillo made combating corruption a national priority, he acknowledged that success in this field would take time.

In May 2000 the head of INCD, Mariano Herran Salvatti, announced the capture of Ismael "El Mayel" Higuera Guerrero, a high-ranking operator of the Arellano Félix cocaine cartel who was taken after a gun battle. This was seen as a major victory against one of the country's most powerful drug gangs. Higuera was wanted for the murder in 1993 of the head of the attorney general's office and was the head of the Arellano Félix brothers' drug-smuggling, execution, kidnapping, and bribery operations. The DEA described this arrest as "a major victory for both Mexican and U.S. law enforcement." The previous month the Mexican authorities had arrested the cartel's alleged financial controller, Jesús "El Chuy" Labra. These two arrests were followed by retaliatory murders, and the cartel was suspected of being behind the murder in May of three anti-drugs agents near Tijuana as well as being responsible for the assassination of the city's police chief.

Controversy is bound to surround the U.S. anti-drugs war if only because of the selective way the DEA and the U.S. government deal with individual countries. In the case of Mexico, the most strategically important of all Latin American countries to the United States—with its long joint border and its membership in NAFTA—this has led the U.S. government to tread lightly in its dealings despite the fact that in April 2000 U.S. officials described Mexico as a "narco-state" in which five major drug cartels operate and have penetrated the highest levels of army and police ranks. The arrest of General Rebollo in 1997 after he had just been appointed anti-drugs czar (to high praise from President Clinton) and his subsequent conviction for working with a leading drug trafficker illustrated the extent to which the military has become corrupt. Critics of U.S. aid for the anti-drugs war suggest that a more likely U.S. motive is to create secure, stable regimes that would approve trade accords favorable to U.S. interests.

The anti-drugs war has a recurring pattern: the arrest of a major drug trafficker, the seizure of a large consignment, the breakup of a cartel, and the announcement by the Mexican or U.S. government or both together of a

significant victory. Yet the flow of drugs continues, new instances of corruption in high places are unveiled, and nothing really changes. The capture
in May 2001 of Mario Villanueva Madrid, a former governor of Quintana
Roo state who had been on the run for two years, illustrates the sameness of
this ongoing drama. Villanueva, suspected of involvement on behalf of the
Juárez drug cartel in the Yucatán, was the highest-ranking Mexican to face a
drugs investigation while still in office. Imprisoned in a maximum-security
jail outside Mexico City, he was due to stand trial first in Mexico and then
to face extradition to the United States. A New York indictment accused
him of conspiracy to smuggle over 200 tonnes (196.84 tons) of cocaine
across the border. Officials were alleged to have received bribes of
$500,000 for each consignment that went through. Mexican charges against
Villanueva included 28 counts of drug trafficking, money laundering, and
protecting organized crime. Better relations between the United States and
Mexico appeared to follow the December 2000 election of President
Vicente Fox Quesada who had vowed to root out corruption. An agreement
between the two countries permits the temporary extradition of criminals
both ways for trial so that an investigation does not grow cold. As President
Fox said: "What we are going to achieve is justice, and what we are going
to end is impunity." Referring to Villanueva, the president said: "If he is ex-
traditable, then he will be extradited."[8]

12
The Golden Triangle

Myanmar (Burma), Laos, and Thailand (Figure 12.1) are collectively one of the world's two traditional sources of opium. Most of Myanmar's opium-producing region has for decades been plagued by warfare between government forces and various ethnic groups and rival drug warlords. The Rangoon government has permitted the drugs trade to continue provided it takes a substantial cut of the profits. Myanmar is the most important of the three Golden Triangle countries. In 1996 Myanmar's opium harvest from 163,100 hectares (403,040 acres) gave a yield of 2,560 tonnes (2,520 tons), and represented a 9 percent increase over the crop for 1995. Through the 1990s Thailand developed one of the most successful crop eradication programs, inspired and largely financed by the United States, although Bangkok is both a drug-transit and leading money-laundering center. Thus, in 1996 it had 2,170 hectares (5,360 acres) producing opium to give a potential yield of 30 tonnes (29.5 tons), while by 1999 only 835 hectares (2,060 acres) produced opium to give a potential yield of six tonnes (5.9 tons). Laos is the world's third-largest producer of heroin after Afghanistan and Myanmar.

According to U.S. government estimates, the potential opium cultivation and production in the countries of the Golden Triangle fell in 1999 for the third year in a row: total opium cultivation fell by 29 percent while yield fell by 35 percent. Altogether, growers in Myanmar, Laos, and Thailand cultivated an estimated 112,135 hectares (277,100 acres) of opium poppy, equivalent to a possible output of 1,236 tonnes (1,220 tons) of opium, with Myanmar accounting for 80 percent of the whole. Even so, Myanmar's production fell sharply from 130,300 hectares (321,980 acres) in 1998 to 89,500 hectares (221,160 acres) for 1999, equivalent to 1,090 tonnes (1,070 tons) of opium gum. Weather conditions were largely responsible for the decreased harvest. The Laos areas cultivated fell from 26,100 hectares (64,500 acres) for 1998 to 21,800 hectares (53,870 acres) for 1999, although production remained the same at 140 tonnes (138 tons). Thailand again reduced the hectares under production dramatically. In the case of Vietnam (not strictly regarded as a member of the Golden Triangle, but discussed later in this chapter), the crop had fallen by 30 percent in 1999 from 3,000 hectares (7,410 acres) of opium poppy cultivation in 1998 to 2,100 hectares (5,190 acres). These reductions of opium harvests in the countries of the Golden

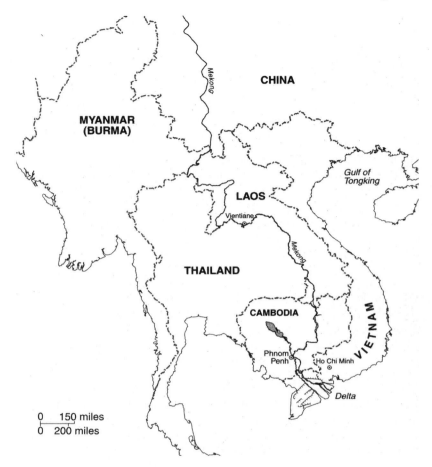

Figure 12.1   The Golden Triangle. (Cartography by Map Creation, Ltd., Maidenhead, Berkshire, U.K.)

Triangle must be offset against new producers, such as Mexico, or the greatly increased output of Afghanistan.

Myanmar (Burma)

At the end of the 1990s the government of Myanmar, the State Law and Order Restoration Council (SLORC), made a deal with the leading drug warlord Khun Sa who retired, while the military wing of SLORC, Tatmadaw, took over his empire so that the government directly controlled

the taxation of heroin production. At the same time, Tatmadaw established
heroin farms manned by forced labor. As a result, SLORC more or less legitimized the drugs trade during the period 1995–1997, while four ethnic
groups involved in heroin production each opened offices and private banks
in Rangoon. By the end of the century the Myanmar economy was under-
pinned by profits from the drugs trade. Since in world terms the country has
largely isolated itself politically, it cannot easily be pressured into a change
of policy over drugs.

The CIA annual, *The World Factbook,*[1] gives a final section for each
country headed "Transnational Issues," and in the case of Myanmar this section includes the following:

> Illicit drugs: world's second largest producer of illicit opium, after
> Afghanistan (potential production in 1999—1,090 metric tons, down 38
> percent due to drought; cultivation in 1999—89,500 hectares, a 31 percent
> decline from 1998); surrender of drug warlord Khun Sa's Mong Tai Army
> in January 1996 was hailed by Rangoon as a major counter-narcotics suc-
> cess, but lack of government will and ability to take on major narco-
> trafficking groups and lack of serious commitment against money
> laundering continues to hinder the overall anti-drug effort; becoming a
> major source of methamphetamines for regional consumption.

This survey sounds all too familiar: scope of drugs business, reduction in
production and reasons for it, surrender of warlord hailed as a major success
but lack of government will to tackle problem seriously, and new drugs
being produced. It could be applied to almost any of the countries of Latin
America or elsewhere for, except in the details, the pattern does not change.

When the SLORC forces captured the last stronghold of the Karen
National Union (KNU) in February 1995, this meant that the Myanmar government could concentrate its full attention and military forces on the only
remaining ethnic militia of any importance, the Mong Tai Army (MTA),
which was controlled by the Shan drug warlord Khun Sa. Early that February, government troops began to probe the MTA's defense perimeter in the
Shan state south of Ho Mong, and on March 14 the Myanmar army launched
an offensive against the MTA. Fighting was concentrated around the border
town of Tachilele, forcing 3,000 civilians to cross the border into Thailand.
The Myanmar army continued its offensive through April, using thousands
of troops in waves of attacks. In May the army drove Khun Sa's forces out of
the western part of his stronghold of Tachilele and also from the Mong Kyut
area. The army claimed that between March 11 and May 4 a total of 65
clashes with the MTA had resulted in the death of 237 members of the MTA
and the capture of 45 MTA camps, in three of which there were heroin-
refining facilities. In the course of these engagements 76 army personnel

were killed and 178 wounded. Then, on November 22, Khun Sa, the drug warlord, announced that he had relinquished command of the MTA (which was ostensibly a Shan nationalist group) and wanted to retire to Thailand, although a split in the MTA, rumored at the time, may have had something to do with his decision. On January 2, 1996, the Myanmar army took control of Ho Mong, the headquarters of Khun Sa and the MTA. The entrance of government troops into Ho Mong was peaceful, giving the impression that a deal had been negotiated, especially as on January 5 a peace agreement was signed between the government and the MTA. On January 28 Myanmar radio claimed that 11,739 MTA had surrendered. Khun Sa was given amnesty and a guarantee against extradition (the U.S. government had offered a reward of $2 million for his capture). On February 9 Myanmar's foreign minister, U Ohn Gyaw, announced that Myanmar would not extradite Khun Sa to the United States where he was wanted on drug-trafficking charges. These events might have signaled a real war on drugs in Myanmar; in retrospect, however, the breaking of Khun Sa and the MTA was rather a question of consolidating SLORC's control over the country.

Nonetheless, in October 1997 when Fidel Ramos, the president of the Philippines, visited Myanmar to meet the chairman of SLORC, General Than Shwe, they signed a number of agreements including one on combating illicit drug trafficking. Over March 31–April 1, 1998, a seminar organized by the UNDCP and the Myanmar and Japanese governments was held in Rangoon to examine strategies for the eradication of opium poppy cultivation. Representatives from 21 countries that included Bangladesh, Cambodia, China, India, Laos, Thailand, and Vietnam participated. Following the seminar the United States and Japan pledged grants worth $3.8 million to help Myanmar eradicate opium poppy cultivation in its border areas. This was the first U.S. grant to Myanmar since the military takeover of 1988. In February 1999 another conference, this time organized by Interpol, was held in Rangoon and attended by 28 countries, but boycotted by Britain, the United States, Belgium, Denmark, France, Italy, the Netherlands, and Norway on the grounds that Myanmar had failed to curb drug production and trafficking and also in protest of its poor human rights record. Richard Dickens, the head of UNDCP in Rangoon, said that recent U.S. government estimates of Myanmar's opium production were exaggerated. An exiled Myanmar opposition radio station, for example, claimed that the figures given by the government of the illicit poppy fields that had been destroyed since the previous November were spurious since, in many cases, the poppies had already been tapped for opium prior to their destruction. On January 16, 2000, the State Peace and Development Council (SPDC, formerly SLORC, until November 1997) announced a plan to combat the production of opium in Myanmar by relocating up to 50,000 people from the opium-producing regions to new agricultural areas. This plan was presented to foreign journalists by Colonel Kyaw Thein, a senior member of the SPDC's committee for drug abuse control. The program aimed to bring an end to opium production in Myanmar by 2005.

U.S. estimates at the end of the century rated Myanmar as the world's second-largest source of illicit opium (after Afghanistan) and the source of 80 percent of all Southeast Asian opium. Although poppy production in 1999 declined for the third year in a row, this was due to severe drought conditions in the poppy-growing areas rather than a sustained government attack on cultivation. Seizures of drugs in 1999 included an increase for methamphetamines but a reduction in the seizure of opium and heroin to well below the 1998 figures. Although a number of arrests of drug traffickers were made during the year, the government was clearly unwilling to take on the most powerful groups. As a U.S. report suggested: "Ceasefire agreements with insurgent ethnic groups dependent on the drug trade implicitly tolerate continued involvement in drug trafficking for varying periods of time." Furthermore, two ethnic armies—the United Wa State Army and the Myanmar National Democratic Alliance Army—remained armed and heavily involved in the heroin trade. Although the government of Myanmar claimed that it favored a program of crop eradication, it allocated only limited resources to the program. Instead, it expected the leaders of the different ethnic groups to find the revenues to spend on social and physical infrastructure. Such an approach seems unlikely to succeed. Despite having the necessary laws in place, the government demonstrated little inclination to deal with either serious money laundering or to seize drug-related assets. Moreover, it appeared likely that the economy of Myanmar derived a considerable boost from drug money that was laundered into legitimate enterprises. Large-scale poppy cultivation continues in Myanmar while the government tolerates money laundering and is unwilling to implement any effective anti-drugs measures.

During 2001 the production of opium and heroin declined for the fifth year in succession, but the production of amphetamines increased dramatically. By 2002 Myanmar had reduced its production of the opium poppy by more than half over the preceding five years and was pledged to end the production of drugs by 2005. Both Japan and Thailand provided assistance for Myanmar's anti-drugs campaign.

Laos

According to the CIA's *The World Factbook 2000*, Laos, one of the three states composing the Golden Triangle, is the world's third-largest illicit opium producer, a potential heroin producer, a transshipment point for heroin and methamphetamines from Myanmar, and a producer of cannabis.

Production of opium in 1999 came to 140 tonnes (138 tons). U.S.-funded crop substitution areas did not show any commercial opium production, though there was some low-level production for local addict consumption. Laos cooperates with both the U.S. government and the UNDCP on crop control and substitution measures, and in May 1999 the government agreed with the UNDCP to aim at eliminating opium cultivation over a period of six years. However, if opium cultivation is to be eliminated, an alternative to opium has to be found and the implementation of such a plan will require different development activities, proper law enforcement, and a reduction in demand. As of 1999 the highland farmers who grow opium have no viable option. At least this UNDCP plan includes the vital requirement that there should be a reduction in demand, though how this is to be brought about is another question altogether. Drug seizures for 1999 fell significantly (compared with 1998), although there was a slight rise in seizures of methamphetamines. The traffickers appeared to have changed both the routes and the methods they employed to meet the U.S. market demands. These changes included, for example, sending many more opium-filled parcels to the United States.

During September 2000 Laos and Thailand were in dispute after Laotian troops occupied two islets in the Mekong and expelled 48 Thai farming families to the Thai riverbank. Laos claimed sovereignty over all islands in the Mekong (dating from a treaty of 1926). In this case the Laotian government alleged that the islands had been used for drug trafficking and as refuges for antigovernment rebels. In April 2001 the Lao National Assembly approved an amendment to the criminal law and introduced the death penalty for heroin traffickers found in possession of more than 300 grams (10.6 ounces) of the drug. Those carrying between 100 and 300 grams (3.5 to 10.6 ounces) would be subject to life imprisonment. At the same time, the U.S. government suggested that Laotian opium output for 2000 had been 210 tonnes (207 tons).

Thailand

In 2000 the CIA ranked Thailand as a minor producer of opium, heroin, and marijuana, but as a major transit country for heroin from Myanmar and Laos en route to the international drug markets. One result of eradication programs was to shift the cultivation and production of cannabis to neighboring countries. Thailand has had considerable success in reducing opium poppy cultivation. However, it is a drug money-laundering center. Ironically, too, as it succeeds in reducing drug cultivation, Thailand is witnessing an increase in indigenous abuse of both methamphetamines and heroin.

In 1999 Thailand was estimated to be cultivating about 1,000 tonnes (9,480 tons) of opium, although crop eradication programs substantially reduced cultivation below this figure in 2000. In March a joint crackdown on drug production was agreed to with Myanmar when Thai Prime Minister Chuan Leekpai met General Than Shwe, the Chairman of SPDC, in northern Thailand. This was followed in June 2001 by Thailand and Myanmar concluding an agreement to cooperate in fighting drug production and smuggling and to resolve their border differences. In November 1999 three people were executed by firing squad in a Bangkok prison for drug-trafficking offenses. One of them, Samai Pan-intara, was the first woman to be executed in the country in 16 years; she had been convicted of trafficking four kilograms (8.8 pounds) of heroin six years earlier.

A significant amount of heroin destined for the U.S. market transits through Thailand. The United States regards Thailand as one of the top three countries in the world in cooperating with Washington on extradition requests. Thailand's success in crop substitution programs and opium eradication operations meant that for 1999 poppy cultivation was down 38 percent from 1998 and opium production was down 62 percent. Altogether, cultivated acreage has been slashed by 91 percent since the eradication program was started in 1984. The Royal Thai Police increased the number of their drug law enforcement units during the year and targeted organizations believed to be involved in drug trafficking. Official corruption remains a major problem, but arrests for corruption appear to be focused on lower-ranking officers and officials. The U.S. DEA regards its cooperation with Thailand as one of its most successful overseas partnerships anywhere in the world.

Cambodia and Vietnam

Two other countries of this region, Cambodia and Vietnam, should also be considered together with Myanmar, Laos, and Thailand; although they are not regarded as members of the Golden Triangle, they are peripheral to it and inevitably affected by the triangle's drug-trafficking activities. In October 1995 the Cambodian government dismissed 85 percent of its higher-ranking police officers in a restructuring exercise of the police force in order to step up its campaign against the consumption of and trafficking in drugs (as well as against illegal immigration). The move was welcomed by the United States. An article in the *Far Eastern Economic Review* of November 23, 1995, alleged that the U.S. ambassador to Cambodia, Charles Twining, had warned Sam Rangsi, the leader of the newly launched Khmer Nation Party, early in 1994 that Theng Bunma, the country's wealthiest businessman, was a major international drug trafficker. The article also claimed that close links existed between Theng Bunma and high-ranking Cambodian politicians and military personnel. The report suggested that Theng Bunma was a "benefactor" of Hun Sen, second prime minister and vice-chair of the Cambodian People's Party, and of First Prime Minister Norodom Ranariddh, as well as a "special adviser" to Chea Sim, the National Assembly president. Such accusations, if true, suggested that drug-related corruption operated at the highest political levels in the land. In March 1996 the United States placed Cambodia on a list of 31 major drug-producing and -trafficking countries. The United States threatened to cut aid to Cambodia unless the government curbed the trafficking activities. However, it was clear by the end of the century that Cambodia had made little progress in this direction. As the CIA's *The World Factbook 2000* recorded: Cambodia was a transshipment country for heroin from the Golden Triangle; was possibly engaged in money laundering; narcotics-related corruption involved members of the government, military, and police; there was small-scale opium, heroin, and amphetamine production; and the country was a large producer of cannabis for the international market.

None of this was surprising given the general state of lawlessness in Cambodia and the country's proximity to the Golden Triangle; as a result the United States designated Cambodia as a major drug-transit country in 1999. Political turmoil has prevented any effective anti-drugs program from being put in place, although the government did take some positive anti-drugs measures in 1999. Thus, the prime minister, Hun Sen, publicly threatened to dismiss provincial governors if they allowed marijuana cultivation to take place in their provinces. There were also several drug seizures (for the first time) at Phnom Penh international airport. At the same time both the president and the chief prosecutor of the Phnom Penh municipal court were removed from their posts for corruption and some judges were investigated. Various government officials emphasized their opposition to synthetic-drug production in Cambodia. The DEA claimed that Cambodian cooperation with the United States was excellent. Corruption in Cambodia appears to be endemic and drug money ensures that such corruption persists. Corrupt officials and police allow drug traffickers and other criminals to slip through the legal net, and as long as such corruption continues there is little chance of mounting an effective anti-drugs war. Despite these considerations, the United States decided in 1999 to certify Cambodia as doing its best to fight the anti-drugs war since it was a vital U.S. national interest to promote democracy in Cambodia and stability in the region. There seemed little prospect at the beginning of the new century that the Cambodian government would become any more effective in combating drug trafficking.

The other country on the periphery of the Golden Triangle is Vietnam. It is a minor producer of the opium poppy and had 2,100 hectares (5,190 acres) under cultivation in 1999 with a potential to produce 11 tonnes (10.8 tons) of opium. It is also a transit country for heroin destined for Europe and the United States. Addiction to opium/heroin appears to be growing in Vietnam, which has probably become a small-scale heroin producer. On the other hand, the government of Vietnam has clearly determined to fight drug trafficking because of the threats it poses to its own people. In May 1997 a high-profile trial for drug trafficking led to eight of the accused being sentenced to death, eight being given life imprisonment, and six receiving prison sentences ranging from 1 to 20 years. Those sentenced included six law enforcement officers who had smuggled 300 kilograms (661 pounds) of heroin into the country. These harsh sentences gave a clear signal that the government was determined to stem the drugs trade and its accompanying corruption. Three years later, in May 2000, a row erupted between Canada and Vietnam because of the execution of a Canadian citizen for drug smuggling. Nguyen Thi Hiep, although born in Vietnam, had become a Canadian citizen in 1982; she had returned to Vietnam on a visit in 1996. Drugs had been found in her luggage. Both the Canadian and Vietnamese police were investigating claims that she had been tricked into smuggling them. Her mother, who had accompanied her, was sentenced to life imprisonment.

The government has given high priority to the fight against drugs and in 1999 implemented a high-profile anticorruption campaign that led to public trials of government and party officials involved in illicit drug smuggling. Law enforcement campaigns against drug traffickers were stiffened and a record number of arrests and convictions were recorded. Vietnam, however, remains a major transit country for opium and heroin from the Golden Triangle, and so the government created a special task force to operate along its borders. In the course of a year the border forces and customs officials arrested 19,010 drug criminals, while drug seizures also increased. Other measures included the creation of a marine police force and greater efforts to control the production of precursor chemicals. Finally, the national assembly approved revisions to the penal code that criminalized money laundering.

13
The Golden Crescent

The second traditional region for the production of the opium poppy for heroin is the Golden Crescent comprising Pakistan, Afghanistan, Iran, and Turkey—countries that extend along the south and southwestern rim of the Asian landmass. The roles of these four countries constantly change: For example, Iran currently is not producing heroin on any scale, while Turkey produces heroin legally for the pharmaceutical trade.

Afghanistan

As *The World Factbook 2000*[1] of the CIA reported of Afghanistan, it had become the world's largest illicit opium producer, surpassing Myanmar (Burma), with a potential production in 1999 of 1,670 tonnes (1,640 tons), while its cultivation of the opium poppy in an estimated 51,500 hectares (127,360 acres) represented a 23 percent increase over 1998 (see Figure 13.1). Afghanistan is also a major source of hashish. The UNDCP suggested a more dramatic increase of opium at 70 percent over 1998. The Taliban controlled reportedly 97 percent of the area that produces opium. The Taliban taxed the opium crop at a rate of 10 percent and allowed it to be sold in the bazaars. Crop taxation confers legitimacy on the cultivation of the opium crop. The Taliban also obtained direct payments from the traffickers.

Over the years 1995–2000 the Taliban on more than one occasion announced that it intended to suppress the opium/heroin trade, though whether these announcements arose out of an ideological conviction that the trade went counter to its strict religious beliefs or were made as a response to Western and UN pressures without any intention of fulfillment was difficult to ascertain. On November 24, 1997, for example, the director of the UNDCP, Pino Arlacchi, announced that an agreement had been reached between the United Nations and the Taliban government to end opium production in Afghanistan; no new land would be placed under poppy cultivation and UN monitors would be allowed free access to those areas where the opium-producing plants were cultivated.[2] Two years later, however, in September 1999 the UNDCP reported that the production of opium in Afghanistan had more than doubled and that farmers had produced 4,600

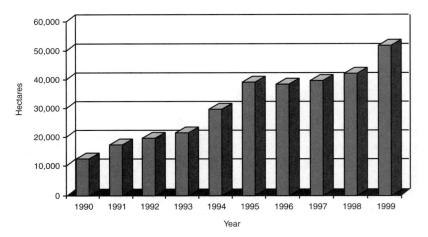

Figure 13.1 Afghanistan opium cultivation, 1990–1999. (U.S. DEA, 2000, UNDCP estimates.)

tonnes (4,530 tons) of opium, three-quarters of the global output, following a period of high prices for the drug. These figures placed Afghanistan way ahead of Myanmar as the world's largest producer of opium and heroin. At this time the Taliban claimed that there was no problem with the drug in Afghanistan and called on the international community to protect itself by providing assistance to Afghanistan in order to prevent the export of opium.

The export of heroin from Afghanistan led to a form of border war with neighboring Iran whose Law Enforcement Force (LEF) tries to curtail the flood of drugs across its borders from Afghanistan and Pakistan on the way to the Western markets. Estimates suggest that in the 13 years to 2000, as many as 2,600 members of the LEF had been killed in clashes with the highly armed traffickers from Afghanistan and Pakistan whose armaments include night-vision equipment, heavy machine guns, and stinger-type missiles. Chuttu in southern Afghanistan has become the largest source of the heroin that reaches the cities of London, Liverpool, and Glasgow in Britain and elsewhere throughout the world. According to a Western drug enforcement officer, Chuttu "is a one-stop shop for heroin traffickers. It has everything they need. In a single day they can buy the opium, arrange for its refinement into heroin, and set up a 10,000-kilogram convoy to the West. And it will almost certainly get there. Chuttu is the smack smugglers' superstore."[3] Drug enforcement officers in Pakistan believe that two-thirds of the heroin sold in Britain passes through the village of Chuttu, that 95 percent of the heroin reaching British streets comes from Afghanistan's opium, and 70 percent of that comes from the south and west of the country and passes through Chuttu. The village is protected by its geographic position in deep hill valleys and is easily defensible. It has adequate water, which is essential for its 20 heroin-processing laboratories. The local tribesmen provide the labor. There were large orders for heroin in the latter months of 2000. The opium that feeds the laboratories in Chuttu and elsewhere in Afghanistan is grown by poor farmers and sold to dealers for about £30 a kilogram and is by far the most lucrative crop grown in Afghanistan. The Taliban taxed the crop but otherwise left the farmers alone. Opium can be stored and then released into the market when prices are high. Late in 2000 the Taliban leader, Mullah Mohammed Omar, decreed that farmers should turn one-third of their fields over to other crops but said that to ask them to do more would undercut support for the regime since a high proportion of its revenues were derived from the drugs trade from which it made huge profits.

Accounts out of Afghanistan tend to be provocatively contradictory. In September 2000, for example, the UNDCP decided to end projects that encouraged Afghan farmers to cultivate alternative crops to opium. The projects had been reported as achieving a 50 percent success rate in reductions of opium production in some provinces. The decision to end them was apparently a response to funding cuts from European countries and the United States. The Taliban government expressed surprise and criticized the move, claiming that the previous July it had met UN demands to halt opium production by issuing a nationwide ban on the cultivation of the poppies used to produce the drug.

According to an article of December 12, 2000, in *The Observer*, the Taliban regime raised taxes on the transit of "white powder" (heroin) as well as opium through the territory it controlled. The opium was bought in huge open markets at different villages. According to the head of the UNDCP mission in Islamabad, Bernard Frahi, one trader in the village of Sangin, for example, had sold 28 tonnes (27.5 tons) of raw opium in a season. A Pakistani drugs officer based in Quetta reported that individual dealers in Chuttu held stocks of up to 10 tonnes (9.8 tons) of refined heroin. Most deals were made from Dubai, in the United Arab Emirates, the orders being placed by satellite phones. Traffickers were Turkish, British, German, or Southern European. After arranging a deal, the smugglers contacted Baloch tribesmen to arrange a caravan of vehicles to take the heroin into eastern Iran. A typical caravan consisted of 12 four-wheeled vehicles and, of those, four would carry heavily armed guards and the rest the cargo of heroin. A single convoy could carry drugs worth as much as £160 million at London street prices of £20,000 for a kilogram of heroin. In November 2000 the British government, which had already lifted its ban on the export of security equipment to Iran, announced a £1.15 million grant to Iran and an additional £300,000 for 1,020 bullet-proof vests for border guards whose task was to intercept the drug caravans. However, this trickle of Western aid and assistance provided through the UNDCP was totally inadequate and made little impact.

In February 2001 international narcotics experts commended the Taliban regime for virtually wiping out opium production, although the ban had brought drastic economic and social hardships to the poppy-growing regions. (Mullah Mohammed Omar had banned the cultivation of the poppy crop in March 2000 as un-Islamic.) In the first two weeks of the month, the UNDCP surveyed the prime growing sites in Afghanistan and concluded that huge areas of poppy fields had been cleared. According to Kenzo Oshima, the UN under-secretary-general for Humanitarian Affairs, "Part of the desperation in Afghanistan has arisen because of farmers being forced to stop cultivation of poppies, and having nothing else to fall back on. There is a policy in place, and it deserves attention and action to support it. The international community should respond comprehensively with funding to pay for the transition from drugs to crops." Mr. Oshima was mainly concerned with Afghanistan's huge refugee camps in Afghanistan itself, Iran, and Pakistan, which had appeared as a result of 20 years of fighting and the worst drought in 30 years. Although the UNDCP had foreseen the difficulty of switching from poppy cultivation to other crops, its program had run out of funding and could obtain no further finance from its main Western sources. As the UNDCP regional head for Southwest Asia, Bernard Frahi, said: "The situation is now clear: There is nothing. No development program —nothing. For many of the farmers, it is purely a question of survival, and that needs to be immediately addressed." Aid workers based in Kandahar supported Frahi's statement and claimed that the ban was causing drastic economic and social problems in local communities. On his return to Pakistan, after carrying out his survey in Afghanistan, Mr. Frahi said: "Whether we like the Taliban or not we have to recognise that they have taken action to solve the problem. In a way, it is a historical event." One result of the ban was a huge rise in the price of opium. Despite the increase in value—as much as tenfold, from $35 to $350 a kilogram—Mr. Frahi optimistically also said of the Taliban: "If they consider it against Islamic values, then in my view they are now completely bound."[4]

Another article in *The Observer* reported that fields, which in 2000 produced three-quarters of the world's heroin supply, had not been planted on the orders of the Taliban, with the result that Afghanistan would probably only produce 200 tonnes (197 tons) of opium during 2001. This success, however, meant a huge rise in the price of opium and could make it more attractive for farmers elsewhere in the world to grow opium. At the same time the UNDCP believed that the Taliban had strategic reserves of opium, although its director, Pino Arlacchi, believed it would be impossible for other opium-growing countries such as Myanmar, Colombia, Iran, and the former Soviet republics of Central Asia to make up the shortfall caused by the

Taliban ban. However, the indifferent international response to the Taliban gesture raised doubts as to how long the Taliban would maintain its ban on growing opium. As Frederick Starr of the Central Asia Institute—Caucasus at Johns Hopkins University in Washington said: "The reduction is probably the most dramatic event in the history of illegal drug markets, not only in scale but also in the fact that it was done domestically, without international assistance." Starr believed that the ban on opium cultivation by the Taliban had been catastrophically mismanaged by both the United Nations and the international community. As he said:

> For years UN delegations have been wandering through Kabul telling the Taliban that cultivating opium was bad and that they should stop it. They talked to the Taliban about aid packages up to £180 million if they would do it, but no agreement was ever signed. By the UN's own estimation the Taliban were making no more than £18 million from taxing the trade that at most was worth £107 million. But the Taliban felt there was a deal in the air, and they were expecting a quid pro quo for stopping opium production. What has happened instead is that since their declaration there has been no aid. Worse than that, new sanctions were introduced against them in December. What we can expect to happen next is for the other countries in the region to quickly take up the slack in opium production. And if the Taliban are not getting anything in return, they are not going to sit by while others corner the trade.[5]

Starr went on to claim: "The international community has got to persuade the Taliban that it is supporting them in this effort." Other arguments advanced at the time fell by the wayside following the terrorist attacks on New York and Washington of September 11, 2001, and the subsequent total isolation of Afghanistan by the world community. Whatever might have happened was profoundly altered and put on hold by the war situation that faced Afghanistan from mid-September onward. Back in June, however, Pino Arlacchi had told the *New York Times*, quite correctly: "Even if in the long term this reduction of supply is a major success, it will be sustainable only with a parallel reduction in the demand in the industrial countries."

At the very end of September 2001, when attacks on targets in Afghanistan by U.S. and British forces appeared imminent, it was disclosed that their troops would target a stockpile of opium and heroin worth an estimated £20 billion that intelligence officials believed the Taliban would release into the world market. This would provide Osama bin Laden and the Taliban with cash resources to carry on the war with the West. The Western intelligence organizations claimed that up to 3,000 tonnes (2,950 tons) of opium, enough to manufacture 300 tonnes (295 tons) of heroin, were concealed in secret bunkers in the north and west of Afghanistan. This would be sufficient heroin to supply the British market (at its 2001 rate of consumption) for

10 years. According to Downing Street officials (the Prime Minister's Office), bin Laden and his organization al-Qaeda have close connections with drug gangs that transport the heroin to its European and North American destinations through Iran, Turkey, and the former Central Asian Soviet republics. By this time in the developing "war on terrorism" it was clear that Afghanistan's drug production was also being seen as a target; according to a British government source, the destruction of the drugs trade was a "long-held ambition" and, therefore, the war on terrorism would be made flexible so that destroying the drugs trade would be a part of it. An official spokesman of Prime Minister Tony Blair stated, "We want to see an end to opium production in Afghanistan." At the time of these speculations it was thought that U.S. and British forces operating in Afghanistan would focus on areas where it was believed the drugs were stored; that is, around Jalalabad and the bin Laden camps of Darunta, Bhesud, and Khost, and that these sites could be targeted by air strikes when the military campaign, named "Operation Enduring Freedom," was launched. Meanwhile, the Taliban lifted its ban on the planting of poppy fields.

According to an official spokesman of the prime minister:

> Assessments suggest that those stocks are now being disposed of because of the threat of war and the need to raise money. Bin Laden has been closely involved in the Afghan drugs trade and has encouraged major traffickers in the past to flood Europe and the U.S. with heroin as a means of undermining and destabilising. There are strong grounds for believing that he has large stockpiles of drugs himself. The Taliban in the past have used money from drugs to fund military action. Bin Laden is actively involved in the Afghan drugs trade and sees these drugs as a means of undermining the West.[6]

In a belated move, Britain, on the occasion of the Foreign Secretary Jack Straw's visit to Iran at the end of September 2001, announced a government grant of £650,000 to President Mohammed Khatami to assist his government's anti-drug-trafficking measures. Although the border with Afghanistan is officially closed, it passes through such rugged and difficult terrain that it is virtually impossible to police adequately. One complication that faced any attempt to eliminate the Afghan drugs stockpile was the fact that up to 5 percent of the heroin held in Afghanistan was under the control of the Northern Alliance, which the United States wanted to enlist as an ally in any military action inside Afghanistan. By early October 2001 conjecture and estimates as to who controlled the flow of heroin from Afghanistan had once more changed; it was suggested that almost half the heroin from Afghanistan in fact came from areas controlled by the Northern Alliance, which the West was busy wooing as a partner against the Taliban. According to the UNDCP, the alliance and its leaders were deeply implicated in the cultivation of the opium poppy and the resulting export of heroin through Tajikistan; any expansion of alliance territory, the UNDCP warned, would result in an increase in the drug supply. Such a development would rebound on the West since at the height of the Cold War, when the Soviet Union had up to 125,000 troops in Afghanistan, the mujahedin, with the full knowledge and connivance of U.S., British, and other intelligence agencies, refined and exported heroin to finance its struggle against the Soviet invaders. There is also evidence that the CIA had encouraged the spread of hard drugs in the hope that they would help demoralize Russian troops in the way that U.S. troops in Vietnam had been affected by the spread of drug abuse.

In the aftermath of the events of September 11, 2001, drugs from Pakistan became available in the streets of its leading cities such as Peshawar and Quetta for as little as £20 a gram. Drugs are certainly likely to complicate the war on terrorism in this part of the world. After the Taliban banned the cultivation of the opium poppy, the price of heroin in Pakistan soared by 10 times from $44 a kilogram to $440. Then it rose again, after September 11, to $746 a kilogram. Suddenly, however, the street price dropped and that was less easy to explain. It may have been the result of a decision by many small traders to realize their stocks. According to a narcotics official:

> Drugs are a currency in Afghanistan and the border areas of Pakistan. Farmers, traders, and ordinary people keep drugs in their homes rather than money in the bank. Today we are in a war situation, so what do people do? They go to the market and sell their assets to realise cash, just as people in the West sell shares. You cannot ignore the socio-economic aspects.[7]

The Taliban, prior to banning the cultivation of the opium poppy, was earning up to $27 million a year from taxing the peasant growers and charging fees for narcotics production.

By late 2001 it was impossible to predict what would happen to opium production in Afghanistan in the aftermath of the terrorist attacks on New York and Washington on September 11 and the subsequent U.S. military action against the Taliban as the host and protector of Osama bin Laden and his terrorist organization al-Qaeda.

However, by mid-February 2002 it was reported that the planting of opium poppies had increased dramatically. In April the new government launched a program to destroy the opium crop. This proved impossible to implement as farmers resisted the destruction of their highly valued cash crop while local warlords protected the revenue source from which they armed their followers. In October 2002 the UN Office for Drug Control and Crime Prevention published a report, which confirmed that since the fall of the Taliban Afghanistan had reemerged as the world's biggest producer of opium.

Pakistan

In 1999 Pakistan's opium poppy cultivation at 1,570 hectares (3,880 acres) represented a 48 percent drop from the figure for 1998. This was the result of a continuing eradication program and alternative development. Pakistan also produces hashish for the international drugs trade. At the end of the century Pakistan was more important as a transit country for heroin from Afghanistan, passing through Baluchistan province on its way to Western markets, than as a drug producer (see Figure 13.2). Pakistan had developed excellent cooperation with the United States and, with assistance from the DEA, had established a Special Investigative Cell within its Anti-Narcotics Force (ANF). During 1999 there was a 57 percent increase in heroin seizures and the arrest of a number of high-profile drug traffickers took place, with the government extraditing four traffickers to the United States. Crucial to any long-term success in fighting drug trafficking must be the extension of government control over the tribal areas of the Northwest Frontier Province and that has yet to be achieved. The region remains fiercely independent, borders Afghanistan, and is affected by the presence of large numbers of Afghan refugees so that it presents formidable problems of control. Nonetheless, 1999 saw a record number of opium and heroin seizures, although it is probable that these seizures indicate as much the extent of the transit trade as they do any success in curtailing it. Both the ANF and the Frontier Corps had clashes with Afghan drug convoys through the year and made a significant number of drug seizures from them. However, the level of drug trafficking, transit activities, smuggling, and

Figure 13.2   Heroin routes into Britain. (*The Independent*, October 1, 2001.)

corruption remains very high. During the 1990s the Khyber Pass became a vital highway in the worldwide drugs trade. Most of Afghanistan's heroin production is in its eastern provinces with easy access to the Khyber Pass and, while a substantial part of the drug crop is exported to Pakistan through the pass, goods to pay for it in the form of weapons have been smuggled back, using the Khyber Railway to the Afghan border. Such arms become part of the drug producers' armory to ensure their semi-independent status against the Taliban (or any other) Afghan government.

Iran

Although Iran has made considerable efforts to stamp out opium or heroin production, it remains a principal transit route for heroin from Afghanistan to European and other markets. At the same time, the country faces a growing domestic problem with a rising consumption of drugs. As of 2000, there were an estimated 1.2 million drug users in the country. Iran's border with Afghanistan is 936 kilometers (582 miles) long and passes through exceptionally rugged terrain that is extremely difficult to police; drug traffickers from Afghanistan cross it all the time as they carry their cargoes toward the markets of Europe and engage in periodic battles with the Iranian border guards. In August 1999 four European tourists—three Spaniards and one Italian—as well as one Iranian were kidnapped by a gang from a hotel in Kerma, which is 880 kilometers (547 miles) southeast of Tehran. The kidnappers were suspected drug traffickers, although in this case they released the five people unharmed two weeks later. At the end of September three Portuguese working on a television network in the southeastern province of Sistan va Baluchestan near the Pakistan border were also kidnapped, though they too were later released. In this case it was believed that they had been kidnapped in retaliation for the government's crackdown on drug trafficking. No concessions had been made to the kidnappers. Then on November 3, 36 Iranian frontier guards were ambushed and killed in a single incident by heavily armed drug smugglers, again in the Iranshahr region of Sistan va Baluchestan. A further incident occurred on November 23 when security forces killed 16 drug traffickers in an operation to free four hostages in a border area of northeast Iran.[8]

Since 1979 nearly 3,000 Iranian frontier guards have been killed in clashes with gangs smuggling drugs (mainly opium, which was destined to be turned into heroin for sale in Europe and North America). The drugs came from either Afghanistan or Pakistan. This border war between the Iranian guards and the drug smugglers is carried on relentlessly; there could be as many as a dozen small battles taking place along the border on any given night. The drug traffickers risk death in such skirmishes but are prepared to do so because for them smuggling is how they earn their living.

These men would not be aware of the huge prices paid for the drugs they transport once these reach the markets of Western Europe, where there are about 2 million hard-drug users. In a collection center for drug seizures in Tehran, a haul of drugs taken in the first eight months of 2001 included a ton of refined heroin, 8 tons of morphine, 90 tons of opium, 5 tons of hashish, and 2 tons of cannabis, representing about half the total seizures by the Iranian antinarcotics forces over that eight-month period. The opium alone, once turned into heroin, would be worth £500 million, although the total value of this haul would be in the region of £1 billion. The Iranian forces seize an average of 16 tons of opium a month. The drug traffickers are heavily armed and use Toyota 4×4 customized high-suspension trucks; for every three jeeps carrying drugs, a fourth carries arms—a heavy machine gun, a mortar, and a multibarrelled rocket launcher. They also carry satellite phones to call up reinforcements if trapped by the Iranians. Drugs are only moved a certain distance by one gang before being transferred to another on their way to Turkey. In a sense Iran is fighting a battle to prevent drugs reaching the West, especially as the traffickers argue that they want to deliver the drugs either to Turkey or north into the Caucasus states for onward passage to Europe. Iran has its own growing drugs problems; poverty ensures that only limited resources are available for the war on drugs. Meanwhile, Afghanistan is estimated to have established about 200 laboratories to process the opium into heroin, which is infinitely easier to transport; once processed, the drug can then be moved by individual runners rather than being transported in convoys and that would make apprehension and seizure of the drug far harder.[9]

Turkey

The trail, or rather one of the trails, of the drug traffickers runs from Pakistan through Afghanistan and across Iran into eastern Turkey and then to Istanbul. Turkey has become a principal transit route for heroin from Afghanistan and Pakistan on its way to Western Europe and, to a lesser extent, to the United States. From Istanbul the heroin is dispatched over land, by sea, or by air. Istanbul is the center from which Turkish, Iranian, and other international drug-trafficking gangs operate. In the remote regions of Turkey, as well as in areas close to Istanbul, laboratories convert the imported morphine base into heroin. Elsewhere in Turkey, the government maintains strict controls over the areas where the opium poppy is cultivated legally for pharmaceutical purposes.

Even a cursory examination of these four countries points to the enormous difficulty of eradicating the drugs trade of the Golden Crescent.

14

The Involvement of All Asia

Active or passive complicity in the drugs trade affects most of the countries of Asia to raise fundamental doubts as to whether any realistic prospects exist for its eradication. Heroin from the Golden Triangle, for example, travels by sea to Vladivostok and then passes overland through Mongolia, the Russian Federation, and Eastern Europe to the main Western European markets. Most of the countries of Southern Asia—Bangladesh and India—as well as the former members of the Soviet Union—Armenia, Azerbaijan, Kazakhstan, Tajikistan, Turkmenistan—have become involved in the transit trade (see Figure 14.1), while Russia is a major market for drugs as well as a transit country. Malaysia and Singapore each have draconian anti-drugs laws: in Malaysia these include flogging and imprisonment for soft-drug offenses and the death penalty for hard-drug offenses, and Singapore has similar laws, although it is known to be a drug money-laundering center. Eighteen Chinese provinces are drug importers, and opium smoking has long been a traditional Chinese practice. India is a major hashish-consuming country. The greater part of the Asian transit business is to supply the European market, and, following the end of the Cold War, various drug cartels moved into Eastern Europe to control access to the market of the European Union. Synthetic drugs are produced in Russia, Poland, the Czech Republic, and Latvia, although the main ecstasy producers are based in Western Europe. The location of Lebanon, strategically situated on the edge of Asia with easy access to both Europe and Africa, makes it an important distribution center. The country has long been in turmoil as a result of civil war and Israeli/Syrian incursions, a fact that has made both drug trafficking and money laundering easier. Lebanon produces both heroin and cannabis, though it is believed that most of its poppy fields in the Bekaa Valley have now been eradicated. More important are its distribution and money-laundering activities.

In May 1998 six Asian countries held a two-day meeting in Hanoi composed of senior drug control experts; they signed a series of agreements aimed at strengthening their cooperation over drugs control. The six countries were Cambodia, China, Laos, Myanmar (Burma), Thailand, and Vietnam. In March 2000 a different group of countries known as the Six-Plus-Two contact group—consisting of China, Iran, Pakistan, Russia,

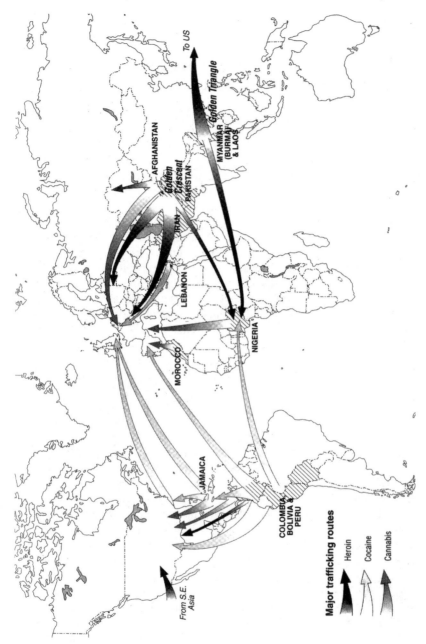

Figure 14.1   Contraband trade routes. (Cartography by Map Creation, Ltd., Maidenhead, Berkshire, U.K.)

Tajikistan, Turkmenistan, the United States, and Uzbekistan—launched an initiative aimed at combating increased drug trafficking from Afghanistan. The meeting followed a United Nations report that highlighted the sharp rise in opium production that had occurred in Afghanistan during 1999. In 2000 the United States refused certification for narcotics control outright to Afghanistan and Myanmar; gave national interest certification (that is, gave certification for reasons of U.S. national interests even though the countries concerned were judged not to have made sufficient effort to combat drug trafficking) to Cambodia; and gave full certification to China, Hong Kong, India, Laos, Pakistan, Taiwan, Thailand, and Vietnam.

China

China historically has long been associated with the practice of opium smoking. Eighteen Chinese provinces are known to be drug importers, and there is a big demand for heroin and other drugs. The Opium War of 1839–1842 between Britain and China, which resulted in the British acquisition of Hong Kong, was the result of a Chinese attempt to put an end to the import of opium, which at the time was being shipped to the Chinese coast from British India. In April 1996 China launched a national campaign against criminal gangs involved in drug dealing and since then has been ruthless in its pursuit and punishment of drug traffickers. On June 27, 1996, the execution of 231 people convicted of drug trafficking was carried out in nine provinces. On June 25, 1999, 71 people were executed by firing squad for drug trafficking to mark the United Nations anti-drugs day. Later that year, on August 13, a meeting between President Imomoli Rakhmanov of Tajikistan and Jiang Zemin of China was held in Dalian on their joint border at which they agreed on combined measures to combat drug trafficking. In June 2000 it was reported that 72 people had been executed for drug trafficking. In general, the high number of exemplary executions of drug traffickers represented a dramatic intensification of the government's war on drugs. Then on June 25, once again to mark the UN International Day for Narcotics Control, 10 executions were carried out. China's State Council issued a white paper detailing its policy on drugs control. The paper acknowledged achievements to that date but admitted that "drugs are still rampant in China, and a long fight remains."

China's heroin seizures in 1999 fell well short of those for 1998 yet nevertheless accounted for the great majority of heroin seized throughout Asia. At the same time there was a significant increase in the seizures of methamphetamines and other amphetamine-type stimulants; seizures of precursor chemicals and opium remained at the level of the previous few years. China provides preexport notification of dual-use precursor chemicals. According to government estimates, about 10 percent of the population of

1.3 billion viewed a nationwide anti-drugs exhibition. China cooperates over a range of operational issues against drug trafficking with the United States, and the U.S. DEA opened an office in Beijing during 1999. The government launched a "Drug Free Communities" program in 1999 with the aim of eliminating drug trafficking and abuse and drug-related crimes. The Chinese government also cooperated with the UNDCP and neighboring states on a range of anti-drugs programs aimed at reducing the demand for illicit drugs and gave its support to crop-substitution programs in Myanmar and Laos. China has acceded to the 1961 UN Single Convention, to the 1971 Convention on Psychotropic Substances, the 1972 Protocol, and the 1988 UN Drug Convention. However, despite its own war on drugs and its readiness to cooperate with the United States, China has been much less open about the money-laundering aspects of drug trafficking and does not rigidly enforce or strengthen its anti-money-laundering legislation. Nonetheless, China has in place one of the toughest anti-drugs programs in Asia. Even so, it remains a major transit country for heroin from the Golden Triangle.

Hong Kong and Taiwan

The geographic location of Hong Kong makes it a natural transit center for drug traffickers, with the vast hinterland of China as both its source and market. It is a major transit center and staging area for shipment to the United States of heroin and methamphetamines. In 1999 Hong Kong drug seizures were impressive: 205 kilograms (452 pounds) of heroin, 35.8 kilograms (78.9 pounds) of cannabis, 16.7 kilograms (36.8 pounds) of cocaine, and 9,811 kilograms (21,630 pounds) of methamphetamines. In addition, 7,620 individuals were arrested during the year for drug-related offenses and the authorities enhanced their drug detection capabilities. They increased the number of drug-sniffing dogs at the airport and border, while high-tech equipment was obtained to be used in detecting illicit drugs in packages and to facilitate the inspection of baggage and cargo. The Hong Kong government also amended its legislation to tighten controls over the transshipment, removal, and storage of potassium permanganate and to require a license from the commissioner of customs and excise before it can be imported, exported, or manufactured. Money laundering was also targeted with sentences for offenses being lengthened. Hong Kong cooperates with the United States law enforcement agencies, and legislation allowing the transfer of sentenced persons to the United States or Sri Lanka has been enacted, as have similar laws in relation to the European Union. There appears to be an increasing domestic problem of amphetamine abuse.

By the end of the century Taiwan had become an important heroin transshipment country while also experiencing major domestic problems with the increasing consumption of heroin and methamphetamines.

India

Apart from being the world's largest producer of licit opium, India's location between the Golden Triangle and the Golden Crescent ensures that it has become a major transit country. Heroin is both produced in India and trafficked through it. The Indian government cooperates with the U.S. DEA and is a party to the 1988 Drug Convention of the United Nations. During 1999, for example, the Indian government uncovered a drug-trafficking network that shipped locally produced heroin from a number of Indian cities to Sri Lanka, as well as seized a heroin laboratory and more than 100 kilograms (220 pounds) of heroin. Heroin from Afghanistan, destined for the American market, is also routed through India. During the latter half of the 1990s, the government made strenuous efforts to prevent the illicit cultivation of the opium poppy and substantially reduced its cultivation. In 1999 India had meetings with both Myanmar and Pakistan to discuss tightening of cross-border controls. India's output of licit opium only just meets demand. This is due, in part, to the diversion of licit stocks to the illegal market. In order to counter this practice, the government raised the prices paid to licit opium farmers and threatened stiffer penalties for those who continued to divert stocks for illicit purposes. India is a major producer of hashish, mainly for home consumption, and also of methaqualone.

Russia and the Central Asian Republics

During the latter half of the 1990s, various agreements between Russia and the former Soviet states of Central Asia were concerned with cross-border cooperation aimed at controlling drug trafficking and money laundering. One such agreement was between Latvia and Russia in 1996. Another similar agreement between Russia and Tajikistan in 1999 also included joint measures to combat drug trafficking. That year Tajikistan carried out an overhaul of its security agencies since it was found that these were "endemically" disposed to participation in crime and drugs. In the course of 1998 about 700 people in Turkmenistan were sentenced to death by firing squad, and of these, 90 percent had been convicted of drug-related crimes. In January 1998 Tajikistan and Uzbekistan made an agreement to cooperate in fighting the drugs trade, which was destabilizing the region. Such agreements, however, probably made little real impact in a region where lawlessness and poverty make controls difficult to impose, especially over a trade—drug trafficking—that provides such lucrative rewards. Thus, for example, the shipment of one kilogram of poppy resin from within Afghanistan to the border with Tajikistan can see its value increase from $25 to $3,000. Since the journey is dangerous, it requires guards, and they require arms. The onward progress of this cargo through Tajikistan to its eventual destination also requires guards and arms as the value increases. This single statistic suggests that the vested interests involved in ensuring that the drug reaches its destination are enormous and that a proportion of the drug money will be used to corrupt border guards or drug enforcement personnel.

The Rest of Asia

Almost no country of the Asian landmass escapes involvement in the drugs trade, although in some cases it may be more by the accident of geographic position on the continent's transit routes than for any other reason. And a number of Asian countries produce drugs such as cannabis almost entirely for their own use. Armenia, for example, cultivates cannabis for its own consumption but, in addition, has become a transshipment point for opium and hashish on its way to Europe and the United States, the drugs being passed on through Iran, Central Asia, and Russia. Armenia's neighbor, Azerbaijan, cultivates cannabis and the opium poppy for its own and the CIS consumption and has also become a transshipment point for drugs on their way to Europe via Iran, Central Asia, and Russia. The Azerbaijan government has a small-scale eradication program in place. Bangladesh, sharing a frontier with Myanmar, has inevitably become a transit center for drugs produced in the Golden Triangle. Belarus, though part of Europe, formed the western extremity of the former Soviet Union; it cultivates the opium poppy and cannabis for its domestic market; it also acts as a transshipment point for drugs both to and from Russia and to the Baltic States and Western Europe. Georgia cultivates both cannabis and opium on a limited scale, mainly for domestic consumption, and is also a transit country for drugs coming from Central Asia on the way to Russia and Western Europe. The growth of casinos in Georgia suggests that in recent years money laundering has become an important additional drug-related activity. Kazakhstan has become a significant producer of cannabis, which is mainly consumed in the CIS. It also cultivates the opium poppy and ephedra, which constitutes the base of the drug ephedrone. There is a small government eradication program. Kazakhstan has become an important transit country for drugs from Southwest Asia en route to Russia, North America, and Western Europe. The same pattern exists in Kyrgyzstan, which cultivates cannabis and the opium poppy for CIS consumption, has a small government eradication program, and is developing into an important transshipment route for drugs from Southwest Asia destined for Russia and Western Europe. Despite its severe anti-drug-trafficking laws, Malaysia is still a transit point for drugs destined for the European and North American markets. Nepal, landlocked between China and India, produces cannabis for both domestic use and the international market and acts as a transit route for drugs en route to the West from

Southeast Asia (the Golden Triangle). Like Malaysia, Singapore is also a transshipment point for drugs from the Golden Triangle destined for North America, Europe, and other countries—the huge number of ships that use the ports of Singapore make it a natural distribution center, while its highly developed banking sector makes it attractive for money-laundering activities as well. Tajikistan cultivates cannabis for domestic consumption. A government eradication program appeared to have all but eliminated opium cultivation at the end of the 1990s. However, Tajikistan remains a major transshipment point for heroin from Afghanistan destined for Russia and Western Europe. Like the other Central Asian republics, Turkmenistan cultivates the opium poppy, mainly for domestic consumption. There is a limited government eradication program (limited as in other cases by lack of funds, inadequate or corrupt law enforcement agencies, and probably also less-than-complete government commitment to the program). Turkmenistan is developing into an important transshipment point for drugs from Southwest Asia (principally Afghanistan) to Russia and Western Europe. In addition it is a route for acetic anhydride destined for Afghanistan. Uzbekistan, of the Central Asian republics, has had an effective government eradication program, although limited quantities of cannabis and small amounts of opium are still produced for the domestic market. However, it is becoming an increasingly important transit country for drugs from Afghanistan en route to Russia and Western Europe and, the other way, for acetic anhydride destined for Afghanistan.

Tajikistan became especially vulnerable to drug-trafficking activities as a result of the civil war of 1992–1997, which led to the emergence of a number of warlords with their personal militias for whom drug trafficking was a source of finance for arms purchases. Some of these warlords established themselves near the Afghan border, in the Pamirs, where the government does not exercise any control. Deep poverty in Tajikistan makes drug trafficking an attractive potential source of extra, illicit income. A major drugs transshipment point in Central Asia is the Ferghana Valley where Tajikistan, Uzbekistan, and Kyrgyzstan meet and where, in any case, there is very high unemployment. In addition, Tajik officials became involved in drug trafficking on a major scale as revealed in May 2000 when two cars from the Tajik embassy were stopped in Almaty, Kazakhstan, and 63 kilograms (139 pounds) of heroin, U.S. $54,000 in cash, and a banker's check for £1.26 million were confiscated.[1]

Russia as a Market

After the United States and Western Europe, Russia is probably the world's third-largest market for drugs. In 1998 there were 500,000 registered addicts in Moscow, 250,000 in St Petersburg, and another 500,000 in Ukraine. Both cannabis and the opium poppy are cultivated in Russia on a limited scale, mainly for domestic consumption, and the government has an active eradication program. However, Russia has become an important transit country for opium or heroin and cannabis from both the Golden Triangle and the Golden Crescent on the way to Western Europe, and possibly the United States, while it also handles cocaine from Latin America en route to Western Europe. Statistics issued by the Russian Interior Ministry indicate that approximately 80 percent of heroin seized in Russia is delivered from points in Uzbekistan, Tajikistan, and Kazakhstan, and one of the most immediate results of this expanding drugs trade through the Central Asian republics and Russia has been a steady rise in the addiction rates in these countries.[2] In addition, Russia is a major source of heroin precursor chemicals. The Ukraine, like Russia, cultivates both cannabis and the opium poppy and most of the drugs are destined for the CIS market. It also produces some synthetic drugs for export to Western Europe. There is a government eradication program, though this has not eliminated cultivation of either cannabis or opium. Ukraine is a major transshipment country for drugs from Africa, Latin America, and Turkey en route to Russia and Europe. Money laundering appears to be a growing problem. By the end of the 1990s increasing evidence of drug trafficking suggested that both Russia and the Central Asian republics had become major transit countries for drugs and, as a consequence, were also becoming deeply involved in the other related problems of increased addiction, the corruption of officials, and money laundering.

On the Pacific extremity of Asia, both Indonesia and the Philippines face drug problems. As yet Indonesia is only involved at the margins of the world drug-trafficking business. It produces cannabis, largely for domestic consumption, and may be developing as a transshipment country for heroin exported from the Golden Triangle. Given Indonesia's vast spread and thousands of islands, it may well become much more important as a transshipment country, especially as the drug-exporting mafias constantly have to find and establish new export routes. The Philippines is an exporter of marijuana and hashish to East Asia, the United States, and other Western markets and is also a transshipment point for heroin and crystal methamphetamine.

At the southwest extremity of Asia, a number of Arab countries are also important to the international drug-trafficking business. Lebanon is a minor producer of hashish and a certain amount of heroin processing takes place in the Bekaa Valley. A joint Lebanon/Syria eradication campaign was launched in the early 1990s and has virtually eliminated the opium and cannabis crops. In November 1997, for example, U.S. President Bill Clinton notified Congress that Syria and Lebanon had been removed from the U.S. government list of countries deemed to be involved in narcotics trafficking. However, Lebanon is probably involved quite substantially in the business of money laundering. Syria is principally important as a transit country for hashish and opium bound for both regional and Western markets. Saudi Arabia imposes the death penalty for drug traffickers yet, despite this, is suffering from an increase in both heroin and cocaine consumption. Its draconian laws have embroiled it, for example, with Turkey when in 1995 the Saudi government had eight Turks executed for smuggling the aphrodisiac drug Captagon. Turkey argued that the Koran made no provision for the death sentence for drug smugglers. The Saudi government was also responsible for the growing number of public executions of women, often foreigners, who had been found guilty of drug smuggling. The United Arab Emirates (UAE) has developed as a transshipment country for drugs from Southwest Asia as well as a growing center for money laundering. The highly successful free-trade zone in Dubai is an obvious center for such activities. During 2001, for example, the UAE courts handed down life sentences to two British women for trafficking in cocaine and hashish, although spared them the death penalty. The women will be in prison for 25 years before qualifying for parole. A British man was given a 10-year prison sentence for intent to traffic. Israel has become increasingly concerned about cocaine and heroin abuse among its population; the drugs enter the country from Lebanon and Jordan. Finally, the east Mediterranean island of Cyprus has become a transit point for heroin and hashish from Asia en route by air as well as container traffic to Western Europe. Most of these drugs come from either Lebanon or Turkey. A certain amount of cocaine also passes through Cyprus en route to Europe from Latin America.

15

The Growing Involvement of Africa

Until relatively recent years, the continent of Africa has not been seen as a major player in the international drugs business, nor has it been a producer of the two leading drugs—cocaine and heroin. However, it is now emerging as a principal source of cannabis and has become widely implicated in the transit business between Asia and Europe and North America and, increasingly, between Latin America and Europe. The U.S. practice of certification is being extended to African countries, and those seen as drug traffickers, especially for transit purposes, may find themselves blacklisted by U.S. aid agencies. Although the process started earlier, it was during the 1990s that the African role in the carriage of narcotics expanded rapidly, with the result that a number of countries in Sub-Saharan Africa became staging points of world importance for heroin en route from Asia's Golden Triangle to the markets of North America and, to a lesser but rapidly growing extent, for cocaine from Latin America to Europe. Exports of narcotics to the Gulf states have also increased. Drug routes change all the time, depending on the effectiveness of counternarcotics campaigns, and traffickers will take shortcuts, open new routes, or revert to old tried ones when pressures relax or countermeasures are concentrated elsewhere. Certain countries, such as Ethiopia in the Horn of Africa and Kenya in East Africa, have established their positions as important staging posts for drug-trafficking activities.

Couriers change their nationalities because of the ease with which legal procedures can be bypassed and false passports or other documents can be obtained. African drug syndicates have become established in Bolivia, Russia, Central Europe, and as far away from the continent as China and have equipped themselves with fronts that allow them to avoid Africa altogether. Syndicates, with no apparent links with others on the continent, have appeared in Algeria, Democratic Republic of Congo (Kinshasa), Ghana, Senegal, and Tanzania. They are active in organizing supplies for Europe and South Africa. The Lebanese diaspora in Africa is also increasingly involved in drug trafficking. In a cutthroat business, African traffickers benefit from their membership of flexible, decentralized communities with a long tradition of commercial expertise in their regions. Other factors operating in Sub-Saharan Africa include the premium that is placed on individual success

—the end justifying the means, while cunning and deception are highly prized qualities.

Apart from these expanding transit activities, the consumption of drugs inside Africa is escalating—amphetamines, cocaine, and heroin in West Africa, and the rapid expansion of the Mandrax market in Southern Africa, with the drug entering the region from India through Mozambique and Namibia. Zambia and Zimbabwe, as well as South Africa, are also growing markets for this drug. As yet there is no obvious incentive, in the form of a pronounced market advantage, for Africa to become a producer of cocaine or heroin, though this may happen at some time in the future. At the end of the twentieth century African traffickers concentrated on transit and money-laundering activities. Another factor that has assisted the spread of both drug cultures and drug trafficking on the continent has been the frequency of its wars; these have encouraged the use of drugs as stimulants for the combatants, as in the Congo (1960–1965), Biafra (1967–1970), and in the 1990s in Liberia and Sierra Leone in West Africa, Burundi and Rwanda in Central Africa, and Somalia in the Horn.

Large quantities of all the main drugs now transit through Africa: hashish from Southwest Asia and from Morocco to West Africa; heroin from Southwest and Southeast Asia; cocaine from Latin America. Most of these drugs are bound for the European markets. In 1992 the INCB found that the drug abuse and illicit trafficking situation in Africa had been worsening for a number of years and that the current year was no exception to this development. If efficient steps were not taken, the INCB argued, the illicit trafficking and abuse would get worse, enhancing the existing problems of poverty, violence, corruption, and general destabilization of communities. Other parallel investigations carried out by the U.S. DEA, Interpol, the Customs Cooperation Council, and the Observatoire Géopolitique des Drogues each came to comparable conclusions: that there was a much wider African involvement in drugs than had earlier been believed. Furthermore, illicit drug activities had become a significant source of foreign exchange to countries always in desperate need of such funds, and once the money from this source had been laundered and recycled, it could be used to meet African obligations to legitimate creditors. Moreover, most African countries that are hungry for investment funds are not too concerned about the origin of funds once these have been deposited in their banks. Similarly, the creditor nations are not particular about whether their money is "clean" or "dirty" provided the debts owed them are serviced. The UNDCP works hard to persuade its members to adopt laws to punish money laundering of drug (and other criminal) finances, but even if such laws are adopted this does not mean that the adopting country will at once see they are enforced or, even if it has the will to do so, possess the means to make such laws effective. Ironically, the process of democratizing Africa also democratized and made easier crime among Africa's elites, many of whom have entered into a range of illicit activities, including drug trafficking. The armed conflicts in Liberia and Sierra Leone in West Africa have created conditions favorable to drug production (chiefly cannabis), trafficking, and drug use. Furthermore, the spread of light weapons, many of which fall into the hands of criminal gangs, has assisted the growth of the drugs trade. The main drug-trafficking countries of West and Central Africa, apart from Nigeria, appear to be Liberia, Sierra Leone, Chad, Congo Brazzaville (among its militias), and Congo Kinshasa, whose drug warlords now engage in widespread trafficking. In the civil wars that dominated much of the 1990s in both Liberia and Sierra Leone, a significant proportion of army officers were drug users, while many of the child soldiers, aged between 8 and 15, were also encouraged to take drugs. Such soldiers, when demobilized, are already drug addicts and consequently are desperate to continue obtaining drugs to feed their habit, a condition that inevitably leads them into lawless activities.[1]

In *Congo–Paris* by Janet MacGaffey and Rémy Bazenguissa-Ganga, the authors examine African transnational traders on the margins of the law and in the course of their investigations touch on the growing prevalence of drug trafficking as part of a greater pattern of activities.[2] As they say of Congo traders in France: "The pervasiveness of drug dealing was a major reason for the difficulty of getting people to trust us." Marijuana first appeared in the Congolese diaspora in France in 1975 and by 1977 and 1978 its prevalence had escalated, especially with the influx of young BaKongo *sapeurs*, a term denoting those who live an elegant lifestyle as a result of making quick money. Many of these *sapeurs* became dealers in marijuana. By the end of the 1980s a hard-drug network for heroin had developed, with the smugglers obtaining the drug from the Netherlands or Britain, or from Arab networks. It was largely through drug smuggling that members of the two Congolese communities (from Congo Brazzaville and what in those years was still Zaïre) got to know each other. As they soon discovered, drug couriers required training in self-presentation to acquire the necessary confidence to pass customs and national entry authorities. When stopped, they would claim to be carrying exotic foods, and once this had been linked to the drugs business, the French authorities insisted that food traders should have certificates issued by the Hygiene and Epidemic Disease authorities. Drug trafficking provided the means by which young people, acting as one-off couriers, got to Paris from Brazzaville or Kinshasa. This trade, like its larger international counterparts, involved a dealer, an associate, the courier, the wholesaler, the retailer, and the end customer. As with any successful business, such smuggling soon became increasingly complex, with the smuggler seeking an associate whose job was to find a wholesaler, and the associate standing between the wholesaler and the courier. The attraction of quick, easy money has drawn many young Africans into trafficking. Young smugglers would decide, "I am young; I must try for a coup. If I am caught, I shall be put away for five to seven years and when I come out of prison, I shall still be young and can start my life all over again."[3] African drug traders operating in Europe justify their activities with the consolation that, "In the past Europeans looted Africa, now it is the turn of Africans to help themselves to the riches of Europe."[4] In 1994, the drugs market was dominated by medium to small players, while the quantity and value of drugs being shipped to the European Union was increasing rapidly. At the same time, the organizations bringing the drugs into Europe were reported to be increasingly violent. Europol, the new European Union drug intelligence unit, had by then already intervened to assist French, Belgian, and Greek drugs officers in raids using computer links.

The Congolese police blame Lebanese traffickers for the increase in the availability of cocaine in Brazzaville. Some of this is imported from Latin America, but part of the supply is produced in laboratories in Kinshasa, the capital of the neighboring Democratic Republic of Congo, which now produces some of its own coca crops. These Lebanese traffickers, who were ousted from Kinshasa by the government of Laurent Kabila because of their previous links to Mobutu, speak Lingala, a language common in both Brazzaville and Kinshasa. They have bought up businesses such as bars and restaurants from the French and Portuguese who fled the country during the violence of 1997 and they use these for their drug or money-laundering activities.

The generally weak structure of African states has meant that the deregulation of trade and the financial markets, coupled with the growing pressures of globalization on their sovereignty and capacities, have led to an increase in corruption, violent conflict, the plunder of natural resources, and growing involvement in the drugs business. The international antinarcotics institutions see Sub-Saharan Africa principally as a transit territory for drugs, although the cultivation of cannabis for local consumption has been a traditional activity subject to controls. By the early 1980s, however, there was a rapid spread of illicit cannabis crops. These were produced to supply the expanding home markets and for the international trade, and from the 1980s such crops have been grown extensively, especially in Ghana, Kenya, Nigeria, and South Africa. Experiments in growing the opium poppy and the coca leaf have also been carried out in Benin, the Ivory Coast, Nigeria, and Togo in West Africa, and Kenya and Tanzania in East Africa.

By the end of the twentieth century, large quantities of the major drugs were known to transit through Africa, and most of them were destined for the huge European market. The scale of the African trade demonstrates just how quickly drugs have come to play a lead role in funding the continent's various conflicts. The growth of drug trafficking mirrors the continent's problems of poverty, economic failure, and debt and its inability to break this pattern except by resorting to illegal means. In the Ivory Coast the cocoa crisis of 1988–1989 acted as the stimulus to desperate farmers who switched to producing cannabis. The attractions of the crop are obvious: The output of 0.1 hectares (0.2 acres) of cannabis in value is equivalent to 16 tonnes (15.7 tons) of cocoa grown on 30 hectares (74.1 acres) by an owner employing 10 workers. So far, only cannabis is produced on any scale in Africa and most of this is still destined for domestic markets and cross-border trading rather than for export outside the continent.[5] In the early 1990s, however, African production of cannabis escalated and much of it was for the European market. In 1993 customs seizures of African cannabis only represented 1.5 percent of world seizures and a tiny share of the European consumer market. By the end of the twentieth century South Africa, Kenya, Benin, and Ghana were producing cannabis and exporting it as marijuana to Europe. Nigeria and Ghana are the main cannabis producers in West Africa, although little information, as yet, is available as far as Nigerian production is concerned. In Ghana the cannabis crop is grown throughout the country and known as "the Devil's tobacco" or "wee," and a ganja farm may be as large as three hectares (7.4 acres) and receive protection from the local police.

West Africa has shown how armed conflicts create favorable conditions for drug production, trafficking, and consumption. The cannabis trade provides a large part of the finances required by the rebels of Senegal's Casamance province. Cannabis was important in Senegal as early as the 1960s, with Casamance acting as the main producer. In the early days of their revolt the Casamance rebels defended the cannabis growers against the authorities, but by the 1990s they were forcing the cannabis growers to pay them, and requiring those inhabitants of Casamance who have left the province to live elsewhere to support them with money donations under the threat of harm to their families if such contributions were not forthcoming. The former president of the Gambia, Dawda Jawara, who was ousted from power in 1994, has claimed that drugs and precious stones from Liberia cross Guinea, Sierra Leone, and Guinea-Bissau to transit Casamance before being shipped from the Gambia. The militias who operated in a deeply troubled Congo Brazzaville during the 1990s would first take control of cannabis plantations when they moved into an area and subsequently encourage the use of drugs by their soldiers so as to stimulate their fighting qualities. Such action helps explain the readiness of soldiers in a number of West African countries to commit atrocities. Charles Taylor, who emerged as the eventual victor in the Liberian civil war, trafficked in drugs through Buchanan port, which he controlled from 1990 to 1992, and exported cannabis grown in the areas controlled by his National Patriotic Front of Liberia. The use of drugs was also widespread among the troops of the Economic Community of West African States (ECOWAS), mainly Nigerian, who acted as peacekeepers in Liberia.[6] War violence provides a natural breeding ground for drug trafficking, and this became clear in both Liberia and Sierra Leone during the 1990s.

According to a report in *African Business* for April 2000,[7] Africa is now a major transit route for drugs from Asia to the United States. Sophisticated gangs, often enjoying high political connections, have little difficulty evading U.S. drug enforcement agencies. West Africans, Kenyans, Ugandans, Somalis, and South Africans risk imprisonment to become couriers since they stand to make a huge fortune—as much as $100,000—for a single successful operation. Like most aspects of drug trafficking, the courier business is now highly organized and departmentalized. Heroin from Asia, for example, will be moved by a number of couriers. One will pick up a shipment in Bangkok and fly to a destination in India, Indonesia, or Egypt where the shipment will be handed over to a second courier who will take it to Kenya. There it will be handed on to a third courier, perhaps the member of a family going to visit a student son in the United States. By this means the final courier will have no obvious connection with the heroin source country. The profits involved in trafficking are so large—a 1,000 percent mark-up for heroin smuggling—that countermeasures often fail or are foiled because of corruption on the part of officials and politicians who facilitate the trade. Furthermore, when they are exposed, the "middle men" are often protected by top politicians in order to prevent the exposure of their own complicity in the trafficking. Although most African countries are signatories of the 1988 Convention against Illicit Traffic in Narcotic Drugs and Psychotropic Substances, few of them take more than token action to prevent trafficking, not least because they simply do not possess sufficiently sophisticated police or customs infrastructure for the task. In addition, many governments, for reasons of complicity among politicians or highly placed officials, are uninterested in any rigid attack on the transit trade. The money attached to the drugs trade often proves more powerful than counternarcotics policies. In 1998 a conference organized by the UNDCP was held in Johannesburg, South Africa, and attended by experts from Botswana, Ethiopia, Lesotho, Kenya, Uganda, Tanzania, and Zimbabwe; the participants hoped to implement a joint anti-drugs program. The UNDCP issued the following statement from Johannesburg: "At a time when national borders are increasingly under assault from drug traffickers seeking to compromise national sovereignty in pursuit of their illicit trade, regional cooperation assumes critical importance."

Africa is now a major source of cannabis for both local consumption and export to Europe. According to the Vienna-based INCB, Nigeria, Morocco, Kenya, Ghana, Senegal, and the Ivory Coast are the leading African producers of marijuana. Vast tracts of forest make it easy to hide marijuana plantations. The U.S. DEA has opened offices in Pretoria and Lagos, although political corruption acts to protect many of the traffickers. At the same time many Africans who see the damage that drugs do to their citizens are becoming more vociferous in demanding that their own counternarcotics agencies do their jobs properly.

Nigeria

In Africa, Nigeria has now achieved a reputation as the country most involved in drug trafficking, although it is possible that U.S. antinarcotics experts overemphasize its role in the international heroin trade. It is certainly regarded with most concern by U.S. drug law enforcement agencies. The attention paid to Nigeria as a drug-trafficking country by the United States and the suspension of direct flights between Lagos and the United States has persuaded drug smugglers to develop new routes. These may pass through a number of other African countries including Cape Verde, the Ivory Coast, Ghana, Liberia, Mauritania, Senegal, and Sierra Leone in West Africa and through South Africa or Zimbabwe in the south. Nonetheless, despite the spread of drug networks, increasingly over a widening range of African countries, Nigeria remains the continent's most prominent drug-transit country. The Ibo are seen as especially important in this trade and are believed to control between 70 and 80 percent of heroin from Myanmar (Burma) reaching the United States and between 35 and 40 percent of heroin from all sources appearing on the U.S. market. Nigeria's drug-trafficking success depends on its highly developed techniques for concealing illicit goods, the recruitment of "mules" or couriers from a number of backgrounds, including a growing number of white couriers from the United States and South Africa, and the ethnic homogeneity of the leading drug syndicates, which makes them impossible to penetrate by outsiders. Individual couriers may carry as much as two kilograms (4.4 pounds) of heroin inside their bodies worth a street value of $2 million in New York. They have established networks that operate at both ends of the drugs trade, thus linking the Golden Triangle with New York and North America, and Europe. Larger consignments of drugs are transported by sea, by road, or by airfreight routes. The drugs trade in Nigeria has been criminalized but more as a result of external pressures than any arising within the country itself. Furthermore, the Nigerian Drug Law Enforcement Agency (NDLEA) is believed to obtain an unofficial tax from the trade it is supposed to police, while much of the Nigerian economy is assisted by inputs of money from drug trafficking. At the same time many politicians are reputed to strengthen their own power and financial positions by participation in the drugs trade.

In 1993 customs worldwide seized 34,631 kilograms (76,350 pounds) of marijuana from Nigeria alone; this included 7.72 tonnes (7.6 tons) hidden in containers destined for Amsterdam. In 1994 seizures of Nigerian marijuana accounted for 28.25 percent of total world seizures. Nigeria now appears to play a comparable role in Africa to that played by Colombia in Latin America. African cocaine networks were first established in 1984; by the end of the century the quantities smuggled through Brazil to Nigeria and Ghana had become a significant proportion of the flow to Europe. A close link has been developed between Brazil and Nigeria. During 1992 and 1993 Brazil tightened its customs controls and on one occasion arrested Nigerians and Ghanaians at São Paolo airport as they attempted to smuggle 270 kilograms (595 pounds) of cocaine to Africa. According to the Customs Cooperation Council, reporting in 1993: "The smuggling of cocaine from Brazil to Nigeria and Ghana has now become a significant trade. The main feature of this illicit trafficking is that it seems to a large extent to call on West Africans residing in Brazil."[8] Nigerian couriers can buy a kilogram of cocaine for between $8,000 and $10,000 in Brazil and sell it in Europe for between $50,000 and $60,000. In 1996 about 100 Africans were held in Brazilian prisons for trafficking offenses. Drug networks controlled by Nigerians have been uncovered and destroyed in Brazil, Colombia, and Ecuador, but when this happens they are likely soon to be replaced.

Nigerians moved swiftly into Eastern Europe following the end of the Cold War and the opening up of the region's borders. In any case they already had good contacts there; these were often the former recipients of scholarships from the old communist regimes. These Nigerians tended to stay in the background, hiring couriers from the host countries. During 1995 and 1996, for example, Czechs working for Nigerian drug syndicates were arrested in Bangkok, Paris, Prague, the Netherlands, and Finland. The Western media as well as its secret services have accused former Nigerian presidents and their wives of complicity in drug trafficking, while the sudden appearance of new young millionaires in Nigeria is almost certainly due to money-laundering profits from illegal activities, much of these from drug trafficking. However, there are exceptions and, for example, while illegal cross-border trade from Nigeria is conducted by Hausa-Fulani networks based in the north of the country, these are said to have eschewed trading in narcotics. Nigerian drug networks are strongly structured and work independently of each other. Thus, " 'Drug barons' allegedly command 'under-barons,' who in turn monitor a team of smugglers. Within this scheme, 3 bosses allegedly supervise 85 cells of about 40 members each. Within each cell, a Nigerian 'lieutenant' allegedly leads from 6 to 20 'soldiers.' "[9] Such networks may employ Lebanese, Indians, Pakistanis, or Filipinos, depending on the place, but they can only function with the aid of accomplices in official circles. According to the Anglican Bishop of Nigeria, the Right Reverend Joseph Abiodun Adetiloye, speaking in 1992: "Nigeria is one of the countries in the world with the largest number of young millionaires without any known source of income."

The Nigerian cartels operating from the United States are highly sophisticated and one such gang, known as the Blackstone Rangers, set up its own training school in Chicago to teach couriers of all nationalities how to avoid detection by customs and border officials. In recent years thousands of smugglers from Nigeria and other West African states have been arrested by U.S. and European authorities. The business was only a trickle in the 1980s but it grew through the 1990s and by the end of the century, according to the DEA, had reached epidemic proportions. Another Nigerian cartel in the United States developed the technique of "shotgunning," whereby a number of couriers travel on the same air flight so that at least some are bound to get through if their destination is an overworked airport such as London's Heathrow.[10]

At the end of the twentieth century the United States saw Nigeria as the hub of African narcotics trafficking, operating global drug networks, dominating the Sub-Saharan drug markets and being responsible for a large proportion of the heroin imported into the United States. In addition, it transported cocaine from South America into Europe, Asia, or other parts of Africa. Furthermore, the United States was critical of the Nigerian approach to the problem of drug trafficking and did not believe that the NDLEA made adequate efforts to combat trafficking activities; though it made regular arrests of individual couriers, few major traffickers were either arrested or prosecuted. On coming to power in 1999, following democratic elections, President Olusegun Obasanjo denounced drug trafficking in strong terms, although there was little enhancement of anti-drugs activities thereafter. Despite an active program to eradicate cannabis, the supply of the drug continues to meet demands and no significant figures concerning the drug are available. After the cocaine-producing countries centered on Colombia in South America and the principal heroin-producing countries of the Golden Triangle and Golden Crescent, Nigeria has emerged as the next-most important country involved in general drug-trafficking activities.

Kenya and Tanzania

Kenya has become the leading drug-trafficking country in East Africa, and the northern Lamu Archipelago bordering Somalia has developed into a major smuggling zone. Heroin from Asia is reexported to the United States where it is sold on streets in those suburbs where there are large numbers of Nigerian nationals. Kenya has also become a significant producer of cannabis and, for example, in 1996 a 243-hectare (600-acre) cannabis plantation was discovered in the southwest Rift Valley. It is a transit country for both heroin and hashish from Asia to Europe and, to a lesser extent, to the United States and is also a transit country for methaqualone (Mandrax) from Asia destined for Southern Africa. Cannabis/marijuana is grown commercially for the illegal domestic market, as is qat, a mild narcotic that is chewed and widely used in the Arabian Peninsula and the Horn of Africa. It is legal in Kenya. The antinarcotics police cooperate with U.S. and other national anti-drugs agencies. Kenya has managed to reduce significantly airborne heroin shipments but has had less success in intercepting shipments of heroin or other drugs entering the country by sea. Kenya's geographic position and well-developed infrastructure—its international airports and Mombasa, which is one of Africa's premier seaports—have made it a natural choice as a transit country, whether for legal or illegal trade. The Anti-Narcotics Unit of the Kenyan police force is the principal organization used to combat drug trafficking.

Tanzania is also well placed geographically to play a significant transit role in the international drugs trade, with major points of entry at its international airports of Dar es Salaam, Zanzibar, and Kilimanjaro, and its seaports of Dar es Salaam and Zanzibar, and the lesser ports of Tanga and Mtwara. Cocaine, hashish, heroin, Mandrax, and opium, in varying quantities, now pass through Tanzania and across its porous borders to points elsewhere in Africa and beyond. And like Kenya it produces both cannabis and qat for domestic consumption. Until the end of the 1980s Tanzania's involvement with drugs was more or less limited to cannabis and qat, but during the 1990s it was drawn into the growing continental involvement in drug trafficking, while drug abuse, especially among the young, was on the increase. The fact that a variety of drugs transit through Tanzania, as well as the development of the tourist industry, have both acted to increase the local demand for drugs. There are strong indications of a growing arms–drugs link between Tanzania and the troubled countries of the Great Lakes region—the Democratic Republic of Congo (Kinshasa), Burundi, Rwanda, and Uganda.

Morocco

As we have seen (in chapter 1), Morocco has become a major producer of cannabis. However, networks separate from the cannabis business have turned to the production of hard drugs and have brought in Colombians and Italians to assist them. Moroccan government efforts to combat drug trafficking are inadequately funded and though the government established a coordination unit to control the fight against drugs—Unité de Coordination de la Lutte Anti-Drogue (UCLAD)—it has achieved only indifferent success. Legislation allows prison sentences of 30 years for serious drug offenses and fines ranging from $20,000 to $80,000, although 10 years is the most likely sentence for drug traffickers arrested in Morocco. UCLAD's coordination measures, however, appear less than effective. There is in Morocco, as in many other countries where drug trafficking has become a significant factor, a conflict between the forces of law and order (in this case backed by European Union pressures) and the value of the drugs trade to the country's economy. Cannabis, which is processed into hashish, resin, or oil, is exported to Algeria and Tunisia and smuggled into the Spanish enclave of

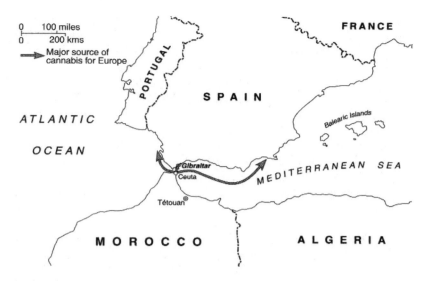

Figure 15.1   Morocco: cannabis to Europe. (Cartography by Map Creation, Ltd., Maidenhead, Berkshire, U.K.)

Ceuta, whose economy depends on such smuggling, and is then moved to Spain from where it is distributed to other European destinations (see Figure 15.1). Given the wealth accruing to this illegal cannabis business, Morocco has no economic motive to stop the trade, no matter what pressures are brought to bear on the government, while stamping out—or trying to eradicate—the trade would lead to major social unrest.[11] Most Moroccans who take drugs use cannabis, though there is now a small domestic market for cocaine and heroin.

South Africa

On August 4, 1996, Rashaad Staggie, a suspected drug dealer, was set on fire with petrol and shot to death by demonstrators opposed to drugs in South Africa. This execution was carried out by the Cape Town Muslim organization known as People Against Gangsterism and Drugs. The demonstrators had approached the drug dealer's home in a motorcade of 500 vehicles. Such an anti-drugs demonstration made little difference to the growth of drug activity in the country as a whole. In 1995, for example, the South African authorities revealed that cannabis was grown on 83,000 hectares (205,100 acres) of land—putting production on a par with that in Morocco—to place South Africa at the top end of the cannabis-producing nations. The cannabis is produced mainly in Transkei but also in Kwazulu Natal. It is also produced in the neighboring countries of Botswana, Lesotho, and Swaziland, and most of it ends up in the urban areas where it is consumed. The South African marijuana market is valued at several billion dollars. Cannabis is exported to Britain and the Netherlands, and in March 1995, for example, two tons of marijuana bound for Holland were seized in the port of Durban. By the mid-1990s, according to the South African authorities, cannabis production had passed that of Mexico, the United States, and Colombia to make the country the world's leading producer. South Africa has also become a major consumer of Asian heroin and a leading African market for hallucinogenic drugs. South Africa is now the largest market for Mandrax (methaqualone), a popular depressant that is widely used by addicts in South Africa, Zambia, Zimbabwe, and Botswana, and is readily available in Johannesburg and Durban. It is mainly imported from India. Although the South African government is committed to the fight against drugs, the country has developed into a significant transit area for both cocaine from South America and heroin from the Far East. Apart from its own growing demand for these drugs, they are principally destined for the European market. Drug trafficking through South Africa received a major boost when the country emerged from the long years of apartheid-induced isolation and was reintegrated into the world free-market economy. This, however, only strengthened a drug culture that had already been in place, partly as a result of apartheid policies. During the hearings of the Truth and Reconciliation Commission and the trial of Wouter Basson, who had had responsibility for the government's chemical and biological warfare, it was revealed that the apartheid government had acquiesced in drug trafficking among certain ethnic groups and had produced illegal drugs, primarily Mandrax, so that these could be used as an instrument of social and political control. By 2000 South Africa had emerged as a transit hub for drug smuggling. This role was greatly assisted by the fact that South Africa has the most advanced transportation, communications, and banking infrastructure in Africa. Its highly developed international telecommunications system, its direct air links with South America and Europe, as well as its 4,830 kilometers (3,000 miles) of porous land borders each contribute to make drug trafficking—and other illegal smuggling activities—a going concern.

Continent-Wide Drug-Trafficking Activities

The development of cannabis production for export out of Africa during the 1990s was one aspect of the spread of drug activities on the continent as a whole. Traditionally, cannabis production had been for domestic or local consumption, but during the 1990s extensive cannabis cultivation for export was undertaken in Ghana, Kenya, Morocco, Nigeria, and South Africa. This change was indicated by the fact that increasingly cannabis crops, which had been grown in association with other crops and so were hidden, were now being grown on their own over substantial areas. Cannabis (and its derivative marijuana) is first intended for the domestic market, then exported across borders for use in neighboring countries, and finally exported to markets outside Africa, mainly Europe. In 1993, for example, the Customs Cooperation Council announced that in 1992 "total quantities of the marijuana seized in Europe and in Sub-Saharan Africa have grown 130 percent in comparison with last year (1991), and reached 3,600 kilograms." Seizures in Europe suggest that Nigeria and Ghana have become the principal sources of Sub-Saharan cannabis reaching European Union countries.

A brief roundup of other African countries shows just how widespread drug trafficking has become. Angola, divided by war up until the beginning of the twenty-first century, is used increasingly as a transit country for cocaine and heroin destined for Western Europe and other African countries. Benin has also become a transshipment point for drugs destined for Europe and the United States; these mainly originate in Nigeria. Some cannabis is also grown in Benin, though seizures have been small-scale, while transit through Porto Novo, which is on the border with Nigeria, allows Benin traffickers to deal with Yoruba smugglers from Nigeria. In any case the Yoruba live on either side of the border and maintain close cross-border links. The Cape Verde islands are another transshipment point for drugs from both Latin America and Africa destined for Europe. The Democratic Republic of Congo (Kinshasa) cultivates cannabis for domestic consumption. By 1996, in the Republic of Congo (Brazzaville), a majority of the cannabis fields found near many of the country's villages were cultivated on behalf of politicians, while areas close to Brazzaville were used as rear bases for private militias to grow cannabis. In ex-President Lissouba's base area of Dolisie, his militia also grew cannabis. Following the cocoa crisis of 1988–1989 in the Ivory Coast, a significant number of farmers turned to the illicit cultivation of cannabis to offset the drastic fall in prices of their usual cocoa and coffee crops. Most of these crops are destined for local consumption, but the Ivory Coast has also become a minor transshipment point for heroin from Southwest and Southeast Asia en route to Europe and for cocaine from Latin America to Europe. Egypt (Cairo) is a major transit point for heroin and opium from the Golden Triangle and the Golden Crescent en route to Europe, Africa, and the United States and is extensively used by Nigerian couriers. Ethiopia is an important transit country for heroin coming from Southwest and Southeast Asia on its way to Europe and North America and for cocaine from South America destined for the markets of Southern Africa. Qat is cultivated, both for local use and for export to Djibouti and Somalia. As well as producing cannabis (the Devil's tobacco) throughout the country for both domestic consumption and the international trade, Ghana has become a transit point for heroin from Asia destined for Europe and North America, and cocaine from South America destined for Europe. When Guinea's Sekou Touré died after ruling the country for 25 years through his military clique, the new president, Lansana Cont, was obliged to open up the control of illicit operations that formerly had been in the hands of the military to a range of power-hungry groups so that drug trafficking was given a boost. During the civil war that eventually brought him to power in Liberia, Charles Taylor turned to drug trafficking to provide him with the finances he needed, and he used the port of Buchanan between 1990 and 1992 as his center for illicit trading. He had Greek and Lebanese trading partners and exported cannabis in return for guns and ammunition. Once the ECOWAS peacekeeping operation had been mounted in Liberia with the ECOMOG forces led by Nigerian troops, there was intense air traffic in and out of Springfield airport between Liberia and Nigeria, and every time a plane landed the airport was cleared of staff and cordoned off by armed Nigerian soldiers while illicit cargoes such as drugs were handled. Liberia has developed into a significant transshipment point for Asian heroin and South American cocaine. On the opposite side of Africa, the island of Madagascar is becoming another transshipment point for Asian heroin. Madagascar also cultivates cannabis, including wild varieties, principally for domestic consumption. The neighboring island of Mauritius has also become a minor consumer as well as transit point for Asian heroin and grows small amounts of cannabis for local consumption. Meanwhile Mozambique, one of the poorest countries in Africa and the world, has developed into another transit hub for South American cocaine as well as methaqualone from India destined for the South African market. In July 1996, after a long and painstaking investigation, seven senior police officers and four magistrates were among 50 people, also including local government figures, who were arrested on drug-related charges in Mauritania. The government claimed it had broken up an extensive drug-trafficking network. Drugs have become closely associated with the guerrilla movement in Senegal's southern breakaway Casamance region. The Diola communities, virtually cut off from the rest of Senegal by the Gambia enclave, began to demand independence in the early 1980s when they formed the Mouvement des Forces Démocratiques de la Casamance (MFDC). The MFDC has been largely bankrolled by the proceeds from cannabis production, which by the end of the twentieth century sold for $80 a kilo at the farm gate. In the early days of its rebellion, the MFDC collected a tax on locally grown cannabis and endeavored to protect the families that grew the crop. Later, however, it forced people to grow the crop so as to finance the revolt. As the export of marijuana from the region became more organized and valuable, so Senegalese drug traffickers began to work with others from the neighboring states of Liberia, Ghana, and Nigeria. Senegal also became a transshipment point for Asian heroin moving to Europe and North America. In Somalia, the warlords who operate to the north of the Kenyan border in that troubled land have come to see the routing of heroin through their territories as their main source of income. Some of the consignments of drugs that these Somali warlords handle are dropped offshore by ships, to be carried inshore by the tides. Nigeria's small neighbor Togo has become a transit state for Nigerian cocaine and heroin traffickers. The Central African state of Zambia is a transshipment point for methaqualone, heroin, and cocaine bound for Southern Africa and Europe and is also a regional center for money laundering. Its neighbor Zimbabwe has become a significant transit point for African cannabis and South Asian heroin, Mandrax, and methamphetamines destined for the South African and European markets.

Over two-thirds of the countries of Africa are now involved in drug trafficking at one or more levels, whether as producers of cannabis (the only homegrown African drug), transit countries, money launderers, or consumers, and the evidence in almost every case is that drug trafficking is on the increase. This is hardly surprising in the world's poorest continent when the large sums of money involved in trafficking operations are taken into account. Moreover, even where African countries have government antinarcotics programs in place, in almost every case these require more money and resources than those which governments are able to make available for the task. Just to take the example of Morocco, a poor country on the doorstep of Europe that can earn as much as $5 billion a year from the export of cannabis, the question that cannot readily be answered by those who would stop the trade is simply this: Why should Morocco ban a trade that brings it such big financial returns as long as Europe is willing to buy the cannabis or marijuana that it can supply?

16
Europe

A drug-smuggling exercise that went wrong for the traffickers and was uncovered in 1992 is typical of the way drugs are brought into Europe, the routes taken, and the nationalities involved, especially once Eastern Europe had opened up to more normal relations with Western Europe following the end of the Cold War. On November 20, 1992, a consignment of 350 kilograms (772 pounds) of cocaine was seized in Hamburg on board a Russian cargo ship from Panama. The drugs were hidden in shipments of fake "Reebok" sports shoes and blue jeans. They were then to transit through Poland and be re-exported to Western Europe. The three Poles who came to pick up the cargo were arrested, as was the mastermind behind the whole operation, a Nigerian who was arrested in Frankfurt.

The European Union summit held in Dublin during December 1996 included recommendations on "strengthening the capacity to deal with the fight against drugs." Earlier in the year a proposed summit meeting set for March between France, Germany, and the Benelux countries to work out a common approach to combat cross-border drug smuggling was postponed indefinitely following a meeting between French and Dutch officials in the Hague. France was highly critical of the tolerant Dutch stand on soft drugs and claimed that this made the Netherlands a conduit for the entry of drugs into the European Union as a whole and that the Dutch government did not do enough to prevent drug trafficking through the port of Rotterdam. In response to demands from its European Union partners, in particular France, the Dutch legislature voted on April 2, 1996, to tighten the country's traditionally liberal attitude to the sale of marijuana by reducing the amount of the drug that could be sold openly in "coffee shops" from 30 to 5 grams (1.1 to 0.2 oz.). The move was the first of a series of measures designed to meet the demands of its neighbors who insisted on tougher anti-drug laws prior to the full implementation of the removal of border controls as outlined in the Schengen Agreement of 1985. Other measures planned included sanctioning tougher police action against drug users convicted of petty crimes, discouraging "drug tourism" by foreigners drawn to the Netherlands by its liberal attitude to marijuana use, and reducing the number of "coffee houses" supplying the drug to 1,000.

Over April 12–16, 1996, the sixth meeting of foreign ministers of the Group of Rio and the European Union was held in Cochabamba, Bolivia. In their final declaration the ministers recognized that drugs posed a global threat and stressed the responsibility of the international community to face the problem together. Also in April a meeting of Lusophone foreign ministers was held in Maputo, Mozambique. Those countries taking part included Angola, Brazil, Cape Verde, Guinea-Bissau, Mozambique, Portugal, and São Tomé and Príncipe. The participants agreed to create a Lusophone Community and to finalize the arrangement at a summit in Lisbon the following July. Their communiqué reflected their growing concern about drug trafficking. The June 1996 contract killing of Victoria Guerin, one of Ireland's best-known investigative journalists, highlighted unease over Ireland's growing drug connections. Organized crime and drug dealing had become of major concern to the Irish public. Prime ministers from the member states of the Central European Initiative (CEI) held a summit meeting in Graz, Austria, on November 8–9; and in an end-of-conference communiqué the CEI claimed the meeting had agreed to coordinate the fight against drug dealing and money laundering, and that members had recognized the importance of cooperating with Russia on matters of "an all-European nature." This calendar of developments in Europe during 1996 is not untypical of the ongoing concern with the drugs problem. Too often, however, although concern about the drugs problem is demonstrated by meetings and pronouncements, there seems to be little change in the rate at which drugs are imported, distributed, and used.

Belgium

In January 2001 the Belgian cabinet approved plans to legalize the use of cannabis, although it resisted calls for the introduction of a drugs regime as tolerant as that in the Netherlands. After a heated debate the coalition government reached a compromise that would make it legal to grow or smoke cannabis but not to buy or sell it. Smoking openly in public places would still render Belgians liable to prosecution under laws to prevent "social nuisances." Only in March 2003, however, did the Senate approve by only 30 votes to 19 the new law legalizing the personal possession of small amounts of cannabis. The selling of cannabis, however, remained illegal, raising curious questions as to how individuals were to obtain their "small amounts." Recent surveys had revealed that up to 40 percent of the country's 10 million population had had some experience of cannabis; since the Dutch border (and a more relaxed drug regime) was only about an hour's distance away from most Belgians, some liberalization seemed inevitable. A spokesman for the Ministry of Consumer Affairs and Health, Paul Geerts, said that plans to allow Dutch-style cafés, where cannabis was legally available, had been judged to "go too far." He said that there were two alternatives for those who wished to obtain cannabis: "You can grow it yourself, or most people in Belgium know where you can buy it in the Netherlands." There would be no limit placed on the amount that people could possess for their personal use. These new Belgian regulations placed cannabis on a par with alcohol and nicotine in terms of the health risks that the drug posed. The prime minister, Guy Verhofstadt, said prosecutors would be instructed not to pursue people for possession. "This is a policy," he said "that is being followed in many of the countries in the European Union." Other European Union countries, however, took a tougher line against the drug. The health minister, Magda Alvoet, said that the new measure was a recognition that the judiciary should no longer interfere in the personal use of cannabis: "The criminal judge won't interfere any more in the lives of people who use cannabis on a personal basis and who do not create harm or do not become dependent. We want to create an extra space of liberty, but we want to do it in a controlled manner."[1]

The Netherlands

In March 1997 President Jules Wijdenbosch of Surinam announced plans to join forces with neighboring countries to establish a multilateral organization to track and prosecute drug traffickers. His government cooperated with the Dutch authorities to increase the level of drugs surveillance over flights from Surinam to Amsterdam. The Netherlands had requested the extradition of Surinam's former military ruler, Desiré "Desi" Bouterse, for smuggling drugs into the Netherlands. In June 2000 the Dutch Second Chamber (lower house) narrowly approved a nonbinding motion calling for the decriminalization of the wholesale trade in cannabis. The motion, which was passed by 73 to 72 votes, did not have cabinet approval. The object of the motion was to remove the anomaly whereby licensed "coffee shops" were allowed to hold and sell small quantities of cannabis while their suppliers remained liable to prosecution. After the vote, Justice Minister Bent Korthals indicated that he would not draw up legislation to comply with the motion. The 60 local authorities, which regulated coffee shops in the Netherlands, were said to be in favor of the change and, following the vote, the mayor of the city of Nijmegen, Edumond d'Hondt, said that he would fight any resistance to the change by the cabinet and threatened to bring a lawsuit if it did not comply with the wishes of the legislature. The debate about "coffee shops" in Amsterdam featured in the magazine *The Free Amsterdam Guide*, for example, and an attempt was made at the end of the century to squeeze out the troublesome coffee shops that dealt in the harder drugs and thereby attracted criminals. The Netherlands approach to drug use is increasingly one that sees it as a health problem rather than a crime, while coffee shops are seen as a way of separating marijuana smokers from the underworld. The Netherlands, with its more tolerant attitude toward drug use, has become something of a whipping boy for those countries that want to prosecute the war on drugs more harshly. President Jacques Chirac of France, for example, has blamed the Netherlands for France's drug problems, even though, according to *Time* magazine, the former has fewer addicts per thousand than France and supplies France with fewer drugs than Spain, Pakistan, and Morocco. On the other hand, U.S. drugs czar Barry McCaffrey described the progressive drugs policy of the Netherlands as "an unmitigated disaster."

Drugs and Sport

There are many anomalies in the attitudes of European countries toward the use of drugs, and sports play an important role in these. On October 24, 2000, the trial opened in Lille, France, of eight persons charged with conspiracy to provide banned substances to three teams in the 1998 Tour de France cycle race. Observers anticipated that the trial would uncover further evidence of widespread use of drugs by competitive cyclists. The trial continued until December 22 when seven of the eight accused were convicted, given suspended sentences, and fined. The French star, cyclist Richard Virenque, was acquitted. Meanwhile, in May 2000 the former head of East Germany's sports confederation, Manfred Ewald, and a sports doctor, Manfred Hoppner, went on trial accused of causing grievous bodily harm to 142 young sportswomen by prescribing a program of anabolic steroids. The trial was seen as an unprecedented public examination of the project, which had aimed to produce superhuman athletes by feeding them with performance-enhancing drugs without their knowledge. Ewald was the most senior former official to be brought before the courts on doping charges since the collapse of the German Democratic Republic. The use of anabolic steroids and other performance-enhancing drugs by sportsmen and sportswomen has become so widespread that testing for drugs has become automatic at all major sports events, though it is debatable whether this is done in order to counsel the competitors against harming themselves or whether the real concern is simply about one team or competitor taking an unfair advantage over rivals.

Liberalization

At the beginning of the new century some member countries of the European Union were setting the pace (ahead of the United States) in decriminalizing certain drugs. On July 6, 2000, the Portuguese assembly voted to decriminalize the use of drugs such as cannabis and heroin and to treat drug use (or abuse) as an illness. By this decision Portugal joined Spain and

Italy in decriminalizing the possession of drugs. The eventual logic of such decriminalization measures must be also to decriminalize the provision of drugs—but that more difficult decision will take some time to materialize.

Spain and Gibraltar

Meanwhile, seizures of large quantities of drugs, which demonstrate the level of police activity, are normally the most dramatic events in the war on drugs, and in July 1999 the Spanish authorities carried out a sea assault on a cargo vessel, the Panama-registered *Tammsaare*, in the mid-Atlantic. Ten tonnes (9.8 tons) of cocaine, Europe's largest ever haul, was seized on this occasion. This was followed a few days later by a series of dawn raids by the police in Madrid and the northwestern region of Galicia, which led to the discovery and seizure of a further 5.2 tonnes (5.1 tons) of cocaine. Some 60 members of the Spanish–Colombian drug ring were arrested in connection with these hauls. This was the world's second-largest haul; 20 tonnes (19.7 tons) of cocaine had been seized back in 1990 in the United States. European anti-drugs initiatives are uneven, especially where other political considerations get in the way. The dispute between Britain and Spain over the future of Gibraltar is a case in point. In March 1995, for example, the chief minister of Gibraltar, Joe Bossano, described Spain's refusal to have direct talks with Gibraltar as incomprehensible and as an impediment to effective implementation of joint initiatives on drug trafficking and money laundering. The following July, however, under joint Anglo-Spanish pressure, the Gibraltar government passed antismuggling legislation. Two days of serious disturbances followed when the police seized high-speed launches used to convey cigarettes and hashish from Gibraltar to Spain. Community and business leaders held mass demonstrations on July 12 and called for an end to smuggling, although the activity provides Gibraltar with a significant part of its income. Britain also threatened Gibraltar with direct rule unless the latter tightened its legislation controlling financial services. Britain was concerned with curbing illegal trafficking to Spain of cigarettes and cannabis, as well as money-laundering activities.

Switzerland

During the latter half of the 1990s, Switzerland took measures to tighten its legislation on drugs. In February 1995, as many as 300 police took part in an operation to clear the notorious "needle park" around the old station of Letten in Zurich; this area had become the symbol of a liberal policy on drugs where thousands of drug dealers and addicts collected daily. The police action was part of a clampdown on foreigners suspected of drug dealing and followed new anti-drug legislation passed in December 1994. In a referendum of September 1997, 71 percent of Switzerland's voters supported the government's anti-drugs policy, which included supplying regular doses of heroin for long-term heroin addicts. The three-year-old program showed that crime levels among addicts had fallen by 60 percent. The referendum had been forced by the "Youth Without Drugs" campaign, which had argued that the state should concentrate on repressing drug use. In April 1999 a government-appointed panel recommended that the Swiss authorities should legalize the consumption of cannabis since, they argued, the prohibition of the drug had failed. Ministers rejected the recommendation, however, as well as the call for the issue of licenses to sell the drug, on the grounds that drug-taking tourists and traffickers would be encouraged to visit the country. In June 1999 the Swiss Federal Tribunal ruled that the drug ecstasy was "in no way a harmless substance" but that it did not pose a serious risk to physical and mental health. Although it remained illegal to use ecstasy in Switzerland, the drug was classified as "soft," with the result that only comparatively mild punishments would be handed out to those found in possession of it.

Ignoring international criticism, in 2001 Switzerland made clear its intention to maintain its liberal drugs policy. It proposed to legalize the consumption of cannabis and allow its production and sale under strict regulations. This would only be for Swiss residents, and there would be a ban on export.

The United States and Europe

The annual report of the United Nations Commission on Narcotic Drugs, published on February 23, 2000, criticized the over-prescription of psychotropic drugs in both the United States and Europe, arguing that the practice tended to undermine efforts to prevent drug abuse. The report drew attention to the contrast between the large quantities of narcotics available in illicit markets with the shortage of pain-relieving drugs in many poor countries. Ten countries accounted for 80 percent of analgesic morphine consumption, while 120 countries had little or no access to analgesic drugs.

In its annual appraisal of the world drug scene for the purpose of the certification procedure, the U.S. government examines countries, first and foremost, in terms of whether their drug activities have an impact on the United States. Drug trafficking covers a number of related but different activities: consuming the drugs—that is, providing a market for them; smuggling them into the markets; acting as transit countries to pass the drugs to markets further along the line; and money laundering. Europe, under such examination, may be divided into three groups of countries: a minority that are not involved in the drugs business at all, at least according to the CIA, although this is hard to believe; the countries of Western Europe that are principally important as one of the world's main drug-consuming groups; and the countries of Eastern Europe whose primary involvement is as transit countries for drugs destined for the big consumers of Western Europe. Of course these roles overlap, and in terms of probability the countries of Eastern Europe will become increasingly important as markets as well as transit points.

The following European countries are given a clean bill of health according to *The World Factbook 2000* published by the CIA: Denmark, Finland, the Holy See, Iceland, Liechtenstein, Luxembourg, the Isle of Man, Monaco, Norway, San Marino, and Sweden.[2] It seems unlikely, given the general propensity in the rich Western world to use drugs, that the five Scandinavian countries—Denmark, Finland, Iceland, Norway, and Sweden—are in fact free of this habit, though it is possible that it is on a limited, controllable scale. The other members of this group of 11 countries are in fact mini-states and of these at least two—Liechtenstein and Luxembourg—would appear likely candidates for money-laundering activities.

Western Europe

The countries of Western Europe form one of the world's two principal markets for drugs: they possess the money and the different population groups most likely to take to drugs—bored middle classes, hyperactive money earners who seek relief in drug relaxation or thrills, a range of fashionable young party-goers, and, at the lower end of the social scale, the dropouts and marginalized for whom drugs have become a way of life for which, if necessary (and it usually is), they will commit crimes in order to finance their habit. Belgium is a source of precursor chemicals for South American cocaine processors and a transshipment point for cocaine, heroin, and marijuana entering Western Europe. France is a major consumer of South American cocaine and Southwest Asian heroin as well as a transshipment point for these drugs. Germany is another major consumer of cocaine and heroin, as well as European-produced synthetic drugs, and also acts as a transshipment point for cocaine and heroin. It is a source of precursor chemicals for South American cocaine processors. Ireland has developed into a major transshipment point for hashish from North Africa destined for Britain and the Netherlands, as well as a growing hashish consumer. It also handles European-produced synthetic drugs. It is still only a minor transshipment point for heroin and cocaine destined for Western Europe. Italy is both an important gateway into Europe for South American cocaine and Southwest Asian heroin entering the European market, as well as a major consumer of these drugs. The Netherlands is a major producer of illicit amphetamines and other synthetic drugs and acts as an important gateway for cocaine, heroin, and hashish entering Europe. It is a major consuming country and has been praised and blamed in equal proportion for its liberal attitude toward drugs and its "coffee shop" experiment. Portugal has developed into an important gateway for South American cocaine entering the European market. It is a transshipment point for hashish from North Africa destined for Europe, and it is a consumer of heroin from Southwest Asia. Spain acts as a crucial gateway into Europe for both South American cocaine and North African hashish. It is also a transshipment point, as well as consumer, for Southwest Asian heroin. Switzerland is a transit country and consumer of South American cocaine and Southwest Asian heroin. The application of more stringent regulations on banks by the government has reduced its role as a money-laundering center. The United Kingdom acts as a gateway country for South American cocaine entering the European market as well as being a major cocaine-consuming country. It is also a major consumer of Asian heroin. It is a producer and major consumer of synthetic drugs and a producer of synthetic precursor chemicals. It is a major money-laundering center. The above countries—Belgium, France, Germany, Ireland, Italy, the Netherlands, Portugal, Spain, Switzerland, and the United Kingdom—may be said to constitute Western Europe, along with the Scandinavian countries.

Eastern Europe

The countries of Eastern Europe and the Balkans are more important as transit countries for Western Europe than as consumers, though this will almost certainly change as they become more prosperous. Albania has become an active transit point for Asian heroin, hashish, and cannabis on their way through the Balkans to Western Europe. On a smaller scale it is also a transshipment point for cocaine from South America destined for Western Europe. Albania produces both opium and cannabis in limited quantities. Albanian narco-trafficking organizations are rapidly expanding their operations in Europe. Austria, which in terms of wealth qualifies as a Western European country, is a transshipment point for heroin from Southwest Asia and cocaine from South America destined for Western Europe. Belarus, part of the former Soviet empire, cultivates both the opium poppy and cannabis to a limited extent for its domestic market, although its output could be expanded. It is also a transshipment point for illicit drugs to and from Russia and to the Baltic States and Western Europe. Bosnia and Herzegovina is a minor transit country for marijuana and opiate trafficking into Western Europe. Bulgaria, on the other hand, has developed into a major transshipment country for heroin from Southwest Asia destined for Western Europe and, to a lesser extent, for cocaine from South America. It is a marginal producer of precursor chemicals. Croatia is another Balkan-route transit country for heroin from Asia destined for Western Europe and a minor transit center

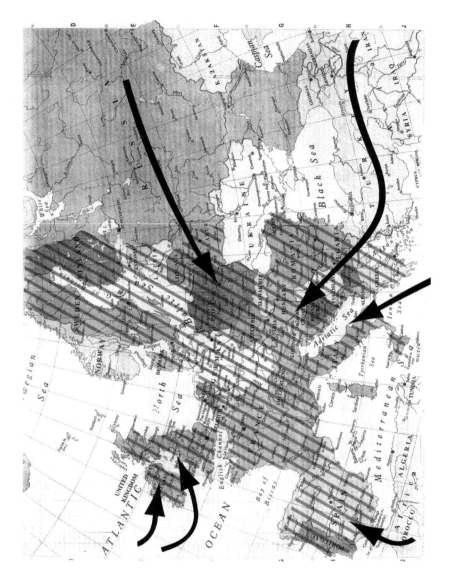

Figure 16.1 Europe is the second-largest market for drugs after the United States and these enter Europe in a variety of ways as indicated. (Cartography by Map Creation, Ltd., Maidenhead, Berkshire, U.K.)

for maritime shipments of cocaine from South America. The Czech Republic is now a major transshipment point for Southwest Asian heroin and a minor transit point for South American cocaine bound for Western Europe. Domestic drug consumption, especially of locally produced synthetic drugs, is on the increase. Estonia is an important transshipment point for opium and cannabis from Southwest Asia and the Caucasus coming via Russia, and cocaine from South America, destined for Western Europe and Scandinavia, as well as synthetic drugs from Western Europe en route to Scandinavia. It may also be involved in manufacturing precursor drugs. Greece acts as another gateway into Europe for traffickers bringing cannabis and heroin from the Middle East and Southwest Asia to Western Europe and smuggling precursor chemicals to the east. A limited amount of South American cocaine enters Greece and is either consumed locally or transits through the country. Latvia is another transit country for opium and cannabis from Central and Southwest Asia to Western Europe and Scandinavia, as well as for cocaine from South America and synthetics from Western Europe en route to the CIS. There is some production of amphetamines, ephedrine, and ecstasy for export. Lithuania is another transit country for drugs from Southwest Asia and South America en route to Western Europe and Scandinavia. Macedonia is developing as a transshipment point for heroin and hashish from Southwest Asia and a minor transit point for cocaine from South America into Western Europe. Malta acts as a minor transshipment point for hashish from North Africa to Western Europe. Moldova, another former Soviet republic, cultivates limited quantities of opium and cannabis, most of which is destined for CIS countries; it is also a transshipment point for drugs from Southwest Asia coming through Central Asia to Russia and Western Europe, and possibly also for the United States. Poland is a major producer of amphetamines for the international market and a minor transshipment country for Asian and South American drugs destined for Western Europe. Romania is another important transshipment point for heroin from Southwest Asia using the Balkan route to Western Europe. It also handles small quantities of South American cocaine destined for Europe. Serbia and Montenegro act as another transit point for heroin from Southwest Asia using the Balkan route to Western Europe. Slovakia has also become a transshipment point for Asian heroin destined for Western Europe. Similarly, Slovenia has become a minor transit point for Asian heroin destined for Western Europe and produces some precursor chemicals.

Russia is in a class by itself and, straddling the whole of Asia as well as being part of Eastern Europe, it is becoming increasingly important as a transshipment route for heroin as well as cannabis from both the Golden Triangle and the Golden Crescent en route to Western Europe, as well as cocaine from South America, destined for either Europe or the United States.

There is some cultivation of both cannabis and opium in Russia, though as yet on a limited scale, and the production of amphetamines, principally for the domestic market. The Russian government has an active drug eradication program. There is a growing domestic market for drugs.

We have already examined the role of Turkey in relation to Asia, but it is of great importance as a major transit route for heroin from Southwest Asia into Western Europe and to the United States, while Istanbul is a major center for drug-trafficking organizations. There is limited cultivation of both cannabis and opium in the Ukraine, mainly for consumption in the CIS countries; there is also some production of synthetic drugs destined for Western Europe. The government eradication program is limited in scope. The Ukraine has become a transshipment point for drugs from Africa, South America, and Turkey to Europe and Russia.

Trends in Europe

The annual report of the European Monitoring Centre for Drugs and Drug Addiction for 2000 provided a rundown of overall trends in Europe at the end of the twentieth century.[3]

Cannabis

At least 45 million Europeans (18 percent of those aged 15 to 64) have tried cannabis at least once. Use is higher among younger age groups and in some countries use has doubled since 1990; in others the rise is less marked, and in a few it has stabilized. Cannabis remains the primary drug in drug offenses, mostly for use or possession rather than trafficking. Numbers of seizures have increased sharply since 1997.

Amphetamines and Ecstasy

These are the second-most commonly used drugs in Europe. Following increases in the 1990s, ecstasy use appears to be stabilizing or even falling, while amphetamine use is stable or rising. Drug use continues to shift away from large dance events to more geographically diffuse club, bar, and private settings.

Cocaine

Although cocaine is less commonly used than amphetamines or ecstasy, its use is rising—particularly among socially active groups—and spreading to a broader population. Between 1 and 6 percent of those aged 16 to 34 and 1 to 2 percent of schoolchildren have tried cocaine at least once, although some surveys show levels of up to 4 percent among 15 to 16 year olds. Higher levels of use are found among socially outgoing, employed young adults in urban centers. Severe problems associated with smoking "crack" have been identified, particularly among female sex workers.

Heroin

Heroin dependence remains broadly stable. Known users are a largely aging population with serious health, social, and psychiatric problems, although indications of heroin use among some younger groups are noted.

Multiple Drug Use

Patterns of weekend and "recreational" drug use increasingly involve combinations of illicit and licit drugs, including alcohol and tranquillizers.

Problem Drug Use and Demand for Treatment

Patterns of problem drug use are changing across the European Union. The European Union has an estimated 1.5 million problem drug—mainly heroin —users (between 2 and 7 per 1,000 inhabitants aged 15 to 64); and of these an estimated 1 million are likely to meet clinical criteria for dependence.

Policy and Strategy Developments

New drug strategies have been adopted by Spain, France, Portugal, and the United Kingdom as well as by the European Union itself. National drug policies are becoming more balanced in approach, with greater emphasis placed on demand reduction relative to supply reduction. The drugs problem is increasingly viewed in a broader social context and common aims include drug prevention, reduction of drug-related harm, and crime deterrence.

The report also devotes a chapter to the drugs problem in Central and Eastern Europe (the Central and Eastern European Countries—CEECs). As the report says, drug-related problems in the CEECs were generally limited until the geopolitical changes of 1989, which led to increased permeability of borders, greater movement of people and goods, and a decline in traditional social values. Since that time, the report claims, the drug phenomenon has spread through all sectors of society. Increasing numbers of seizures of marijuana and cannabis plants suggest that both trafficking and local production are escalating in most of these countries. Opiates used in the CEECs include heroin, whose use in the region was negligible until the early 1990s. Although cocaine use in these countries is relatively rare, its availability has increased, as has its use, trafficking, and seizures. Over the last four years of the twentieth century, the popularity of all synthetic drugs grew, particularly in the three Baltic States, the Czech Republic, Hungary, Poland, Slovakia, and Slovenia, to become an integral part of youth dance culture. Despite increased law enforcement measures against illicit drug use and trafficking, drug demand reduction remains a low priority in most CEECs.

According to the CIA, almost all the countries of Europe, both East and West, are involved to some extent, and often very deeply, in the illicit drugs business. Western Europe shares with the United States the dubious distinction of being one of the world's two largest markets for all kinds of drugs, while Eastern Europe is deeply involved in the transit trade. It is unrealistic to suppose that countries that first become involved as transshipment countries will not, in due course, also become consumers. Given that this huge group of countries with common borders, highly developed systems of transport and communications, and sophisticated criminal mafias are all involved, often very heavily, in drug trafficking, the possibility of reducing the size of the European markets for the variety of drugs offered under such conditions seems extremely slim.

17
Money Laundering

Profits from drug trafficking can only be usefully employed by the criminal underworld when the money has been legitimized. Drug traffickers must convert their illicit gains into acceptable, respectable money before it can be used and before they can branch out into legitimate occupations that allow them to enjoy their wealth without fear of investigation. The major end process in drug trafficking, therefore, is money laundering. Consequently, one of the principal tasks of the UNDCP is to tackle this problem. Thus, to deprive drug traffickers of their illicit power and influence, UNDCP assists governments in efforts to counter money laundering and confiscate assets gained from drug trafficking. It is supporting a $4.3 million global program to improve the capacity of legal and law enforcement systems, which includes the creation of financial intelligence units to reduce the vulnerability of financial systems.[1]

The end objective of all drug trafficking is to make money; and the way to curtail successful drug trafficking, therefore, is to make the legitimization of drug-trafficking profits increasingly difficult, if not impossible. The task is a daunting one since there are always crooked bankers and businessmen who will turn a blind eye to the source of finances that come their way provided they themselves are able to make a profit out of handling such money.

The "war on terrorism" that followed the events of September 11, 2001, in the United States lent new urgency to the problem of combating money laundering when, at the end of October 2001, the 29 member countries of the FATF met in Washington to consider U.S. proposals to reinforce the international crackdown on financing for terrorist groups. FATF was founded in the 1980s as the principal intergovernmental body responsible for promoting policies to combat and curtail money laundering by drug traffickers. Its policy has been to curb money laundering by blacklisting countries that fail to adopt strong laws to end the flow of criminal money through their banks. Formerly, the United States had been reluctant to support fully the blacklisting efforts of FATF, but post-September 11, 2001, the Bush administration decided to embrace FATF as a tool in its war on terrorism. New measures proposed to deal with terrorists could equally be applied to drug traffickers. And new legislation to be passed by the U.S. Congress will outlaw smuggling of bulk cash and give the treasury secretary new powers to punish foreign banks that do not cooperate in stopping or trying to stop money laundering.

The end of the 1990s had witnessed multilateral support for stronger measures against those countries that failed to deal with money laundering effectively when FATF considered what steps to take against states, including FATF members, that did not provide effective international administrative and judicial cooperation in this matter. Three steps were involved: first, to define noncooperative countries; second, to identify governments that fell into this category; and third, to decide what international action should then be taken. FATF expressed its concern about Austria, which is a member of FATF, because of its failure to eliminate the anonymous passbook savings accounts that were available there. FATF warned Austria to eliminate such accounts or face suspension from the organization. In 1999 FATF invited three leading countries of Latin America—Argentina, Brazil, and Mexico—to join as observers, to be given full membership when they had satisfied FATF membership requirements. Also in 1999 the G-7 finance ministers formed the Financial Stability Forum. At its first meeting the forum agreed to focus on three issues: the implications of highly leveraged institutions, the offshore financial services sector, and short-term capital flows and their possible relation to money laundering. In December 1999 the UN General Assembly adopted the International Convention for the Suppression of Terrorist Financing, which requires states to criminalize the provision or collection of funds to be used to conduct terrorist activities. At the same time a UN Convention against Transnational Organized Crime was being negotiated for adoption. There is, then, an increasing range of machinery, both national and international, to tackle money laundering. As the U.S. INCSR for 2000 made plain:

> People who commit crimes need to disguise the origin of their criminal money so that they can use it more easily. This fact is the basis for all money laundering, whether that of the drug trafficker, organized criminal, terrorist, arms trafficker, blackmailer, or credit card swindler. Money laundering generally involves a series of multiple transactions used to disguise the source of financial assets so that those assets may be used without compromising the criminals who are seeking to use the funds. Through money laundering, the criminal tries to transform the monetary proceeds derived from illicit activities into funds with an apparently legal source.[2]

Huge profits from drug trafficking remain largely worthless unless these can be moved into legitimate financial and commercial activities. This is not easy to do and, at the very least, requires legitimate organizations to cooperate in the process, passively by turning a blind eye to any questions about the source of such funds or, more actively, by becoming partners in the money-laundering venture. Given the size of the funds seeking legitimate outlets, it is not surprising that major financial institutions, such as banks, as well as countries, have been prepared to accept large inputs of what they must have known to be the profits of crime without asking any questions.

Money laundering is a growing part of the global "black economy" in which more and more countries are involved. Financial speculations are an increasingly important aspect of shadow economies, and market deregulation has led to huge increases in Western speculative financial transactions:

> Of the trillions of dollars that daily flow around the global marketplace, less than 10 percent are connected with the real economy. The remainder are largely concerned with gambling on the future performance of stocks and markets. While its magnitude is unknown, it has been argued that money laundering by criminal networks has become part of such huge speculative flows. Indeed, given its willingness to take risks, it has probably amplified the turbulence and volatility of such movements.[3]

Revelations concerning the fact that during the 1990s some $20 billion of International Monetary Fund aid to Russia left that country and was laundered in Europe and the United States gives little hope that the practice can be prevented when sums on such a scale are involved. The Bank of New York, it turned out, was deeply implicated in this huge ex-Russian money-laundering operation, and it was shown that some of Russia's giant natural resource and energy utilities were linked to illicit trade, tax evasion, and money-laundering networks.[4]

The various stages through which money has to pass before it has been effectively laundered indicate the problems involved in detection. These stages begin with the placing of such money in the financial system, for example, in offshore banks or other financial institutions in countries that have, or exercise, few controls. The next stage is to separate these funds from their source by means of currency swaps, investments in stocks, or using the money for loans for legitimate businesses. The third stage in the process is to conceal the linkage of the money with its original criminal source. This can be done by employing a variety of techniques such as multicountry registration, packing boards with accomplices or relatives, or exploiting loopholes in the laws of countries where the money is being placed. Given the fact that the rapid movement of money around the world is now accepted as a normal part of the global economy, such dirty money can be legitimized very quickly and the more quickly it is legitimized, the harder it is to track down. According to one authority, Western Europe is thought to have some of the weakest money-laundering regulations of the developed economies.[5] Like the constantly changing routes that are employed by drug traffickers, money launderers have to be innovative and ready to change their methods and adapt quickly to new regulations or attempts to control their activities.

The total acceptance by the West of "market forces" has made money laundering easier than it was in a more financially regulated age. Thus, the liberalization of the movement of capital since 1974 has greatly facilitated the recycling of "dirty money"—from the sale of drugs and arms to the pickings of white-collar criminality—in legalized tax havens and, thanks to banking secrecy, through the financial and industrial organizations otherwise respected in countries "of excellence" reputed for their professionalism and democratic institutions.[6]

At its 14th regular meeting in Quito, Ecuador, during May 1995, the Group of Rio foreign ministers called for a hemispheric agreement, to include the United States, to fight drug-related money laundering. There were a good many such calls over the last years of the twentieth century, but money laundering, and not just from the proceeds of drug trafficking, is clearly a growth industry and it appears to be outstripping efforts to curtail it. Illicit trading of all kinds makes a significant contribution to the acquisition of foreign currencies for national economies. As a former World Bank adviser has pointed out: "Once they have been laundered and recycled in the international banking system, narco-dollars can be used by the governments of developing countries in order to meet their obligations with their creditors." The international community (in this context, the West) strives through the UNDCP to pass laws to punish money laundering, yet for most creditor nations, "As long as the service of the debt is assured, creditors do not make any difference between 'clean money' and 'dirty money.'"[7] It is, in any case, unrealistic to expect poor, deeply indebted countries to be squeamish about demands for forms of "rectitude" from the rich countries. In such circumstances African countries—generally the world's poorest and most indebted —are unlikely to take effective anti-drug-trafficking measures. Nigeria, in particular, which is the leading drug-trafficking country in Africa, is able to launder money from this source easily since its banks have branches all over the world and it does not have anti-money-laundering laws in place. Nigerian money launderers operate global networks to repatriate the proceeds of drug trafficking and, though in 1995 the Nigerian government enacted a decree to combat money laundering from the proceeds of drug trafficking, enforcement has been uneven, and there have been few seizures of laundered money and no convictions.

Tom Nevin, a respected South African journalist who has examined the growth of money laundering on the African continent, says that no one knows how much "dirty money" circulates through the world's financial system every year, although there is probably much more than even the most generous calculations would suggest. Probably half of all the laundered money is derived from the illicit drugs trade, while the rest comes from all other organized crime. Africa, he claims, is rapidly emerging as the "washing machine" of illegal money as criminals and mafias seek new places through which to launder their illegal gains. As new measures are put in place in the developed world to make money laundering increasingly difficult, so Africa, which lacks similar legislation or regulations, has become a principal target area for money laundering. The continent has a reasonably sophisticated banking system, while there is also plenty of "loose" legal money about since most African communities operate cash economies and a large proportion of the people prefer to keep their income in cash rather than banking it—a practice that makes it easy for money launderers to operate. Moreover, "The worldwide integration of financial systems and the freedom to move capital across international boundaries has made money laundering possible on an extensive basis, simply because it becomes difficult to trace assets and paper trails are easy to destroy."[8] Although the UNDCP is, apparently successfully, encouraging the development of anti-money-laundering legislation in a majority of countries in the world, it is the financial institutions that are obliged to carry out most of the preventive work. They must, therefore, pay strict attention to the fundamental principle of business practice, which is to know your customer—a practice that many banks have not adhered to when large sums of money have been involved. Only when a customer's business and his or her transactions are fully understood does it become possible for bank staff to recognize attempts at money laundering.

The 1988 South African Prevention of Organized Crime Act became a leader in the fight against money laundering. It defines the circumstances that constitute the offense of money laundering and lays down heavy penalties for it. In addition, it creates an obligation on anyone involved in business to report suspicious transactions. In 2000 the South African government created a new regulatory body, the Financial Intelligence Service. And South African penalties, of fines up to 100 million rand or 30 years in prison "should serve as notice of the government's intent not to let South Africa become a haven for money launderers." Although there is nothing new about money laundering, it is the recent increased integration of the world's financial systems and the removal of barriers that now allow criminals to move their money easily from one country to another while at the same time making the tracing process more difficult.

The growth of money laundering and the parallel efforts to curtail it vary enormously around the world. The proliferation of casinos in the poor Caucasus state of Georgia makes more sense when they are also seen as convenient means of covering money-laundering activities by that country's mafias. Hong Kong has introduced new legislation in an effort to strengthen its anti-money-laundering regime and this includes new reporting requirements for financial transactions, while sentences for money laundering have been increased. In March 1999 Jamaica amended its 1996 Money Laundering

Act to require the reporting of suspicious transactions in an effort to meet international standards. The government has devised a financial analysis unit to identify money-laundering activities, though it has to find trained staff to run it. China, though it has draconian laws against drug traffickers and regularly executes offenders, has so far failed either to enforce properly or strengthen its anti-money-laundering laws and has remained outside the Asia-Pacific group on money laundering. In 1995 the Supreme Court of the tiny island state of Vanuatu confiscated $1.5 million from international drug traffickers who had laundered the proceeds through Australia in 1989 and then moved the money to trust companies in Vanuatu.

The Commonwealth heads of government, law, and finance ministers have called on all member states to combat money laundering and eliminate corruption. The Commonwealth secretariat assists member countries to implement the 40 recommendations on money laundering of the FATF. The secretariat also collaborates with three regional groups—the Caribbean FATF, the Asia-Pacific Group on Money Laundering, and the Eastern and Southern African Anti-Money Laundering Group. The secretariat was responsible for setting up this last group and continues to give it support. It facilitated the group's first meeting in Dar es Salaam in April 2000 and, with FATF and the UN Global Programme on Money Laundering and collaborating countries, helped develop the group's work program. The secretariat provides experts to help these groups. The techniques of money launderers constantly change as they try to evade preventive measures. They are becoming ever more sophisticated and use complex ways to manage their finances so as to legitimize their assets, obscure profits, and hide the identity of transferred funds. In response to their increasing professionalism, the secretariat has published a model of best practice for combating money laundering in the financial sector, which is an updated version of an earlier set of guidance notes originally published in 1996. This manual is intended for use by Commonwealth policy makers, regulators, and financial institutions. Commonwealth assistance in combating money laundering is funded by the Commonwealth Fund for Technical Cooperation.[9]

The CIA's annual *The World Factbook 2000*[10] lists more than 20 countries that it considers to be involved in money laundering, though this is not to say that the practice is not carried on in many other countries as well. These, however, are either countries where major money laundering is practiced or small territories, often islands, which are ideally placed to attract offshore financial activities. The CIA list provides an interesting slant on money laundering, with the majority of the countries it names falling into the small, island category, most especially in the Caribbean region. These countries include Antigua and Barbuda, which is seen as more important for money laundering than for the transshipment of drugs; Aruba, which fulfills both roles; the Bahamas; Belize; the Cayman Islands, described as "vulnerable to drug money laundering and drug transshipment"; Dominica, which is a drug transshipment point and also "vulnerable" to money laundering; the Netherlands Antilles, described as a money-laundering center; and Panama, which is described as a major money-laundering center, and though the monitoring of financial transactions is seen as improving, Panama has yet to prosecute anyone for money laundering. Three South American countries are singled out as money-laundering centers: Chile, Ecuador, and Venezuela. Asian money-laundering centers pinpointed by the CIA are Cambodia; Hong Kong, whose position (part of China yet with separate financial institutions that have special ties with the West) gives it immense money-laundering potential; Singapore, whose position as a hub of Far Eastern trade and finance also makes it a natural choice as a money-laundering center; and Thailand, whose membership in the Golden Triangle naturally places it in the forefront of likely money-laundering activities. Other countries considered include Switzerland in Europe, though it is suggested that the introduction of more stringent government regulations means it is now used significantly less as a money-laundering center; the Ukraine, still a minor player but becoming more important; the United Arab Emirates, which benefits from both its proximity to the Southwest Asian drug-producing countries and the free-trade zone in Dubai; and Zambia for Southern Africa. Finally, and most important as major money-laundering centers, are Britain and the United States. This is clearly a selective list; money laundering, whether connected with the illicit drugs trade or any other criminal activities, is a universal phenomenon. However, two broad distinctions can be made. At the top level are banking and financial centers such as New York and London, Hong Kong, and Singapore, whose financial tentacles stretch worldwide and whose wealth offers endless opportunities for investment once money has been legitimized. At the other end of the scale are the tiny offshore economies where poverty and corruption both work to make illegal transactions attractive.

In the aftermath of the September 11, 2001, terrorist attacks in New York and Washington, the United States has paid increased attention to the informal money-changing operations that are common throughout the Middle East and known as "hawala." In November 2001, U.S. investigators decided to crack down on Barakat, a Somali-based financial and telecommunications conglomerate that operates in 40 countries worldwide; the investigators believed that Barakat had funneled tens of millions of dollars to the al-Qaeda organization of Osama bin Laden. Hawala operations are difficult to control. As an example:

> A Somali . . . who wants to send home money from Minneapolis in the United States, where there are more than 50,000 Somali nationals, takes the cash to a local hawala agent, who issues a receipt of payment. Details

of who is to receive the money and the sum is then telephoned, faxed, or e-mailed to another agent in the network and handed over to the recipient. Over time, payments in one direction will be matched by those in the opposite direction, avoiding the need for cross-border transfers.[11]

Such networks have long been seen as a potential problem and as possible conduits for the proceeds of crime.

The UN Office for Drug Control and Crime Prevention (ODCCP) has highlighted the money-laundering potential of offshore financial havens and centers and has suggested a number of areas that require further attention and investigation. These include:

- the misuse of a state's sovereignty to provide safe havens for criminal proceeds.
- the proliferation of international business corporations that are routinely used in money-laundering schemes because they provide an impenetrable layer of protection around the ownership of assets.
- the abuse of offshore trusts.
- the role played by some professionals protected by legal privileges.
- the effect of the "dollarization" of the global market and the likely effect of the introduction of the euro.
- the usefulness of free-trade zones for legitimate purposes, since tariffs have declined.
- the vulnerability of casinos to money laundering and the need for the industry to be more carefully regulated.
- the need to develop and more efficiently exchange financial crime intelligence.
- the proposal that financial-center countries publish data, including information on both the asset holdings and the flows of funds through accounts of all types, in a reasonably coordinated way to form a basis for informed answers to police questions.
- the quasi-absence of regulation of offshore banking, and excessive bank secrecy protection, that sometimes even blocks regulators in a country from effectively supervising branches of their home country's financial institutions.
- the importance of improving financial investigators' training in order to equip them to deal with complex schemes.[12]

This is a formidable list of areas to be investigated and regulated and demonstrates not only how complex a process it is to combat money laundering, but also the scale of institutions and interests that are involved and will resist any close examination of their connections with dirty money as long as they are able to do so.

However, attitudes to problems, once established, remain in place for a long time before any significant change takes place. For example, following the assassination of the Colombian presidential candidate Luis Carlos Galán Sarmiento in 1989, his brother Alberto commented on the approach to the drugs war by the new Bush administration (George H. W. Bush had been President Reagan's "drugs czar") and pointed out that Washington's strategy avoided "the core of the problem"—"the economic ties between the legal and illegal worlds," the "large financial corporations" that handle the drug money. According to Noam Chomsky, George Bush had been instrumental in terminating the main thrust of the real "war on drugs." Thus, officials in the enforcement section of the Treasury Department monitored the sharp increase in cash inflow to Florida (later Los Angeles) banks as the cocaine trade boomed in the 1970s, and "connected it to the large-scale laundering of drug receipts." They brought detailed information about these matters to the DEA and the Justice Department. After some public exposés, the government launched Operation Greenback in 1979 to prosecute money launderers. It soon foundered; the banking industry is not a proper target for the drug war. The Reagan administration reduced the limited monitoring, and Bush "wasn't really too interested in financial prosecution," the chief prosecutor in Operation Greenback recalls.[13]

In other words, then as later, money laundering through U.S., British, or other European banks is too valuable a business to be curtailed; and the fact that these countries have not seen fit to tackle this problem properly makes nonsense of the rest of the war on drugs.

18
The Cannabis Debate

The debate about the legalization of cannabis raises important issues: should the drug be legalized in the major consumer countries of the West, for example, the impact on the whole drug scene would be incalculable. Most crucially, it would highlight the much-quoted argument that soft-drug users automatically graduate to hard drugs.

In December 1997 the teenage son of Britain's home secretary, Jack Straw, was caught buying cannabis from two reporters from the *Daily Mirror*. Much discussion of the scam and the laws relating to drugs subsequently appeared in the British press. The home secretary's son could have purchased over twice the amount he obtained from the *Mirror* reporters openly in a Dutch "coffee shop." The Dutch approach to the problem is markedly different from that of other Western consumer countries. The Dutch authorities see drug use as a health and education issue, and though cannabis is illegal, the police turn a blind eye to its use in order to keep soft-drug consumers away from hard drugs and dealers. Bob Keizer, head of drug care at the Netherlands Health Ministry, said at this time: "We do not believe in punishing young people for using cannabis for a short period of their life. We think it is irresponsible to give a young person a criminal record for something most will outgrow."[1] In contrast, both Britain and the United States treat all drug use as a law-and-order issue and have "drugs czars" to ensure the law is applied. Some drug experts in Britain have argued that the Americans—with their high rates of addiction, death, and drug-related crime—lost the war against drugs years ago; and, they suggest, Britain, which has moved into the top place in Europe as a consumer of drugs, is in danger of losing the war, too, unless it changes its approach. In December 1997 it was estimated that four out of every ten 15 year olds had tried cannabis and that two in ten took it regularly. According to an in-depth study by the development charity, the Joseph Rowntree Foundation, many British drug users are independent, confident people who lead active lives and come from "good" families. There were signs that more European countries were considering following the Dutch lead, and, for example, some German regions were considering allowing cannabis to be sold in chemists' shops.

In November 1996 a majority of Californian voters passed Proposition 215, which allowed seriously ill people or their "primary caregiver" to grow and use marijuana on a doctor's recommendation. This was followed by the appearance of marijuana clubs, which, however, rapidly became prime targets for government officials determined to prevent the legalization of the drug.[2] Meanwhile, activists in six other states and Washington, DC, were pushing to put the issue to the ballot; President Clinton's administration increased its efforts to prevent medical marijuana use becoming a national phenomenon. In Britain a House of Lords Committee on Science and Technology considered two questions: How strong is the scientific evidence in favor of permitting medical use (of cannabis)? and How strong is the scientific evidence in favor of maintaining prohibition of recreational use? It was pointed out: "The recreational use of alcohol and tobacco are attached by risks. There is no ban on either at the moment." This naturally led to the question: "At what level of risk should people be allowed to make their own judgment about whether they are prepared to take that risk?"[3] During March 1998 supporters of the campaign to decriminalize cannabis, led by the *Independent on Sunday* newspaper, met in London's Hyde Park and marched to Trafalgar Square, where they were addressed by a number of European campaigners for a reform of the drug laws. At the same time the Home Office was being pressed to introduce a new penalty that would force people found taking cannabis to submit to antidrug counseling, while first-time offenders would be given the choice of either being prosecuted or receiving a caution and some treatment. These ideas were promoted by the Association of Chief Police Officers in an attempt to clamp down on the use and availability of cannabis. At this time there were an estimated 500,000 illegal cannabis plants being grown in Britain, while cautions for the possession of the drug had risen tenfold over 10 years, from 4,048 in 1986 to 40,391 in 1995.[4] The debate about cannabis made a substantial impact during March 1998, but the views of medical professionals were mixed. By late April 1998 the British Medical Association (BMA) threw its support behind MPs who were campaigning for cannabis to be legalized for therapeutic purposes. At the same time, the BMA said that the smoking of a cannabis joint could be five times more carcinogenic than a tobacco cigarette and came down firmly against the legalization of cannabis for recreational use, claiming that "because of the way in which it is smoked, a single cannabis joint delivers the equivalent in carbon monoxide, irritants, and carcinogens of 4 to 5 cigarettes and carries similar cardiovascular and respiratory health risks including the risk of lung cancer."[5] Later in 1998 the medical journal *The Lancet* claimed that cannabis was less harmful than alcohol or tobacco.

In August 1999 the new leader of Britain's Liberal Democrat Party, Charles Kennedy, called for a radical overhaul of Britain's drug laws and suggested that a royal commission should be set up to look at the decriminalization of cannabis and other soft drugs. Then, in January 2000 researchers at New York's Memorial Sloan-Kettering Cancer Center published research which showed that regular smokers of cannabis can be more than 30 times as likely to get cancer of the neck, throat, mouth, and larynx than those who have never inhaled. It was the first study to make a definite link between smoking of cannabis joints to full cancers of the head and neck. Adding to the debate, Eugenia Calle of the American Cancer Society said, "One joint is more dangerous than one cigarette, but the effect of cigarettes on health is probably greater because people just smoke so many more cigarettes." As soon as one "expert" produced a theory or evidence on one side of the debate, another "expert" would come up with equally weighty evidence to support the other side. Thus, in October 2000 Dr. Leslie Iversen of the University of Oxford's Department of Pharmacology published a book, *The Science of Marijuana*, in which he exposed the "myths" surrounding marijuana and found that cannabis was an inherently "safe drug" that did not lead to cancer, infertility, brain damage, or mental illness. He found that cannabis was far less toxic than other drugs and had "an impressive record" compared with heroin, cocaine, tobacco, or alcohol.[6] However, when in November 2000 the British politician Mo Mowlam, who was the cabinet office minister responsible for drugs, suggested that using cannabis might not be "an addictive process" and hinted at the possibility of a government rethinking of its drugs policy, a Downing Street (prime ministerial) comment denied any such possibility: "We have absolutely no plans to decriminalize or legalize any drugs that are currently illegal."

In February 2001 new research in the United States indicated that smoking cannabis could affect the fertility of both men and women. And so the debate—a Western rather than a world debate—continued with governments, and especially those of Britain and the United States, maintaining their hard antilegalization lines. And yet, these governments could find they are losing the battle. In Britain cannabis users sought to be prosecuted in an effort to break down the laws on prohibition, with some even proposing to run for office in Britain's 2001 general election. The police and the Crown Prosecution Service have become increasingly unwilling to prosecute for the possession of cannabis. Pro-cannabis users want to be prosecuted in order to plead under the new Human Rights Act, which prevents the government from unduly interfering in the private life of an individual. At the same time, campaigners are becoming increasingly open about using and growing the drug. In March 2001 the British House of Lords recommended that cannabis-based drugs for medicinal purposes should be legalized. A member of the Alliance for Cannabis Therapeutics, Claire Hodges, said: "The law is nonsense. People are prosecuted for using something that eases their pain and distress, which is appalling."[7]

The Independent, a liberal British newspaper, has featured interviews or stories by a range of relatively high-profile people who have "outed" themselves as "pot" or cannabis smokers. In a feature article of March 2000 by Nick Lezard, he suggested: "The number of people who smoke dope or take ecstasy is probably incalculable. The number who don't, but who do not mind if you do it around them, is even larger. At times, it feels as if lighting a cigarette is more frowned upon at the dinner table these days than sparking up a doobie."[8] The same writer goes on to suggest that the real menace to both user and spectator is the violent drunk. What he suggests is that "between the poles of complete abstinence and slavish addiction lies a bell curve of reasonably responsible self-medication."

It had become plain by the beginning of the new century, if not much sooner, that the drug laws were simply not working. Moreover, the Runciman *Report of the Independent Inquiry into the Misuse of Drugs Act 1971* provided the government with the opportunity to change them. One of the myths created by opponents of any relaxation of drug laws has always been the argument that smoking cannabis must lead to injecting heroin. During 2001 Britain was subjected to a kind of high-class farce: Politicians, who up to that point had never admitted to taking drugs, now did so but insisted that they had not enjoyed the experience. As Anne McElvoy argued: "Teenagers are not fools. They know that the reason so many people take narcotics is that they like the effect of them."[9] The Labour government of Tony Blair showed great caution over the issue of cannabis or any other relaxation of the existing laws. The Home Office minister, Charles Clarke, said that, "Any relaxation of the drugs laws would send the message that taking drugs is OK." Such attitudes simply did not take into account what is actually happening in the clubs across the country, where many thousands of young people regard cannabis and ecstasy as a normal aspect of their lives. The publication in March 2000 of Runciman's report came to the conclusion that the 1971 act was the least successful on the statute book and needed to be reviewed. As Anne McElvoy wrote: "It makes criminals out of otherwise lawabiding people, needlessly strains relations between police and community, and wastes the time and resources of the judicial system." A Mori poll at this time showed that 50 percent of respondents favored a change in the law that would stop its targeting cannabis users, while a second BBC-sponsored poll showed the figure to be closer to 70 percent. The debate was to continue throughout the year, with inevitable comparisons being made with the Dutch experiment in a regulated market where cannabis may be consumed in "coffee shops," or the Spanish practice of not enforcing the law.

By mid-2001 health arguments were being advanced, for example, to suggest that smoking cannabis put middle-aged users at a higher risk of heart attacks. Researchers in Boston, Massachusetts, claimed that the chances of having a heart attack increased nearly five times in the first hour after smoking marijuana. They studied 3,882 patients, aged 20 to 92, and found that of the 124 patients who had used marijuana during the past year, nine had taken the drug in the hour before their heart attack. The researchers found that on average the risk of a heart attack was 4.8 times greater in the first hour after smoking marijuana and 1.7 times during the second hour. But as Dr. Murray Mittleman, the director of the Cardiovascular Epidemiology Department at Beth Israel Deaconess Medical Center, said: "The risk associated with marijuana use is about the same as the risk we found for strenuous physical exercise, and a little higher than that observed for sexual intercourse."

The political breakthrough came in mid-2001 when Britain's home secretary, David Blunkett, said that he was interested in radical new police proposals on cannabis possession. He said that hard drugs such as heroin and crack cocaine should be the "absolute priority" for police resources. He was reacting to a scheme run by the police in Lambeth, south London, where they had decided to caution rather than arrest those found in possession of cannabis. He took this line at the time when all the contenders for the leadership of the Conservative Party (they sought to replace William Hague, who had announced his resignation as party leader) called for a national debate on Britain's drug laws. At last it seemed that a British politician was prepared to break the taboos about drugs that, for example, treated cannabis and heroin use as though they were in the same category. As it became clear that the government was seriously considering changing its approach to the drugs problem, groups and individuals lined up on one side of the debate or the other. The medical debate about the impact of cannabis on health remained controversial, with supporters of the drug claiming it had few harmful effects and opponents arguing that it could do serious damage and that its long-term side effects included distorted perception, lower reaction times, impaired coordination and driving skills, and lack of motivation. At the same time it was revealed that more adults used cannabis in Britain than in any other European state and that almost half the nation's teenagers had smoked the drug by the time they left school. It had become clear, however, that support for liberalization of the cannabis laws stretched across the political spectrum from Tory libertarians to hard left socialists. The call for zero tolerance, on the other hand, came from politicians on the right of the Conservative Party, led by its former chairman, Lord Tebbit.

The relaxation of the approach to cannabis was forced by the action of a policeman rather than a politician when the borough police commander in

Brixton, south London, Brian Paddick, launched an experiment: those caught with small amounts in the Lambeth area would not be arrested but instead would be given a warning, have the cannabis confiscated, and their names kept in a file that could not be cited in court proceedings. This approach was generally welcomed in Brixton, where cannabis is widely smoked, especially by the black community. The Brixton experiment, apart from its common-sense approach, aided the national debate and led to a number of politicians expressing forthright views. Thus Peter Lilley, a former deputy conservative leader, said early in July 2001: "What we have actually is the perverse situation that by making cannabis illegal it is only available through illegal sources which are the same channels that handle hard drugs. So we are forcing cannabis users into the arms of hard drug pushers. More people actually try cannabis in this country than in states where it is legally available." By this time the debate was increasingly about when cannabis would be decriminalized. The government, however, still demonstrated an extraordinary unwillingness to debate the issue while the outworn argument that cannabis was bound to lead on to hard drugs was still deployed. As the medical journal *The Lancet* noted: "Moderate indulgence in cannabis has little ill effect on health, and decisions to ban or legalize cannabis should be based on other considerations." Finally, the home secretary, David Blunkett, in line with the government's 1998 drug strategy, signaled the shift in the government's stance when he called for an "adult intelligent debate" on the subject, thus taking a contrary stand to his predecessor, Jack Straw. As Blunkett made this move, the outgoing chief inspector of prisons, Sir David Ramsbotham, called for the decriminalization of cannabis. He said: "The more I think about it, and the more I look at what's happening, the more I can see the logic of legalizing drugs, because the misery that is caused by the people who are making criminal profit is so appalling. I think there is merit in legalizing and prescribing, so people don't have to go and find an illegal way of doing it."[10] He, in turn, was joined by two former home secretaries, Lords Jenkins and Baker, calling for a change in the law.

And so, in a dramatic relaxation of its drugs policy, the British government decided to abandon hunting for cannabis smugglers and dealers; instead, law enforcement officers, including customs officials and police, were instructed to target "hard drugs" such as heroin and cocaine. Large-scale seizures of cannabis and subsequent prosecutions would be a by-product of investigations into Class A drugs. As a customs official explained: "It is not that we plan to stop seizing cannabis when we come across it. However, the need to focus on Class A drugs means cannabis seizures will now take place as a by-product, not as an end in themselves." And a chief police officer said: "Overall, the government strategy is about reducing harm. That has to mean placing a priority in reducing the supply of Class A drugs." This change of emphasis had undoubtedly been assisted by the release of figures of British consumption of cocaine and heroin, which showed that Britons use twice as much cocaine as the previous official estimates for the whole of Western Europe. During 2000 British hard-drug users consumed between 28,000 and 36,000 kilograms (61,730 to 79,370 pounds) of heroin and 35,000 to 41,000 kilograms (77,160 to 90,390 pounds) of cocaine.[11] The next step for cannabis appeared to be the creation of a system of outlets similar to the "coffee shops" used in the Netherlands.

The cannabis debate raised other interesting issues. The right-wing conservative commentator Bruce Anderson, for example, claimed: "The greatest social ill, moral hazard, and health hazard confronting modern Britain are not heroin, cocaine, and marijuana. They are illegitimacy, abortion, and tobacco." Politicians generally, however, remained defensive; having for years taken hard-line stances against all drugs, they found it difficult either to admit that they had ever taken drugs, or if they did admit to doing so in their youth, they accompanied the admission with an assertion that they had not enjoyed the experience. In October 2001, a Labour MP, Jon Owen Jones, launched a bill to "legalize and regulate the sale, supply, and use of cannabis for recreational and therapeutic purposes" and suggested users could be allowed to smoke soft drugs in "cannabis cafés." He claimed that the illegal cannabis trade in Britain was worth an estimated £1.5 billion a year and suggested that struggling farmers (affected by the devastations of foot-and-mouth disease) should be allowed to grow cannabis as a cash crop. At least Mr. Jones admitted enjoying cannabis in his youth. He said: "All over the world it is becoming clear cannabis use is a fact of life and trying to deal with it through the criminal justice system is absurd."[12]

An immediate and welcome result of relaxing the law on cannabis consumption was the likelihood that more police could be drafted onto the streets of London. It was estimated that 74,000 man-hours a year could be saved by allowing the London police to concentrate their resources on tackling more serious crimes. It was also estimated that a typical case of cannabis possession would take a police officer off the streets for five hours and cost £10,000 to bring the offender to court, where he would receive an average fine of £45.

The saga of cannabis in Britain, a drug that is certainly no more harmful than tobacco, was highlighted in the mid-1960s when the police raided the home of Rolling Stones guitarist Keith Richards, where a group of people was found under the influence of marijuana. Richards was sentenced to a year in prison and fined £500, while Mick Jagger, then the most popular icon of the young, got three months in prison for possessing four "uppers" that had been bought legally in Italy. This high-profile case signaled the beginning of a long debate that was to last until 2001 and the relaxation of the law.

Other pop stars, including John Lennon of the Beatles, were also to be raided and fined for the possession of cannabis, but, if anything, such attention to the most popular youth icons merely served to make the drug more attractive, and by the turn of the century 40 percent of children aged 15 or 16 had tried it, while up to 50 percent of adults may also have used the drug, more adults than in any other country in Europe. Although a substantial number of people in authority at any time have probably believed that the drug should be legalized, almost none were prepared to say so during the 1980s when drugs were seen as politically taboo. During the 1990s, however, an increasing number of campaigners called for a change in the law and claims for the drug's therapeutic uses began to be advanced. As the debate grew, examples of the drug's use in other parts of the world as long ago as 500 BCE were advanced to show that it has always been around. In 1997, for example, the BMA concluded that the drug helped people suffering from multiple sclerosis, while it was also suggested that it might be beneficial for people suffering from epilepsy, glaucoma, asthma, high blood pressure, and weight loss associated with AIDS.

In general, the announcement by the home secretary that he wanted cannabis to be recategorized as a Class C drug was welcomed as a concession to reality, which among other results would lessen the antagonism between otherwise law-abiding citizens, particularly the young, and the police. (In July 2002 the home secretary announced that cannabis would be downgraded from a Class B to a Class C drug, making its possession for personal use a nonarrestable offense, by July of 2003.) Cannabis, however, would remain a classified drug, while smuggling and dealing in it would remain criminal offenses. The government, in a typical one-step-at-a-time approach, had decided that cannabis should be treated in the same way as anabolic steroids, as undesirable but no worse. The next step would have to be that of reconciling tolerance of consumption with punishing suppliers. Comments by three of the country's leading newspapers on October 24, 2001, were in favor. The *Daily Telegraph*, Britain's leading conservative broadsheet, said: "Mr. Blunkett is to be congratulated on venturing into this debate on drugs and the law, territory that many of his colleagues have found too inhospitable to enter. But now he should show his confidence in his assessment that cannabis is not an unacceptably dangerous substance, and have the courage to take the next logical step forward by legalizing the drug for an experimental period." The liberal paper *The Guardian* said: "Where Mr. Blunkett falls short is in failing to downgrade LSD and ecstasy from A to B class, as recommended last year [2000] by the Police Foundation's national commission, and rejecting its suggestion that possession of B and C drugs should be made nonimprisonable. The reason was pragmatic: Prison does more harm than good." The populist tabloid the *Daily Express* said: "A huge amount of police time is wasted enforcing the laws on this largely harmless drug. People are taken to court for possession of small amounts of it kept for personal use. Otherwise law-abiding people get a criminal record, courts are clogged up, and policemen diverted from more useful activities."

The debate moved on to the drug ecstasy, which is ranked as a Class A drug and is probably taken by over half a million young people every weekend. According to the charity DrugScope, 66 percent of its 900 member bodies, which include drug treatment agencies, police, probation services, researchers, and academics, wanted ecstasy to be reclassified as a Class B drug. The reclassification of ecstasy and LSD from Class A to Class B was recommended by the Runciman report produced for the Police Foundation in 2000. According to a spokesman for the Police Foundation, fewer people die each year from using ecstasy than from taking aspirin.

Meanwhile, a British pharmaceutical firm, GW Pharmaceuticals, was testing a cannabis-based painkiller. The company's chairman, Geoffrey Guy, said: "The greater liberalization being practiced by governments across the world gives me hope that we will be able to look at using cannabis for less serious conditions, such as mild rheumatoid arthritis."

It has become clear from actions taken in a number of countries that the time to accept the use of cannabis in the same way that we accept the use of tobacco is approaching rapidly in those countries where its use is currently a criminal offense. In Belgium in 1998, for example, the country's nine chief prosecutors issued a circular declaring that the crime of possessing marijuana was to be regarded as one of their lowest priorities. This decision led to legislation, due to come into effect in 2002, that Belgians will be able to possess cannabis for their own consumption but not to purchase it. Surveys showed that 40 percent of the country's population of 10 million had experience of cannabis. In Jamaica, the National Commission for Ganja recommended that adults should be allowed private use and possession of cannabis. The commission's report stated that cannabis has a "reputation among the people as a panacea and a spiritually enhancing substance [which] is so strong that it must be regarded as culturally entrenched." The report went on to argue that in small amounts, moderate use of the drug caused no short- or long-term health effects among most users. Jamaican officials rejected a threat of punishment from the United States should they decide to follow the commission's proposals. A senior government official said: "This is a matter that will be decided by the Jamaican parliament, and the island's sovereign parliament will not be swayed by any external threats."[13] A new Portuguese drug law, which came into effect on July 1, 2001, removed the threat of prison for possession of small amounts of any drug.

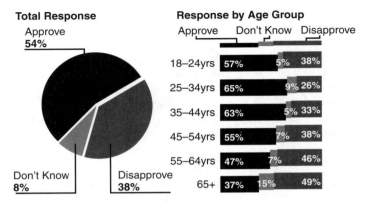

Figure 18.1   Public opinion on cannabis. (ICM/*The Guardian*, October 31, 2001.)

An Independent Communication and Market Research (ICM)/*The Guardian* opinion poll, taken at the end of October 2001, revealed that 54 percent of those polled approved of Home Secretary David Blunkett's decision to relax the laws in relation to cannabis (see Figure 18.1).

The change in the law in relation to cannabis and, more importantly, the changes of attitude by those in authority that this revealed, at once widened the whole drugs debate and posed questions that, sooner or later, must be addressed in relation to other drugs and the way in which they are currently regarded by the law and by the country's establishment.

19
Conclusions

Those who debate the problems that surround the drugs business in all its ramifications should never forget the freedom of the individual. This is a concept that is constantly taken for granted in the West and then conveniently forgotten. In East Harlem, for example, Puerto Rican crack dealers are high spenders, including what they pay for their own drugs, and they regard the money they earn from the trade as "something only I can control. No one could tell me what to do with it."[1] Such an attitude among a group generally seen as impoverished tells us a great deal about the need for human dignity. The current attitude toward the expanding drugs trade is to treat it as an illicit aberration that can be circumscribed and then policed. This approach makes no sense in relation to what has become one of the world's major activities: "The continuing growth and mutation of the global drug economy, for example, despite extensive international policing, is a good example of the adaptability of parallel and grey trade."[2] As the author of this statement also claims: "If history tells us anything, it is to be skeptical of the effectiveness of global policing." Figures for 1997 (assembled by the UNDCP) suggest that $17 billion is spent on food for domestic pets in Europe and the United States, $50 billion on cigarette consumption in Europe, $105 billion on alcohol consumption in Europe, $400 billion on drugs, $780 billion on military expenditure, and $1,000 billion on advertising.

Health services in Britain and elsewhere are far readier to treat those suffering from cancer, one of the ill effects of smoking, than they are to treat hepatitis C, which results from the employment of dirty needles by drug users.

The generally enlightened attitude toward drug addicts began to change in the 1970s:

> Until the early 1970s, Britain was a haven of enlightenment: every doctor in the country had the right to prescribe heroin for the welfare of patients. This reflected the idea, powerfully proposed by the Rolleston committee in 1926, that drug use should be seen as a problem which needed help, not as a sin which needed punishment. There were fewer than 500 addicts in the country, most of them musicians or Chinese. With a clean legal supply of their drug, they remained healthy and were able to live normal lives. Then three London doctors were caught selling inflated prescriptions; there was a moral panic; and Britain's resistance to prohibition started to crumble

under political pressure, some of it from the United States which was already committed to imposing a global policy of prohibition.[3]

The United States has exerted overt pressures on European countries not to deviate from policies of prohibition. Thus, when the Swiss held a referendum on limited heroin legalization in 1997/1998, the U.S. Congressional Subcommittee on National Security, International Affairs, and Criminal Justice openly intervened. "We wholeheartedly oppose this sort of government gambit," the committee declared as though it had some sort of jurisdiction in Switzerland.[4]

In the nineteenth century John Stuart Mill defined one concept of freedom in relation to religion:

> It remains to be proved that society or any of its officers holds a commission from on high to avenge any supposed offense to omnipotence which is not also wrong to our fellow creatures. The notion that it is one man's duty that another should be religious was the foundation of all the religious persecutions ever perpetrated and if admitted, would fully justify them.

Substitute drug taking in the above passage for religious observance and we approach the freedom anomaly inherent in the war on drugs.

Wars always lead to rapid changes in the rules. Hitler injected himself with methamphetamine eight times a day; Churchill, under the advice of his doctor, Lord Moran, took both amphetamines and barbiturates; Anthony Eden did battle with Suez on Benzedrine; and John F. Kennedy sped his way through the Cuban missile crisis, while an estimated 15 percent of Vietnam veterans returned to the United States as heroin addicts.[5] In 1987 it was reported that one in three bills in U.S. circulation had been used in cocaine transactions and 94 percent of American paper currency was said to be contaminated with traces of cocaine. According to author Sadie Plant: "Cocaine and American capitalism are only the most recent examples of a complex history of commercial activity and government control that says as much about the increasingly fraught relationship between markets and the state as about drugs themselves."[6]

The U.S. war on drugs may be dated from 1968, when President Lyndon B. Johnson established the Bureau of Narcotics and Dangerous Drugs with a mission "to enforce the laws and statutes relating to narcotic drugs, marijuana, depressants, stimulants, and the hallucinogenic drugs." Later, when President Richard Nixon threatened to suspend economic and military aid to Turkey if it did not eradicate its opium crop, the Turkish response was to argue that the problem was America's demand for heroin, not Turkey's ability to supply it. In 1973 Nixon created the DEA, which remains the primary anti-drugs agency of the United States. Unfortunately, the response by proponents of the war on drugs to any criticism of their aims appears all too easily to resolve itself into arrogant rejection. Thus the open letter addressed to UN Secretary-General Kofi Annan, in 1998 (see chapter 2) in which 500 leading international figures said, among other things, "We believe that the global war on drugs is now causing more harm than drug abuse itself" was dismissed by General Barry McCaffrey, President Clinton's director of national drugs policy, as "a 1950s' perception" without any attempt to address the issues. The U.S. policy of certification of countries, according to whether or not they are deemed by Washington to be taking effective measures against drug trafficking, acts as an open invitation to two-way blackmail. The United States offers aid on condition that particular anti-drug policies are adopted and threatens sanctions if they are not; the country concerned insists that it is doing its best, but a best that, too often, is designed to ensure the continued flow of U.S. aid rather than to curtail drug activities that are often of great economic value to the state. The process of certification, moreover, becomes a sham when it is argued, as is frequently the case, that U.S. national interests require certification to be granted even when the country in question is clearly not making any real effort to curtail drug trafficking. It then becomes clear that the war on drugs and certification measures are as much about a mechanism that enables the United States to intervene in the internal affairs of a sovereign country as they are about curtailing the drugs trade. Brazil is estimated to launder $50 billion a year from the drugs trade, a figure equivalent to 10 percent of the annual worldwide turnover. Money on such a scale represents the principal reason why demonizing drugs has not worked; instead, the war on drugs has produced one of the largest criminal fraternities in the history of crime. And on the home front in the United States (as discussed in chapter 7), both alcohol-related and tobacco-related deaths are on a greater scale than drug-related deaths, despite the fact that of these three only drugs are prohibited.

There are too many anomalies in the war on drugs for it to make logical sense. Thus it is legal in both Britain and the United States to prescribe Ritalin to hyperactive children. Critics of this drug claim it is creating classrooms of "zombies," and the justifications for its use would appear to be dubious in the extreme. Belated moves toward legalizing cannabis that occurred in Britain during 2001 and 2002 suggested, at last, how the argument that taking a soft drug must inevitably lead on to the use of hard drugs is in the process of being discarded. But Brian Paddick, the head of Lambeth police who pioneered a new approach to cannabis, was not to have everything his own way. Giving evidence before the Home Affairs Select Committee of the House of Commons, he said:

My view is that there are a whole range of people who buy drugs (not just cannabis, but cocaine and ecstasy) with money they have earned legitimately. They use a small amount of this drug, a lot of them just on weekends. It has no adverse effect on the rest of the people that they are with. They go back to work on Monday morning and are unaffected for the rest of the week.[7]

Paddick's views, however, were not held by many of his colleagues; and there was a clash of cultures in the police over the drugs issue as Paddick discovered when he was called before the metropolitan police assistant commissioner, Mike Todd, to explain his comments to the Home Affairs Select Committee. The metropolitan police commissioner, Sir John Stevens, meanwhile, had just announced a police crackdown on middle-class cocaine users in London bars and restaurants. The result, healthy enough, was to reveal deep divisions in the police about how to tackle the drugs problem. Paddick, however, probably came closer to the public mood than his superiors when he said: "If I felt my officers were going into nightclubs looking for people who were in possession of ecstasy, then I would say to them, and I would say publicly, that they were wasting valuable police time."[8] In December 2001 police reformers called for the mass prescription of heroin to addicts on the National Health Service and the consequent creation of safe injecting rooms or "shooting galleries" where heroin users could inject under controlled conditions in a move that would lead to the decriminalization of drugs. Such an initiative, so the police believed, would break the link between addicts and property crime. The Association of Chief Police Officers, which represents chief constables in England, Wales, and Northern Ireland, was preparing to announce this revolutionary change of policy in January 2002. By the end of 2001 it had become clear that Britain's drug laws were not working. The announcement by Home Secretary David Blunkett that he wanted to relax the laws on cannabis was no more than an acknowledgement of the failure of such laws to operate and the futility of pursuing a policy that was consistently ignored by the people at whom it was directed.

Drugs are big business, on a par with the oil trade, and to assume that such a business can be controlled by police action has become increasingly unrealistic. This assertion may be justified by examining one small aspect of the worldwide business. British gangsters, for example, make a turnover of £90 million a year supplying the drugs market for Ibiza's clubs in Spain, which are annually frequented by 450,000 British tourists. Ecstasy is the principal drug supplied, followed by cocaine, amphetamines, cannabis, and LSD. The dealers are a law unto themselves, and the local Spanish police admit they can do little to stop the trade. In any case, the Spanish police class ecstasy as a soft drug.[9]

The provision of drugs, at all levels, constitutes a worldwide industry; and if governments and law enforcement agencies began to view it in this light, they might make more sense of the efforts to control the trade, which, to date, have manifestly failed. If the structure of the drugs business—from raw materials to drugs to movement and supply to street sales—is examined, then it is as much a business as any other and perhaps should be treated as such and legalized. As a professor from Manchester University, Enid Mumford, has argued:

> Legalization would make price and quality subject to regulation, as in other businesses such as alcohol and tobacco. Decriminalization, on the other hand, although removing punishment for personal use, would leave the business in the hands of criminals, with all the associated uncertainty and dangers. Leaving things as they are while discussion focuses more on customers than on producers seems the least desirable option. If we are sticking with this strategy, the debate and action should at least be extended from the drug users to the total drug management system.[10]

When the war on terrorism got underway in Afghanistan following the terrorist attacks on New York and Washington of September 11, 2001, one target for U.S. and British troops operating in the country was said to be the £20 billion stockpile of opium and heroin which, it was claimed, Osama bin Laden and the Taliban would release onto world markets. The estimated 3,000 tonnes (2,950 tons) of opium then held in Afghanistan would be enough to manufacture 300 tonnes (295 tons) of heroin, which would be sufficient to supply the British market for 10 years. A spokesman for British Prime Minister Tony Blair said, "We want to see an end to opium production in Afghanistan." The chance of doing anything of the kind, even with the total defeat of the Taliban, seems remote. Members of the Northern Alliance have been as much involved with the production and marketing of opium as the Taliban, and they are unlikely to forego the trade once the situation in Afghanistan returns to some form of normality. As the head of the UNDCP in Islamabad, Bernard Frahi, said at the beginning of October 2001:

> There are very serious doubts about the future. We are seeing all the ingredients for illicit opium cultivation: civil war, an absence of law and order, and no alternative for farmers. The criminal gangs which control the refining and shipment of heroin are still very much in place. Opium provides credit and savings for farmers, while wheat fetches only two-thirds of the price, and there is no guarantee that you can sell your crop when it is ready. If farmers have a choice, they grow opium.[11]

On the other hand, should a successful coalition manage to stop all opium cultivation in Afghanistan, heroin producers in Myanmar (Burma), Colombia, and elsewhere would move rapidly to make up the shortfall in the world supply. And no one should be surprised because that is how international business enterprises have always worked.

A number of developments during the early months of 2002 did suggest both that the spread of drugs was increasing and that the war on drugs was failing. Disturbing indications of the growth of cocaine smuggling from Jamaica to Britain suggested that tighter airport security regulations in the United States had closed American destinations to "mules" from Jamaica, at least for the time being, and that instead they were concentrating on the British market, with as many as 1 in 10 passengers on flights to Britain attempting to carry drugs. The Narcotics Division of the Jamaican Constabulary admitted that it required help to deal with the increasingly sophisticated drug-smuggling operations that work out of the island. At the beginning of 2002 it was estimated that 65 percent of all the cocaine available in Britain was smuggled through Jamaica. The head of the Jamaican Narcotics Division, superintendent Gladstone Wright also admitted, what sadly has become normal, that corrupt police officers are part of the problem.

At the beginning of February 2002 a British chief constable, Richard Brunstrom, head of the North Wales Police, called for heroin to be prescribed free to Britain's 300,000 addicts. He said pure heroin should be provided on prescription for addicts since this would remove the need for addicts to commit crimes to pay for their habit. He told the *Police Review* magazine: "Heroin does not make you commit crime; it gets you addicted. If you could get free heroin, you wouldn't commit crime. We know that a third of all crime is committed by people to get money to support their drug habit." It was his view that the policy based on a war on drugs was "an almost unqualified disaster." Other senior police officers were known to support Brunstrom's views. But many people, including some senior police officers, were fiercely opposed to any relaxation of the laws toward cannabis, let alone the Class A drugs such as ecstasy or heroin. Meanwhile, it was estimated that every British drug addict cost the taxpayer £11,000 a year in health, court, and benefit costs, even though hundreds of thousands of "recreational" Class A drug users represent a burden of only £20 each per year, according to government research. As a result the annual economic cost of drug addiction has risen to between £10.9 billion and £18.8 billion, according to the Home Office minister, Robert Ainsworth. Other research at York University found that drug addicts cost the National Health Service, the state benefits system, and the criminal justice system £6.8 billion a year while social costs, mainly to victims of crime, came to a further £12 billion a year. More than 1 million people over the age of 25 and at least 400,000 people under 25 are believed to use Class A drugs but cost society less than £20 a year each. Such figures led Roger Howard, the chief executive of the charity DrugScope, to say: "The government seems to accept that over 95 percent of drug users do not have a drug problem and account for less than 1 percent of the total social and economic cost of drugs use in the country, yet it still persists in subjecting many to the costly and punitive criminal justice system."[12]

Logic, as opposed to politicians, would suggest that we have lost the war on drugs. This is so for a number of reasons, the first of which is human perversity. A substantial number of people worldwide like using drugs and intend to continue doing so no matter what prohibitions are imposed by governments. Second, as a direct result of the war on drugs and the criminalization of the drugs trade, "All the police and prisons in the world cannot buck a market where the tax-free profit on a kilo of cocaine is 20,000 percent."[13] In the same article as the one from which this statement is taken, Phillip Knightley argues:

> Drugs off-license would save Britain the £800 million a year spent on enforcing anti-drug laws. If drugs were taxed at the same rate as alcohol and tobacco, they would provide the Treasury with revenue of at least £1 billion a year. They would cut the prison population by 10 percent at a stroke, reduce crime and violence, and put the drug bosses out of business.

The same advantages would accrue on a commensurate scale in the United States and any other country that followed such a path. On the other hand, every seizure of drugs simply exerts an upward pressure on the street price and, as a result, increases the incentive for trafficking.

Taking part in the "Cannabis: Shaping a New Agenda" conference at Liverpool in February 2002, the Dutch government drugs adviser talked of his country's drugs policy, which had been formulated in the mid-1970s. He claimed that Dutch policy did not moralize but was based on the assumption that drug use is a fact and must be dealt with as practically as possible. "Our most important objective," he said, "is to prevent, or to limit, the risks and harm associated with drug use, both to the user himself and to his environment." The task fell to the ministry of health. The drugs advisor continued:

> Thanks to a high standard of care and prevention, including the large-scale dispensation of methadone and clean hypodermics, the number of hard drug [heroin or cocaine] addicts stabilized about 10 years ago at the level of 2.5 per 1,000 inhabitants. This means that the Netherlands is among the three countries, after Finland and Germany, with the smallest number of problem addicts in the European Union. Although not an ideal policy, bearing in mind our objective of harm limitation, our drugs policy is reasonably successful.[14]

In spring 2002 the British government's drugs advisory body found that cannabis was less addictive than alcohol or tobacco. In October 2001, Home Secretary David Blunkett had paved the way for the first relaxation of the drug laws in 30 years when he had said that it was important that Britain's laws were taken seriously by young people. Then in March 2002 the Advisory Council on the Misuse of Drugs (ACMD) upheld the home secretary's recommendation for reclassification of cannabis, but claimed that the "dependence potential" of cannabis was substantially less than that of Class B drugs such as amphetamines or, indeed, that of tobacco or alcohol. This finding was warmly received by DrugScope, whose chief executive Roger Howard said: "The ACMD has provided the hard scientific evidence that backs up the move to reclassify cannabis, and we hope the home secretary will quickly implement its advice."[15] It seemed clear that Britain would soon witness the appearance of cannabis cafés along Dutch lines.

Meanwhile, following the collapse of the Taliban government in Afghanistan and the presence in that country of U.S. and British combat troops, as well as a British-led peacekeeping force, British Prime Minister Tony Blair set up a secret specialist unit to target drugs production in Afghanistan and combat the flow of Afghan opium and heroin into Britain. Whether this initiative would prove any more successful than others in the war on drugs remains to be seen. What had become clear, as soon as the Taliban collapse had occurred, was the determination of elements in the Northern Alliance to resume the profitable production of heroin for the international drugs market.

For more than 30 years the United States, Britain, and Europe have spent billions fighting a war on drugs and in more or less direct proportion, as the effort to fight this war has increased so has the incidence of drug taking risen. Prohibition has not worked. As Metropolitan Police Commissioner Sir John Stevens admitted in June 2001, the cocaine business in London was too profitable to beat. When the police reach such conclusions it is time to reexamine the laws relating to drugs and, more important, to question the political philosophy behind the war on drugs. As Milton Friedman argued in the *Tyranny of the Status Quo:* "Revising our police and our courts from having to fight losing battles against drugs will enable their energies to be devoted more fully to combating other forms of crime. We would thus strike a double blow: reduce crime directly and increase the efficacy of law enforcement and crime prevention."[16]

As with so many other international problems, what is decided and executed by the United States has an impact worldwide. The United States is the largest market for drugs; it has waged a "war on drugs" for decades without success—if success is measured by the number of people who abandon as opposed to adopt the drug habit; it has used the war on drugs as an excuse to intervene in a number of countries in Latin America, where it has raised very real fears that its interventions have a wider purpose than simply curtailing the flow of drugs; and with Europe it is one of the two major centers for money laundering the proceeds of the illicit drugs business. The U.S. readiness to intervene and exert pressures in drug-producing countries is not matched by an equal readiness to address the social problems connected with drug use inside the United States. In a fiercely competitive world in which the United States is the chief protagonist of so-called market forces, it is naïve to imagine that supply will be curtailed, whatever incentives are offered or police actions mounted, as long as the demand for drugs continues to rise. As the British are beginning to discover, draconian anti-drug measures do not work. In the United States, where such measures are pursued, it is the poorest and the ethnic minorities that end up in prison, while too many of the leading criminals—whether the organizers of the trade, corrupt law enforcement personnel, or bankers who turn a blind eye to money laundering —escape unscathed. Given 30 years of the war on drugs, matched by steadily rising demand and vast profits, the time has come for a radical new approach. More than most issues, moreover, the drugs business is especially mobile and an open, nondraconian policy in one country or region will result in a closed, tough policy somewhere else. This raises the acute political question: Do U.S. governments want to solve the drugs problem by decriminalizing drug use and destroying the market, or do they want to use the war on drugs as a mechanism for intervention abroad and controlling their ghettos and underclass at home?

Given the failure of the war on drugs to reduce the habit and the fact that the illegal drug business has grown in proportion as the war on drugs has escalated, it is clearly time for a major re-evaluation of worldwide policy. The simple answer would be to legalize all drugs and then use a proportion of the huge sums of money now employed in the failing war on drugs, first for education and second for medical and welfare help for addicts.

Notes

Introduction

1. As reported in *The Independent*, February 22, 1999.
2. Quoted in *The Observer*, March 25, 2001.
3. Christopher Hitchens, columnist for *Vanity Fair*, in the London *Evening Standard*, January 11, 2001.

Chapter 1

1. International Narcotics Control Board, *Report 1997*, New York: United Nations, 1998.
2. Parts of this chapter have been taken from Chapter 45, "The International Drugs Trade" in *World Strategic Highways* by Guy Arnold (London and Chicago: Fitzroy Dearborn, 2000), pp. 283–95.

Chapter 2

1. *International Narcotics Control Board Report,* 1998, p. 5.
2. Quoted in *The Independent on Sunday*, June 7, 1998.
3. International Narcotics Control Board, *Report 1999* (New York: United Nations, 2000).
4. United Nations Office for Drug Control and Crime Prevention, *World Drug Report 2000* (Oxford and New York: Oxford University Press, 2000).

Chapter 3

1. As reported in *The Independent*, November 15, 1997.
2. Quoted in *The Independent*, February 1, 1997.
3. Quoted in *The Independent*, January 29, 1998.
4. As reported in *The Observer*, October 17, 1999.
5. Quoted in *The Independent*, March 25, 1998.
6. Quoted in *The Independent,* October 20, 2000.

Chapter 4

1. The figures and references quoted are taken from John Charlton and Mike Murphy, editors, *The Health of Adult Britain: 1841–1994*, Decennial Supplement No. 12 (London: Stationery Office, 1997).
2. "Deaths Related to Drug Poisoning: England and Wales, 1995–1999," *Health Statistics Quarterly 9* (Spring 2001): 70–72.
3. Alcohol Concern, London, *Britain's Ruin? Meeting Government Objectives via a National Alcohol Strategy* (May 2000) and *Alcohol's on Everyone's Lips* (2001), www.alcoholconcern.org.uk/Publications/Publications_Intro.htm
4. Department of the Environment, Transport, and the Regions, *Road Accidents Great Britain 1999: The Casualty Report* (London: Stationery Office, 2000).

Chapter 5

1. Working Party of the Royal College of Psychiatrists and Royal College of Physicians, *Drugs: Dilemmas and Choices* (London: Gaskell, 2000).

2. The historical sketch of drug developments in Britain is taken from Chapter 3 of *Drugs: Dilemmas and Choices.*
3. As reported in *The Independent*, March 21, 1997.
4. As reported in *The Independent*, August 8, 1997.
5. *Evening Standard*, September 7, 1997.
6. Quoted in the *Evening Standard*, August 7, 1997.
7. Quoted in *The Independent*, November 14, 1997.
8. As reported in the *Evening Standard*, April 9 and 10, 2001.
9. As reported in *The Observer*, April 29, 2001.
10. Danny Kushlick, "An Eloquent Silence: Evidence for Prohibition," *Druglink 16:*1 (January/February 2001): 20–22.
11. *Drugs and the Law: Report of the Independent Inquiry into the Misuse of Drugs Act 1971,* Police Foundation (Chairman: Viscountess Runciman), 2000.
12. *The Observer*, June 17, 2001.
13. Quoted in the *Daily Telegraph*, November 8, 2001.
14. Quoted in *The Independent*, November 10, 2001.

Chapter 6

1. As reported in *The Independent*, July 1, 2000.
2. As reported in *Keesing's Record of World Events*, April 2000.
3. As reported in *The Independent*, April 23, 2001.
4. As reported in *Keesing's Record of World Events*, April 1998.
5. Quoted in *The Observer*, August 27, 2000.
6. Quoted in *The Independent*, February 1, 2001.
7. John Kenneth Galbraith, *The Culture of Contentment* (London: Sinclair-Stevenson, and Boston: Houghton Mifflin, 1992), 38.
8. As reported in *The Observer*, March 4, 2001.
9. Quoted in *The Independent*, May 1, 2001.
10. Joan Smith, "Easy Targets," *Druglink 16:*1 (January/February 2001): 14–16.
11. Quoted in *The Independent*, November 9, 2001.

Chapter 7

1. Substance Abuse and Mental Health Services Administration, *1999 National Household Survey on Drug Abuse* (Rockville, Maryland: U.S. Department of Health and Human Services, 2001).
2. http//:drugwarfacts.org/causes.htm
3. National Council on Alcoholism and Drug Dependence, "Alcoholism and Alcohol-Related Problems," Factsheet, www.ncadd.org/facts/index.html
4. Human Rights Watch, *Punishment and Prejudice: Racial Disparities in the War on Drugs 12:*2 (G) (May 2000), www.hrw.org/reports/2000/usa
5. Human Rights Watch, *Punishment and Prejudice: Racial Disparities in the War on Drugs, 12:*2 (May 2000).

Chapter 8

1. The White House, Office of the Press Secretary, "Text of a Letter from the President to the Chairmen and Ranking Members of the House Committees on Appropriations and International Relations and the Senate Committees on Appropriations and Foreign Relations," December 4, 1998.
2. Bureau for International Narcotics and Law Enforcement Affairs, *1999 International Narcotics Control Strategy Report* (Washington, DC: U.S. Department of State, March 2000).

3. *International Narcotics Control Statistical Report*, 2000, pp. 21–22.
4. *The World Factbook 2000* (Washington, DC: Central Intelligence Agency, 2000), 14.

Chapter 9

1. International Narcotics Control Board, *Report 1999* (New York: United Nations, 2000).
2. United Nations Office for Drug Control and Crime Prevention, *World Drug Report 2000* (Oxford and New York: Oxford University Press, 2000).
3. Mark Bowden, *Killing Pablo, The Hunt for the Richest, Most Powerful Criminal in History* (London: Atlantic, 2001); and *Killing Pablo: The Hunt for the World's Greatest Outlaw* (New York: Atlantic, 2001).
4. As reported in *The Independent*, August 28, 2000.
5. For developments 1995–2000, see *Keesing's Record of World Events* monthly issues for this period.
6. As reported in *The Independent*, February 9, 2001.
7. *The Observer*, June 17, 2001.
8. As reported in *The Observer*, July 1, 2001.
9. Quoted in *The Independent*, May 25, 2001.
10. Quoted in *The Independent*, August 26, 2000.
11. Quoted in *The Independent*, August 30, 2000.

Chapter 10

1. As reported in *Keesing's Record of World Events*, July 2000.
2. Bureau for International Narcotics and Law Enforcement Affairs, *2000 International Narcotics Control Strategy Report* (Washington, DC: U.S. Department of State, March 2001).
3. Rodrigo de Castro and Juan Gasparini, *La delgada línea blanca* [The Thin White Line] (Buenos Aires: Ediciones B Argentina, 2000).
4. As reported in *The Observer*, December 10, 2000.

Chapter 11

1. As reported in *The Observer*, December 21, 2000.
2. Bureau for International Narcotics and Law Enforcement Affairs, *2000 International Narcotics Control Strategy Report* (Washington, DC: U.S. Department of State, March 2001).
3. As reported in *The Independent*, December 30, 1996.
4. Quoted in *The Observer*, December 24, 2000.
5. Justin Davenport, *Evening Standard*, September 11, 2001.
6. Quoted in article by Jason Burke, *The Observer*, September 9, 2001.
7. See *Keesing's Record of World Events*, monthly issues 1995–2000.
8. Quoted in *The Independent*, May 28, 2001.

Chapter 12

1. *The World Factbook 2000* (Washington, DC: Central Intelligence Agency, 2000).

Chapter 13

1. *The World Factbook 2000* (Washington, DC: Central Intelligence Agency, 2000).
2. As reported in *Keesing's Record of World Events*, September 1997.

3. Quoted in *The Observer*, December 12, 2000.
4. Quoted in *The Independent*, February 17, 2001.
5. Quoted in *The Observer*, June 17, 2001.
6. Quoted in *The Observer*, September 30, 2001.
7. Quoted in *The Independent*, October 6, 2001.
8. See *Keesing's Record of World Events*, August 1999, October 1999, and November 1999.
9. As reported in *The Observer*, September 9, 2001.

Chapter 14

1. Tamara Makarenko, "Getting to Market," *Druglink 16:*5 (September/October 2001): 19–22.
2. Ibid.

Chapter 15

1. Daniel C. Bach, editor, *Regionalisation in Africa: Integration and Disintegration* (Oxford: James Currey, and Bloomington: Indiana University Press, 1999).
2. Janet MacGaffey and Rémy Bazenguissa-Ganga, *Congo–Paris: Transnational Traders on the Margins of the Law* (Oxford: James Currey, and Bloomington: Indiana University Press, 2000).
3. Ibid., 77–78.
4. Ibid., 80.
5. Daniel C. Bach, editor, *Regionalisation in Africa*, 89–91.
6. Ibid., 198.
7. Milan Vesely, "Africa—Highway to Drug Hell," *African Business* (April 2000): 8–10.
8. Daniel C. Bach, editor, *Regionalisation in Africa*, 194.
9. Ibid., 195.
10. Vesely, "Africa—Highway to Drug Hell."
11. Guy Arnold, *World Strategic Highways* (London and Chicago: Fitzroy Dearborn, 2000), 293.

Chapter 16

1. Quoted in *The Independent*, January 20, 2001.
2. *The World Factbook 2000* (Washington, DC: Central Intelligence Agency, 2000).
3. *European Monitoring Centre for Drugs and Drug Addiction,* 2000 Annual Report on the State of the Drugs Problem in the European Union (Luxembourg: Office for Official Publications of the European Communities, 2000).

Chapter 17

1. Department of Public Information, United Nations, *Basic Facts About the United Nations* (New York: United Nations, 1998), 190.
2. Bureau for International Narcotics and Law Enforcement Affairs, *2000 International Narcotics Control Strategy Report* (Washington, DC: U.S. Department of State, March 2001).
3. Mark Duffield, *Global Governance and the New Wars: The Merging of Development Security* (London and New York: Zed Books, 2001), 158.
4. Ibid., 180–81.
5. Ibid., 181.

6. François Houtart and François Polet, editors, *The Other Davos: The Globalization of the Resistance to the World Economic System* (London and New York: Zed Books, 2001), 28–29.
7. Daniel C. Bach, editor, *Regionalisation in Africa: Integration and Disintegration* (Oxford: James Currey, and Bloomington: Indiana University Press, 1999), 192.
8. Tom Nevin, "Has Africa Become the World's Washroom for Dirty Money?" *African Business* (March 2000): 20.
9. Commonwealth Secretariat, *Report of the Commonwealth Secretary-General 2001* (London: Commonwealth Secretary-General, 2001).
10. *The World Factbook 2000* (Washington, DC: Central Intelligence Agency, 2000).
11. As reported in the *Financial Times*, November 8, 2001.
12. Al J. Venter, "Dirty Money and the Laundering Loophole," *International Police Review* (January/February 2000).
13. Noam Chomsky, *Deterring Democracy* (London: Vintage, and New York: Hill and Wang, 1992), 116.

Chapter 18

1. Quoted in *The Observer*, December 28, 1997.
2. As reported in *The Independent*, February 27, 1998.
3. As reported in *The Independent*, March 6, 1998.
4. As reported in *The Independent*, March 25, 1998.
5. Quoted in *The Independent*, April 22, 1998.
6. As reported in *The Independent*, October 20, 2000.
7. Quoted in *Metro*, March 22, 2001.
8. Nick Lezard, *The Independent*, March 29, 2000.
9. Anne McElvoy, *The Independent*, March 29, 2000.
10. Quoted in *The Independent*, July 9, 2001.
11. As reported in *The Observer*, July 8, 2001.
12. Quoted in *The Independent*, October 19, 2001.
13. "Ganja Posssession May Be Legalised in Jamaica," *Druglink 16*:5 (September/October 2001), 5.

Chapter 19

1. Philippe Bourgois. *In Search of Respect: Selling Crack in El Barrio.* (Cambridge: Cambridge University Press, 1995), 118.
2. Mark Duffield, *Global Governance and the New Wars: The Merging of Development Security* (London and New York: Zed Books, 2001), 196.
3. As reported in *The Guardian*, June 15, 2001.
4. Ibid.
5. Sadie Plant, *Writing on Drugs* (London: Faber, 1999; New York: Farrar Straus Giroux, 2000), 116–17.
6. Ibid., 207.
7. Quoted in *The Observer*, November 25, 2001.
8. Quoted in *Metro*, November 21, 2001.
9. As reported in *The Observer*, August 15, 1999.
10. Quoted in *The Observer*, March 25, 2000.
11. Quoted in *The Independent*, October 2, 2001, by Raymond Whitaker in Islamabad.
12. Quoted in *The Independent*, February 13, 2002.
13. Phillip Knightley, *Sunday Times Magazine*, May 27, 2001.
14. Bob Keizer, quoted in "PODIUM," *The Independent*, February 25, 2002.
15. Quoted in *The Independent*, March 15, 2002.
16. Milton Friedman and Rose Friedman, *Tyranny of the Status Quo* (San Diego: Harcourt Brace Jovanovich, and London: Secker and Warburg, 1984).

Index

A

Abaroa, Ronald MacLean, 124
Action on Addiction (charity), 58
Addicts
    in Britain, 51, 61–62, 229–230
    deaths among, 62, 231
    decriminalization of drugs and,
        33, 55, 56, 62, 72–73,
        133–134, 234, 235
    in Europe, 206
    in prisons, 55, 74
    in psychiatric homes, 54–55
    public opinions and images of,
        33–34, 229–230
    research on, 34
    in Russia, 175–176
Adetiloye, Joseph Abiodun, 186
Afghanistan, 2, 5, 6, 18, 19–20, 37,
        87, 173, 175, 233
    certification denied to, 90
    conflicts with Iran, 160, 167
    heroin from, 35, 61
    opium production in, 23, 29, 89,
        91, 159–161, 171
    Taliban rule of, 6, 19, 91,
        160–161, 161–163, 233,
        236
Africa. See also individual countries
    cannabis production in, 17, 179,
        183–185, 189
    drug smugglers of, 181–182,
        186–187
    drug transport through, 7–8,
        16–17, 179–185, 190–193
    drug use in, 180
    INCB 1999 annual report on,
        16–17
    money laundering in, 212–213
African Americans, 71–72

African Business, 184
Ainsworth, Robert, 66, 234
Albania, 130, 202
Albright, Madeleine, 69
Alcohol abuse
    in Britain, 42–45
    in Europe, 206
    and religious revivalism, 45
    in the United States, 79f, 80,
        81–82
Alcohol Concern, 42–43
Algeria, 179
Alliance for Cannabis Therapeutics,
        221
Alvarado Linares, Willem, 127
Alvares, Elcio, 129
Alvarez, Gladys, 113
Alves Marchezan, Valdenor, 128
Alvoct, Magda, 197
American Cancer Society, 221
Amphetamines, 27, 205, 232
    use in Europe, 38
Anderson, Bruce, 225
Angola, 16, 97, 191, 196
Annan, Kofi, 14, 15, 231
Antigua, 214
Argentina, 120, 121, 132–133
Arlacchi, Pino, 13–14, 162, 163
Armenia, 7, 19, 169, 174
Aruba, 87, 91, 137, 214
Ashcroft, Michael, 54
Asia. See also Golden Triangle, the;
        South Asia; West Asia; indi-
        vidual countries
    cannabis production in, 174
    Central, 174–175
    eradication programs in, 92,
        169–171

heroin transport through, 6–7
INCB 1999 annual report on, 18
Attention deficit/hyperactivity dis-
    order (ADHD), 31–32
Australia, 20, 214
Austria, 202, 210
Azerbaijan, 7, 19, 169, 174

B
Bahamas, the, 87, 90, 91, 214
Balkans, the, 61, 88, 202, 204, 206
Bangladesh, 7, 19, 152, 174
Banks, Tony, 66
Bánzar Suárez, Hugo, 124, 125
Baramdyka, Frankell Ivan, 133
Barbados, 4, 36, 138
Barbuda, 214
Basson, Wouter, 190
Batlle Ibáñez, Joge, 133–134
Bazenguissa Ganga, Rémy, 181
Bean, Philip, 55
Beatles, the, 226
Belarus, 174
Belgium, 35, 130, 202, 227
    legalization of cannabis in,
        196–197
    synthetic drug use in, 38
Belize, 87, 91, 122, 214
Benin, 182, 191
Berger, Sandy, 119
Bernal Cuellar, Jaime, 110
Bin Laden, Osama, 163–164, 215,
    233
Blair, Tony, 53, 66, 164, 222, 233
Blunkett, David, 25, 64, 223, 224,
    226, 228, 232, 235
Bolivia, 87, 90, 99, 108, 120, 121,
    127, 130, 179
    cocaine production in, 2–3, 3, 88
    Cochabamba department,
        124–126
    eradication programs in, 23, 91,
        122–126

farmers of, 123–126
INCB 1999 annual report on, 18
Bosnia, 35, 202
Bossano, Joe, 199
Botero Zea, Fernando, 104,
    105–106, 110
Botswana, 184, 190
Brauer, Werner Walter, 129
Brave New World, 32
Brazil, 8, 87, 90, 112, 119, 121, 125,
    127, 196
    drug trafficking in, 128–129
    eradication programs in, 92
    money laundering in, 231
Britain
    alcohol abuse in, 42–45
    amount spent on illegal drugs
        in, 64–65
    anti-drug efforts in, 1–2, 29–30,
        51–57, 130, 138, 140,
        141–143, 199, 222
    cannabis use in, 25–26, 55,
        59–60, 219–228, 232
    Channel Tunnel drug trafficking
        into, 64–65
    cocaine use in, 59–60, 61, 225,
        232
    drug use and abuse in, 219,
        229–230
    drug use compared to the
        United States, 84–85
    ecstasy use in, 27–28, 53, 59–60
    growth in number of addicts in,
        51, 61–62
    heroin use in, 35, 52–53, 59–60,
        61–62, 181, 224–225
    high-profile drug use cases in,
        54, 225–226
    Jamaican drug trafficking into,
        141–143
    legalization debate in, 219–228
    LSD use in, 26, 232

money laundering in, 202

police activity against drug use and trafficking in, 60–61, 63–64, 223–224, 231–232, 234

prevalence of alcohol abuse in, 45

prevalence of drug abuse in, 40–42, 57–59

psychiatric homes in, 54–55

smuggling of drugs from the Golden Crescent into, 61–62, 160–161, 166f

smuggling of drugs through Ireland into, 10

social attitudes toward drugs in, 51–52, 61, 66, 228

street prices of drugs in, 32–33

surveys of alcohol use, 44–45

surveys of drug use in, 40–41

synthetic drug use in, 38, 201

temperance movement in, 44–45

tobacco smoking in, 45–50

youth drug use in, 51, 57–59, 226

Britain's Ruin?, 45

British Crime Survey, 58–59

British Medical Association (BMA), 26, 220, 226

British Medical Journal, 56, 57

British Virgin Islands, 3

Brunstrom, Richard, 234

Bulgaria, 2, 35, 36, 38, 202

Bunma, Theng, 155–156

Burns, Nicholas, 106

Burundi, 188

Bush, George H. W., 101, 217

Bush, George W., 70, 72, 74, 116, 135, 209

C

Cable, Vincent, 45

Cachique Rivera, Abelardo, 126

Cali cartel, 2, 101, 103–108, 137

Calle, Eugenia, 221

Calvani, Sandro, 138

Calvini, Sando, 4

Cambodia, 37, 87, 152, 169, 215

anti-drug efforts in, 155–156

certification given to, 90

corruption in, 92

government corruption in, 155–156

Campaign to Legalise Cannabis International Association, 55

Canada, 17, 157

Cancer and smoking, 49, 221

Cancinco, Antonio José, 104

Cannabis, 7, 8, 25–26, 174

California legalization of, 220

cancer and, 221

grown in the United States, 70

health risks of using, 221, 223

INCB 1999 annual report on, 18–19

legalization, 33, 55, 72–73, 196–199, 219–228, 235–236

production in Africa, 17, 179, 183–185, 188–193

public opinion on, 228

use in Asia, 174

use in Britain, 55, 59–60, 232

use in Europe, 37–38, 205

use in North America, 17

use in Oceania, 20

use in the United States, 25–26, 80–81

Cano, Alfonso, 119

Cape Verde, 185, 191, 196

Cardoso, Fernando Henrique, 129

Caribbean islands, 3–4, 17, 87, 90, 138–141. *See also* individual countries

cocaine trade in, 36
  eradication programs in, 91,
    92–93
  money laundering in, 214–215
Carrillo Fuentes, Amado, 144
Castañon, Paulina, 141
Castrillon Henao, José, 137
Castro, Fidel, 4
Cayman Islands, 214
Central African Republic, 98
Central America, 17, 88. *See also* in-
    dividual countries
  anti-drug efforts in, 135–137
  eradication programs in, 93, 96
Central Intelligence Agency (CIA),
    97–98, 151, 153, 156, 159,
    201, 207, 214–215
Centre for International Crime
    Prevention (CICP), 12
Chad, 181
Chambers, Andrew, 67–68
Channel Tunnel, drugs trafficking
    in the, 64–65
Chavarria, Isaac, 123
Chávez Frías, Hugo, 102–103
Chile, 120, 122, 132–133, 215
China, 87, 90, 152, 169, 174, 179,
    215
  anti-drug efforts in, 171–172
  drug importation in, 6, 11
  eradication programs in, 92
  INCB 1999 annual report on, 18
  money laundering in, 214
  opium production in, 11, 22,
    171
Chirac, Jacques, 198
Chomsky, Noam, 217
Chronic obstructive lung disease
    (COPD), 49
Churchill, Winston, 230
Clarke, Charles, 222
Clee, William, 56

Clinton, Bill, 15, 69–70, 73, 75, 107,
    147, 176, 220, 231
  certification of Mexico by, 144
  determination of countries of
    concern by, 87–88
  emergency aid to Peru author-
    ized by, 127
  Plan Colombia and, 112–120
Cocaine
  advocates for legalization of,
    133–134
  from Africa, 185–186
  from Colombia, 36, 68, 88–89,
    99, 111–112
  largest single seizure of, 102–103
  rise and fall in production of,
    21, 28, 88–89
  source countries for, 2–3, 7, 8,
    9f, 18, 68, 111–112,
    138–141, 185–186
  use in Britain, 59–60, 61, 225,
    232
  use in Europe, 36–37, 117–118,
    201–206, 205–206
  use in the U. S., 68, 117–118
Cohen, William, 111
Colombia, 2, 5, 8, 87, 90, 127, 130,
    145, 233
  Cali cartel, 2, 101, 103–108, 137
  cannabis production in, 37
  cartels of, 2–3, 100–101,
    103–105
  certification of, 92, 108
  cocaine production in, 36, 68,
    88–89, 99, 111–112
  Ecuador and, 115–116, 117
  extradition agreements with the
    United States, 109–110,
    112
  financial aid received by,
    110–111, 112–113,
    118–120

government corruption in, 104–105

INCB 1999 annual report on, 18, 99

largest single seizure of cocaine from, 102–103

negotiations between guerrillas and the government in, 115–116

peasant farmers of, 103, 107

political power in, 100–102, 104

Russian mafia connection to, 114

spraying of coca crops in, 103, 114, 116–117

U. S. anti-drug efforts in, 70–71, 110–111

violence in, 100–102, 112–115, 217

Commission on Narcotic Drugs, 12

Congo Brazzaville, 181, 191

Congo Kinshasa, 16, 179, 181, 188

Congo-Paris, 181

Convention against Illicit Traffic in Narcotic Drugs and Psychotropic Substances of 1988, 11, 13, 16, 87, 172, 184

Convention on Psychotropic Substances of 1971, 11, 13, 16, 172

Cook, Robin, 54

Corruption, government, 90–91, 92

in Cambodia, 155–156

in Chile, 133

in Colombia, 104–105

in Mexico, 144–145

in Peru, 127–128

in Venezuela, 130

Costa Rica, 88, 111, 122, 136

Crack, 28, 60, 101, 229. *See also* Cocaine

Crime

alcohol abuse and, 43

costs of drug-related, 234, 236

drug abuse and, 55, 82–83

gangs and, 61–62

government corruption and, 90–91, 92, 104–105, 127–128, 130, 133

and violence in Colombia, 100–102, 112–115, 217

Croatia, 35, 36, 202

Cuartas, Belisario Betancur, 101

Cuba, 4, 88

Culture of Contentment, The, 72

Curaçao, 137, 215

Customs Cooperation Council, 180

Cyprus, 177

Czech Republic, 2, 7, 35, 38, 169, 202, 204, 206

D

Daily Express, 227

Daily Mirror, 219

Daily Telegraph, 65, 226

Dallaglio, Lawrence, 54

Dangerous Drugs Act (Britain), 51, 52

Davenport, Justin, 141

De Castro, Rodrigo, 133

Decriminalization of drugs. *See* Legalization of drugs

De Cuellar, Perez, 14

De la Torre Marquez, Alfredo, 146

Demand for drugs, United Nations efforts to reduce, 13–16

Denmark, 35, 201

Dennis, Walter Guiteras, 124

D'Hondt, Edumond, 197

Diodato, Marino, 124

Djibouti, 191

DOB, 28

Dominica, 215

Dominican Republic, 87, 90, 122, 140

eradication programs in, 92–93
Dorfman, Ariel, 14
Douglas, Michael, 72
Drug Enforcement Administration
        (DEA), the, 1, 2, 60,
        117–118, 130, 140, 147,
        156, 173, 180, 184, 230–231
    corruption in, 67–68
Druglink, 63, 75
DrugScope (charity), 63, 227, 234,
        236
Drug trafficking
    amounts spent on, 64–65, 229
    biggest markets for, 10, 117–118,
        201–207, 229–230,
        236–237
    government corruption and,
        90–91, 92, 104–105,
        127–128, 130, 133,
        144–145, 155–156
    profits from, 1, 64–65, 163–164,
        209–217 (*See also*
        Money laundering)
    terrorism and, 69, 163–164,
        209–210, 215–216, 233
    transport routes in, 166f, 170f,
        174–175, 181–182,
        184–185, 191–192,
        201–205
    volatility of routes, 1, 3–10, 90
Dubai, 215

E
Economic and Social Council
        (ECOSOC) of the United
        Nations, 12–13
Ecstasy, 10, 27–28, 200, 229, 232
    use in Britain, 53, 59–60
    use in Europe, 38, 205
    use in the United States, 70, 117
Ecuador, 87, 90, 112, 114, 119, 120,
        137, 212
    anti-drug efforts in, 131

and Colombia's drug war,
        115–116, 117
    eradication programs in, 93
    money laundering in, 215
Eden, Anthony, 230
Egmont Group, 92
Egypt, 7, 11, 191
Eid Franco, Oscar, 123
Eleazar Pombo, Roger, 110
Elias Nader, Jorge Ramón, 109
Ellison, Edward, 14
El Salvador, 88, 122, 136
Escobar Gavirira, Pablo, 100–102,
        112
Estonia, 204
Ethiopia, 179, 184, 191
Europe. *See also* individual coun-
        tries
    alcohol abuse in, 206
    anti-drug efforts in, 1–2,
        195–196
    cannabis use in, 37–38, 205
    cocaine use in, 36–37, 117–118,
        201–206, 205–206
    drug market in, 34–38, 201
    Eastern, 202–205, 206
    ecstasy use in, 205
    heroin use in, 35–36, 201–206,
        206
    INCB 1999 annual report on, 20
    money laundering in, 211–212
    new policy and strategy devel-
        opment in, 206–207
    smuggling of illegal drugs into,
        7–8, 10, 169, 181–182,
        188–189
    synthetic drug use in, 38, 201
    trends in drug use in, 205–206
    use of anabolic steroids in, 198
    Western, 201–202
European Monitoring Centre for
        Drugs and Drug Abuse
        (EMCDDA), 62

Evening Standard (London), 56, 59, 141
Ewald, Manfred, 198
Extradition agreements, 109, 112, 155

F
Farabundo Marti National Liberation Front (FMLN), 136
Far Eastern Economic Review, 155
Farmer, Melvin, 71
Farmers, coca, 103, 107, 123–126
Félix, Arellano, 147
Financial Action Task Force (FATF), 92, 209–210
Finland, 35, 201
prohibition in, 45
Flynn, Paul, 66
Fo, Dario, 14
Forbes, 100
Forbes, James, 142
Fox Quesada, Vicente, 148
Frahi, Bernard, 161, 162, 233
France, 35, 37, 198, 201, 202
Frechette, Myles, 108–109
Free Amsterdam Guide, The, 197
Freedom, personal, 229–230
Friedman, Milton, 135, 236
Fujimori, Alberto, 120, 127

G
Gacha, José Rodríguez, 100
Galán Sarmiento, Alberto, 217
Galán Sarmiento, Luis Carlos, 101, 217
Galbraith, John Kenneth, 72
García Abrego, Juan, 141
Gasparini, Juan, 133
Gaviria Díaz, Carlos, 106
Gaviria Trujillo, César, 101–102
Geerts, Paul, 196
Gelbard, Robert, 107

Georgia, 19, 35, 213
Germany, 2, 3, 198, 201, 202
heroin use in, 35
synthetic drug use in, 38
Ghana, 7, 179, 182, 185, 190–191, 191–192
Gibraltar, 199
Girling, Jack, 55
Glue sniffing, 27
Golden Crescent, the
countries of, 6, 159, 204–205
heroin smuggling into Britain from, 53, 61–62, 160–161, 166f
opium production in, 29–30, 159–160
Golden Eagle, 28
Golden Triangle, the. *See also* Asia
countries of, 5–6, 96, 97, 149–150, 169–172, 204–205
heroin from, 5–6, 35
INCB 1999 annual report on, 18
money laundering in, 215
opium production in, 149–150
yaba production in, 30
Goodman, Mike, 58
Greece, 35, 192, 204
Grewer, Lawrence, 56
Guardian, The, 62, 226, 228
Guatemala, 22–23, 87, 90, 122
anti-drug efforts in, 135–136
eradication programs in, 93
Guerin, Victoria, 196
Guinea-Bissau, 196
Gutiérrez Rebollo, Jesús, 144
Guy, Geoffrey, 227
Gyaw, U Ohn, 152

H
Hague, William, 223
Haiti, 87, 90
certification of, 140–141

eradication programs in, 93
Hallucinogens, 26
Hashish, 173, 174
Hassenteufel, Oscar, 124
Hatch, Orrin, 72
Health of Adult Britain, The, 41, 46,
    47–48
Health Statistics Quarterly, 41
Hellawell, Keith, 53–54, 54, 62, 63
Henry, John, 27–28
Herbicides, 116–117
Heroin, 2–3. *See also* Opium
    from Africa, 185, 187
    from the Golden Crescent, 6, 53,
        159–168
    from the Golden Triangle, 5, 154
    HIV/AIDS and, 17, 29
    legalization, 198–199, 200
    physical effects of, 28–29
    trafficking routes for, 6–7,
        160–161, 166f, 191–192
    use in Britain, 52–53, 61–62,
        160–161, 181, 224–225
    use in Europe, 35–36, 201–206,
        206
    use in the United States, 79–80,
        89
Herran Salvatti, Mariano, 144
Herrera Buitrago, Helmer, 107
Hiep, Nguyen Thi, 157
Higuera Guerrero, Ismael, 147
Hill, Janice, 32
Hitler, Adolf, 230
HIV/AIDS
    in Britain, 41
    heroin injection and, 17, 29
    United Nations research on, 24
Hodges, Claire, 221–222
Holland, Julie, 75
Holy See, the, 201
Honduras, 88, 122
Hong Kong, 87, 90, 172, 215
    eradication programs in, 93

money laundering in, 213
Hoppner, Manfred, 198
Hough, Mike, 60
Howard, Roger, 234, 236
Hughes, Simon, 66
Human Rights Watch, 82–83, 112
Hungary, 2, 35, 206
Huxley, Aldous, 32

I
Ibero-American Summit, 122
Iceland, 201
Independent, The, 49, 55, 63, 220,
    222
India
    drug trade in, 7, 11, 19, 87, 90,
        152, 173, 174, 180
    eradication programs in, 93–94
Indonesia, 176
International Narcotics Control
    Board (INCB), 1, 11,
    12–13, 180
    1999 annual report of, 16–20, 99
International Narcotics Control
    Strategy Report (INCSR),
    88, 89, 137, 210
International Opium Convention,
    11
Interpol, 180
Iran, 2, 6, 7, 19–20, 35, 37, 61, 91,
    169
    conflicts with Afghanistan, 160,
        167
    designation as a country of con-
        cern by the U. S., 87–88
    eradication programs in, 22–23
    opium production in, 29,
        167–168
    U. S. war on drugs and, 69
Ireland, 10, 202
Isle of Man, 201
Israel, 7, 169
Italy, 35, 37, 198, 202

Iversen, Leslie, 221
Ivory Coast, 7, 182, 183, 185, 191
Izquieredo, Maria, 105, 107

J
Jagger, Mick, 225
Jamaica, 3, 87, 90, 227
    cannabis production in, 37, 227
    eradication programs in, 94
    impact of trafficking in Britain,
        141–143
    money laundering in, 213–214
Japan, 152
Jawara, Dawda, 183
Jimenez, Alvaro, 136
Johnson, Lyndon B., 230
Jones, Jon Owen, 225
Joseph Rowntree Foundation, 219
*Journal of the American Medical
    Association*, 31

K
Kazakhstan
    designation as a country of con-
        cern by the U. S., 88
    drug trade in, 19, 36, 169, 174,
        175, 176
Keizer, Bob, 219
Kelly, Raymond, 130
Kennedy, Charles, 220–221
Kennedy, John F., 230
Kenya, 7, 179, 182, 184, 187–188,
    190
Ketamine, 31
Khatami, Mohammed, 164
Khyber Pass, 6
Killing Pablo, 100
Knightley, Philip, 235
Korthals, Bent, 197
Kushlick, Danny, 63
Kyrgyzstan
    designation as a country of con-
        cern by the U. S., 88

drug trade in, 19, 174, 175

L
Labra, Jesús, 147
Lampreia, Luiz Felipe, 120
Lancet, The, 224
Landivar, Jorge, 124
Laos, 5, 18, 23, 87, 90, 152, 169, 172
    cannabis production in, 37,
        153–154
    dispute with Thailand, 154
    eradication programs in, 94
    opium production in, 94,
        149–150
Lara Nausa, Jaime Orlando, 112
Latvia, 7, 169, 173, 204
Lebanon, 7, 91, 169, 192
    designation as a country of con-
        cern by the U. S., 88
    eradication programs in, 22–23
    traffickers in Africa from, 176,
        182
Leekpai, Chuan, 155
Legalization of drugs, 62, 133–134,
    233
    in Belgium, 196–197
    government studies on, 55,
        220–221, 223, 235–236
    in the Netherlands, 33, 197–198
    newspaper editorials advocat-
        ing, 56, 222
    police viewpoints of, 223–225,
        231–232, 235
    in Portugal, 198–199
    in Spain, 198–199, 232
    in Switzerland, 199–200
    in the United States, 72–73
Lennon, John, 226
Leshner, Alan, 34
Lesotho, 184, 190
Lezard, Nick, 222
Liberia, 16, 180, 181, 183–184, 185,
    192

Liechtenstein, 201
Lithuania, 204
Los Angeles riots, 71–72
Lozano, Antonio, 141
LSD, 26, 232
Lucio, Carlos Alonso, 103, 104–105
Luxembourg, 201

M
MacGaffey, Janet, 181
Madrazo Cuellar, Jorge, 144, 145
Malaysia
    designation as a country of con-
        cern by the U. S., 87–88
    drug trade in, 18, 91, 169, 175
Malherbe de Leon, Oscar, 144
Malta, 204
Mandrax, 8
Marijuana. *See* Cannabis
Marky, Tomás, 127
Marques do Amaral, Leopoldo, 128
Marshall, Donnie, 117
Martinez Santa Maria, Jaime,
    118–119
Marulanda Vélez, Manuel, 115–116
Mauritania, 185, 192
McCaffrey, Barry, 15, 77, 111, 198,
    231
McElvoy, Anne, 222
Medellín cartel, 2
Medina, Santiago, 104, 107
Mercado, Julio, 102
Methaqualone, 8, 173, 187, 190
Mexico, 4–5, 87, 90
    anti-drug efforts in, 141–148
    banking system, 144–146
    cannabis use in, 17
    eradication programs in, 94,
        146–147
    government corruption in,
        144–145
    relations with the United States,
        141, 146

Miami Herald, 145
Michelsen, Alfonso López, 100
Middle East, the
    drug trade in, 7, 176–177
    money laundering in, 215–216
Mill, John Stuart, 230
Misuse of Drugs Act (Britain), 52,
    222
Mittleman, Murray, 223
Moldova, 204
Monaco, 201
Money laundering
    in Africa, 212–213
    amount of money involved in,
        211–212
    areas to be investigated and reg-
        ulated in controlling,
        216–217
    in Asia, 213, 214, 215
    in the Caribbean region,
        214–215
    international agreements to
        fight, 212
    in the Middle East, 215–216
    reasons for, 210–211
    in South America, 215, 231
Mongolia, 6, 169
Mong Tai Army (MTA), 151–152
Monsanto Corporation, 117
Montenegro, 35
Montesinos Torres, Vladimiro, 120,
    126, 128
Morales, Evo, 122–123, 126
Morocco, 8, 11, 37, 91, 180, 190, 198
    cannabis production in,
        188–189, 193
    designation as a country of con-
        cern by the U. S., 88
Mowlam, Mo, 221
Mozambique, 180, 196
Mumford, Enid, 233
Mushrooms, hallucinogenic, 26

Myanmar, 5–6, 7, 11, 18, 54, 87, 94,
      169, 172, 173, 185, 233
   certification denied to, 90
   eradication programs in,
         152–153
   government turmoil in, 150–153
   opium production in, 89, 94–95,
         149–150

N
Nadelmann, Ethan, 75
Namibia, 180
National Academy of Sciences, 17
National Addiction Centre, 56
National Council on Alcoholism
         and Drug Dependence, 81
*National Household Survey on Drug
      Abuse*, 77
National Institute on Drug Abuse,
         81
National Institutes of Health
         (NIH), 17
National Prohibition Act (U. S.), 44
Needle park, Switzerland, 199–200
Nepal, 174
Netherlands, the, 2, 3, 7, 10, 36, 130,
         190, 195, 202
   anti-drug efforts in, 197–198
   cannabis use in, 33, 37, 219, 235
   designation as a country of con-
         cern by the U. S., 88
   heroin use in, 35, 181
   synthetic drug use in, 38, 201
Netherlands Antilles, 137, 215
Nevin, Tom, 212–213
*New Heroin Outbreaks Amongst
      Young People in England
      and Wales*, 61
News of the World, 54
New York Times, 144, 163
New Zealand, 20
Nicaragua, 88, 122, 136

Nigeria, 3, 7–8, 17, 87, 181, 182,
         183–184
   cannabis production in, 37
   certification given to, 90, 95
   cocaine transport through,
         36–37, 185–186
   drug trafficking through,
         185–187, 190–193
   eradication programs in, 95
   money laundering in, 212
Nivia, Elsa, 117
Nixon, Richard, 230
Noriega, Manuel, 136
North America. *See also* individual
         countries
   cannabis use in, 17
   cocaine distribution in, 36
   Free Trade Agreement
         (NAFTA), 141
   Organization of American
         States (OAS) anti-drug
         efforts in, 69–70
Norway, 35, 201

O
Obasanjo, Olesugun, 187
O'Brian, Charles, 34
Observatoire Géopolitque des
         Drogues, 180
Observer, The, 31, 116, 117, 133,
         142, 161
Oceania, 20
Ochoa Vásquez, Fabio, 112
Omar, Mullah Mohammed, 161,
         162
Opium, 11, 174. *See also* Heroin
   destruction by spraying, 29–30,
         103, 107, 123–126
   Golden Crescent production of,
         23, 29, 89, 91, 159–168
   Golden Triangle production of,
         89, 93–95, 149–157

INCB 1999 annual report on,
        18–19
    rise and fall in production of,
        20–21, 22, 89
Organization of American States
        (OAS), 69–70
Orlandez Gamboa, Alberto, 110
Oshima, Kenzo, 162
Overload Support Network, 32

P
Paddick, Brian, 64, 224, 231–232
Pakistan, 2, 6, 19–20, 61, 87, 90, 94,
        160, 165, 169, 173, 198
    eradication programs in, 23,
        95–96, 166–167
    heroin from, 35
    opium production in, 23, 29,
        166–167
Palma Salazar, Héctor Luis, 141
Panama, 3, 87, 90, 112, 114, 119,
        136–137, 195, 215
    anti-drug efforts in, 137
    eradication programs in, 96
Paniagua Corazao, Valentìn, 127
Pan-intara, Samai, 155
Papndreou, George, 14
Papua New Guinea, 20
Paraguay, 87, 131–132
    certification of, 90, 132
    eradication programs in, 96
Pastrana Arango, Andrés, 110–111,
        118
    negotiations with guerrillas,
        115–116
Pataki, George, 74–75
Paz Zamora, Jaime, 123
Peñaherrera, Demetrio Chávez, 126
Penrose, Roy, 54
Pérez Balladres, Ernesto, 137
Peru, 87, 90, 99, 109, 112, 119, 120,
        121, 130

    cocaine production in, 2–3,
        68–69, 88
    eradication programs in, 23, 96,
        126–128
    government anti-drug opera-
        tions in, 3
    government corruption in,
        127–128
    INCB 1999 annual report on, 18
Philip Morris, 49
Philippines, the, 88, 152, 176
Pinochet Ugarte, Augusto, 133
Plant, Sadie, 230
Poland, 3, 7, 38, 169, 204, 206
Police Review, 234
Portugal, 4, 196, 201–202, 202
Pou, Pedro, 133
Powell, Colin, 72
Principal illicit drugs
    amphetamines, 27
    cannabis, 7, 8, 17, 18–19, 20,
        25–26
    cocaine, 2–3, 7, 8, 9f, 18, 21
    ecstasy, 10, 27–28
    hallucinogen, 26
    heroin, 2–3, 5, 6–7, 17, 28–30
    ketamine, 31
    LSD, 26
    ritalin, 31–32
    solvents, 27
    yaba, 30–31
Príncipe, 196
Prisons
    drug abuse in, 55, 74
    women in, 83–84, 141–142, 155
Profits for drug trafficking, 1,
        64–65, 163–164, 209–217
Prohibition in various countries,
        43–44
Psychiatric homes, drug abuse in,
        54–55

Punishment and Prejudice: Racial Disparities in the War on Drugs, 82

Q
Qat, 191
Quintero Payán, Juan José, 146

R
Race and the war on drugs, 71–72, 82–84
Raistrick, Duncan, 56
Ramos, Fidel, 152
Rangsi, Sam, 155
Ratliff, William, 135
Reagan, Ronald, 101, 217
Release (charity), 57, 58
Religious revivalism, 45
Rengifo López, Almabeatriz, 109
Reno, Janet, 68, 106
Report of the Independent Inquiry into the Misuse of Drugs Act 1971, 222
Revolutionary Armed Forces of Colombia (FARC), 102, 107, 110, 111–112, 114, 115–116, 118–119, 135
Richards, Keith, 225
Ritalin, 31–32, 231
Rivas, Carlos Lehder, 100
Rocas, Jorge, 71
Rocha, Michael, 125
Rockefeller, Nelson, 74–75
Rodríguez Gacha, José, 113
Rodríguez Orejuela, Gilberto, 103, 108, 110
Rodríguez Orejuela, Jorge Elieser, 103
Rodríguez Orejuela, Miguel, 101, 103, 104, 108, 110
Rodriquez, Eloy, 26
Rolleston, Humphrey, 51
Romania, 35, 204

Roundup Ultra, 116–117
Ruíz Massieu, Mario, 144, 146
Ruíz-Tagle, Eduardo Frei, 122
Runciman Report, 60, 63, 64, 222, 227
Russia, 6, 19, 169, 179
drug use in, 175–177
mafia connection to Colombia, 114
money laundering in, 211
synthetic drug production in, 38
trafficking routes through, 36, 169, 173–175, 204–205
Rwanda, 16, 188

S
Sa, Khun, 5, 150, 151–152
Salinas de Gortari, Carlos, 141, 144, 145
Salinas de Gortari, Raúl, 141, 145
Samper Pizano, Ernesto, 103–104
cartel funding of, 105
corruption charges against, 105–107
extradition agreements signed by, 109
Sandoval, José Manuel, 111
San Marino, 201
Santacruz Londoño, José, 104, 105–106, 109
Sao Tomé, 196
Saudi Arabia, 7, 177
Science of Marijuana, The, 221
Sen, Hun, 156
Senegal, 7, 179, 183, 185, 192
Serbia, 204
Serpa, Horacio, 108–109
Shalala, Donna, 15
Short, Clare, 57
Shultz, George, 14, 135
Shwe, Than, 152, 155
Sierra Leone, 180, 181, 184, 185
Singapore, 6, 169, 175, 215

Single Convention on Narcotic
        Drugs of 1961, 11, 12, 16,
        172
Slovakia, 2, 35, 206
Slovenia, 35, 206
Smith, Joan, 75
Sniffing, 27
Social attitudes toward drug use,
        51–52, 61, 66, 228
Soderbergh, Steven, 70
Solvents, 27
Somalia, 98, 184, 187, 191, 193
Soros, George, 14, 15
South Africa, 7, 8, 180, 182, 184,
        185
    cannabis production in, 37,
        189–190
    designation as a country of con-
        cern by the U. S., 88
    Prevention of Organized Crime
        Act, 213
South America. *See also* individual
        countries
    drug trafficking in, 2–3, 5, 8,
        121–122
    eradication programs in, 88–89,
        91–93, 93, 96, 122–134
    INCB 1999 annual report on, 18
    money laundering in, 215, 231
    Organization of American
        States (OAS) anti-drug
        efforts in, 69–70
South Asia. *See also* Asia; individual
        countries
    cannabis production in, 37
    eradication programs in,
        152–153
    heroin production in, 35
    INCB 1999 report on, 18–19
Spadafora, Winston, 137
Spain, 4, 33, 198, 202
    anti-drug efforts in, 199
    cannabis use in, 37

cocaine use in, 36
decriminalization of drugs in,
        198–199, 232
heroin use in, 35
synthetic drug use in, 38
Sri Lanka, 19, 172
St. Valentine's Day Massacre
        (Chicago), 44
Staggie, Rashaad, 189
Starr, Frederick, 163
Steroids, anabolic, 198
Stevens, John, 232, 236
Strang, John, 56, 58
Straw, Jack, 54, 164, 219
Straw, William, 54
Stuart, Gisela, 45
Substance Abuse and Mental
        Health Services
        Administration, U. S.
        (SAMHSA), 77
Surinam, 197
Suzman, Helen, 14
Swaziland, 190
Sweden, 33, 201
    cannabis use in, 37
    heroin use in, 35
Switzerland, 33, 202, 215, 230
    heroin use in, 35
    needle park in, 199–200
Symington, Fyfe, 73
Synthetic drugs, 38, 201
Syria
    designation as a country of con-
        cern by the U. S., 88
    drug trade in, 7, 91, 169, 176

T
Tablante, Carlos, 130
Tackling Local Drug Markets, 64
Taiwan
    drug trade in, 87, 89, 90, 172
    eradication programs in, 96

Tajikistan, 7, 19, 169, 171, 173, 175, 176
   designation as a country of concern by the U. S., 88
Taliban, the, 6, 19, 91, 160–161, 161–163, 233, 236. *See also* Afghanistan
Tanzania, 179, 182, 184, 188
Taylor, Charles, 183, 192
Temperance movements, 44–45
Terrorism and drug trafficking, 69, 163–164, 209–210, 215–216, 233
Thailand, 5, 18, 23, 87, 90, 152, 169, 215
   cannabis production in, 37
   dispute with Laos, 154
   eradication programs in, 22–23, 96, 155
   opium production in, 149–150, 154–155
   yaba seizures in, 30–31
Thein, Kyaw, 153
Thompson, Jon, 55
Tobacco use
   in Britain, 45–50
   in the United States, 78, 79f
Todd, Mike, 232
Togo, 182
Toledo, Alejandro, 128
Touré, Sekou, 192
Traffic, 33, 70–71
Trainspotting, 61
Treaties on illegal drugs, United Nations, 11, 12–13, 13, 16
Turkey
   designation as a country of concern by the U. S., 88
   drug trade in, 6, 8, 19, 35, 37, 61, 168, 177, 205, 230–231
   opium production in, 29
Turkmenistan, 7, 36, 37, 169, 171, 173, 175

Turkmenistan, 19
Twining, Charles, 155
Tyranny of the Status Quo, 236

U
Uelman, Gerald, 68
Uganda, 184, 188
Ugaz, José Carlos, 127
Ukraine, 36, 176, 205, 215
United Arab Emirates (UAE), 177, 215
United Nations
   Centre for International Crime Prevention (CICP), 12
   Commission on Narcotic Drugs, 12, 200
   Convention against Illicit Traffic in Narcotic Drugs and Psychotropic Substances, 11, 13, 16, 87, 172, 184
   Convention on Psychotropic Substances of 1971, 11, 13, 16, 172
   Economic and Social Council (ECOSOC), 12–13
   efforts to reduce the demand for drugs, 13–16
   1999 INCB annual report, 16–20
   International Drug Control Programme (UNDCP), 4, 11, 12–13, 138, 159–160, 161–162, 172, 180, 209, 213, 233
   Office for Drug Control and Crime Prevention (ODCCP), 11–12, 99, 165, 216
   research on HIV/AIDS and drug use, 24
   research on the demand for drugs, 21–22

response to global anti-drug ef-
    forts, 13–16
Single Convention on Narcotic
    Drugs of 1961, 11, 12,
    16, 172
treaties regarding drug traffick-
    ing, 12–13
World Drug Report 2000, 20–24
United States, the
African Americans in, 71–72,
    82–84
alcohol abuse in, 79f, 80, 81–82
anti-drug efforts in, 1–2, 29–30,
    68–70, 74–75, 171,
    230–231, 236–237
attempts to cut flow of heroin
    into, 89
cannabis use in, 25–26, 80–81
Central Intelligence Agency
    (CIA), 97–98, 151, 153,
    156, 159, 201, 207,
    214–215
certification process, 87–98, 176,
    231
cocaine use in, 68, 117–118
and Colombia, 70–71, 110–111,
    112–113, 118–120, 135
determinations on countries in-
    volved in drug traffick-
    ing or production,
    87–88
difficulties in keeping up with
    globalized drug traffick-
    ing, 90
Drug Abuse Warning Network
    (DAWN), 81
Drug Enforcement
    Administration (DEA),
    1, 2, 60, 67–68, 117–118,
    130, 140, 147, 156, 173,
    180, 184, 230–231
drugs produced in, 70

drug use compared to Britain,
    84–85
ecstasy use in, 70, 117
extradition agreements with for-
    eign countries, 109–110,
    112, 155
gross domestic product com-
    pared to international
    drug trade, 1
heroin use in, 79–80, 89
INCB 1999 annual report on,
    17–18
legalization of marijuana in,
    72–73
pressure on foreign countries,
    2–3, 105
prohibition in, 45
promotion of institutional
    changes in drug produc-
    ing and transit coun-
    tries, 89–90
race and the war on drugs in,
    71–72, 82–84
rates of drug abuse by
    racial/ethnic groups, 78
relations with Mexico, 141, 146
religious revivalism in, 45
surveys of drug abuse in, 77–80
tobacco use in, 78, 79f
Urrego Cárdenas, José Nelson, 110
Uruguay, 133–134
Usher, Alan, 142–143
Uzbekistan
designation as a country of con-
    cern by the U. S., 88
drug trade in, 7, 19, 29, 36, 37,
    171, 173, 175, 176

V
Valdivieso, Alfonso, 108
Vanuatu, 214
Vargas Arias, Waldo Simeón, 109
Vasquez Velasquez, Orlando, 106

Venezuela, 87, 90, 112, 119, 121, 135
  anti-drug efforts in, 130
  eradication programs in, 96–97
  government corruption in, 130
  money laundering in, 215
Verhofstadt, Guy, 197
Vicente Rangel, José, 135
Vietnam, 18, 87, 91, 119, 152, 169
  anti-drug efforts in, 157
  eradication programs in, 97
  heroin production in, 156–157
  opium production in, 149,
    156–157
  veterans, 230
Villanueva Madrid, Mario, 146, 148
Virenque, Richard, 198
Volkow, Nora, 31, 32, 34
Volstead, Andrew J., 44

W
Waage, Jef, 30
Wall Street Journal, 145
War on drugs, the
  costs of, 63, 110–111, 112–113,
    118–120, 152–153, 236
  failure of, 137, 147–148,
    235–237
  personal freedom and, 229–230
  and Plan Colombia, 112–120
  police viewpoints of, 60–61,
    63–64, 223–225,
    231–232, 234
Washington Post, 120

West Asia, INCB 1999 annual re-
    port on, 19–20. *See also*
    Asia
Western Hemisphere Drug
    Elimination Act, 110
White House Office of National
    Drug Control Policy
    (ONDCP), 77
Wijdenbosch, Jules, 197
Winterburn, Diane, 55
Wise, Roy, 34
World Drug Report 2000 (United
    Nations), 20–24, 99
World Factbook, 97–98, 151, 153,
    156, 159, 201, 214–215

Y
Yaba, 30–31
Youth drug use
  in Britain, 51, 57–59, 226, 234
  and deaths, 57
  government attitudes towards,
    56–57
  prevalence of, 51, 58–59
  in the United States, 77–80
  young people's attitudes toward,
    57–58, 206

Z
Zaire, 181
Zambia, 180, 190, 215
Zedillo Ponce de Léon, Ernesto,
    145, 146, 147
Zimbabwe, 180, 184, 185